# European Heritage
# Planning and Management

Edited by
## Gregory Ashworth
## Peter Howard

**intellect**™
EXETER, ENGLAND
PORTLANDOR, USA

First Published in Paperback in 1999 by
**Intellect Books**, FAE, Earl Richards Road North, Exeter EX2 6AS, UK

First Published in USA 1999 by
**Intellect Books**, ISBS, 5804 N.E. Hassalo St, Portland, Oregon 97213-3644, USA

| | |
|---|---|
| Consulting Editor: | Masoud Yazdani |
| Cover Illustration: | Mark Mackie |
| Copy Editor: | Lucy Kind |

A catalogue record for this book is available from the British Library

ISBN 1-84150-005-4

## Planning Team

Professor Gregory Ashworth,
Department of Geography, University of Groningen, Netherlands
Professor Giuseppe Fera,
Department of Town Planning, University of Reggio Calabria, Italy
Professor Brian Graham,
Department of Geography, University of Ulster, Coleraine, UK
Dra Ascension Hernandez-Martinez,
Department of Art History, University of Zaragoza, Spain
Dr Peter Howard,
Heritage Department, University of Plymouth, UK
Joao Loucao,
Department of Geography, New University of Lisbon, Portugal
Professor Christian Prioul,
Department of Geography and Management, Université de Nantes, France

Printed and bound in Great Britain by Cromwell Press, Wiltshire

# Contents

# Preface

*European Heritage Planning and Management* is the outcome of international co-operation over several years, by a group of seven universities within the European Union. Heritage as a field of academic study is now established in several countries, springing from a variety of departments, some of which are represented in this volume. The book is, therefore, not only international in its writing and European in its scope, but also from a multi-disciplinary background. The most exciting element of that experience has been the extent to which similar debates are occurring in several heritage areas, and that the built heritage specialist, the museum curator and the landscape conservationist have much to learn from each other. Many new developments use all these areas of expertise.

The product of the discussions over several years, funded by the Erasmus and Socrates programmes of the European Union, has been two-fold. From September 1999 each of the institutions will be running a one-year post-graduate course in European Heritage Planning and Management. The course will have many different titles and precise regulations will obviously depend on the host university, but students will spend one semester at their home university studying principles of Heritage Management and Planning before going abroad to one of the other cooperating institutions in the second semester, to study courses in which that university is specialist. English is used as a common language, hence the second major product has been this text-book, primarily intended to be the core text of the first semester of that course. However, the field of Heritage Studies is now growing fast all over Europe, and beyond, and the team hope the book will be of much wider application than the students for whom it was originally written.

## Editors

Professor Gregory Ashworth was appointed to the chair of Heritage Management and Urban Tourism in the Faculty of Spatial Sciences of the University of Groningen in 1994. He was educated in economics and geography at the Universities of Cambridge, Reading and London and has research and teaching interests in heritage, urban tourism, place marketing and city centre management. He coordinated the international consortium in European Heritage Planning and Management.

Dr Peter Howard leads the degree programme in Heritage at the University of Plymouth in Exeter. Trained as a geographer, he has worked extensively in the perception of landscape, and was Vice-Chair of Landscape Research Group, publishing *Landscapes: the Artists' Vision*, (Routledge, 1991). Since setting up a Heritage course at Exeter, working with art historians and sociologists, he has edited the *International Journal of Heritage Studies*.

## Contributors

Giuseppe Fera is an architect, and Professor of Town Planning at the University of Reggio Calabria. His studies on heritage have mainly been concerned with rural landscape and heritage and its management, especially within National and Regional Natural Parks. He is involved also in studies and research on planning for natural risk reduction (mainly earthquakes), and on the theme of people's participation in urban rehabilitation planning.

Brian Graham is Professor of Human Geography, School of Environmental Studies,University of Ulster at Coleraine. He has published widely on research topics concerned with the cultural and historical geography of Europe. Recent edited books include: *In Search of Ireland: A Cultural Geography*, London: Routledge, London, 1997; *Modern Europe: Place, Culture, Identity* London: Arnold, 1998; and *Modern Historical Geographies* (with Catherine Nash) Harlow: Pearson, 1999. In addition, he is co-author of *A Geography of Heritage: Power, Culture and Economy* (with G. J. Ashworth and J. E. Tunbridge), London: Arnold, 2000.

Ascension Hernandez Martinez holds a PhD in History of Art and works in the Department of History of Art, University of Zaragoza, where she teaches Artistic Techniques, and Conservation and Restoration of Artistic Heritage. Specialising in contemporary art, her thesis analyses the work of a Spanish architect, Ricardo Magdalena. She is interested in theoretical and practical aspects of the conservation of cultural heritage, and recently edited a reader: *Documentos para la historia de la restauración*, Universidad de Zaragoza, 1999.

Christian Prioul is Professor of Geography and Management at the University of Nantes, and part of the CNRS team 'Geolittomer'. His main interests are littoral, in the historical geography of the European and African Atlantic, hence his 'Aires de Vents sur l'Atlantique' in *Historiens Geographes* of 1998.

# 1. Europe, heritage and management

Throughout Europe, and much of the world, heritage has become a matter of concern. For well over a century national governments have conserved monuments, built museums, designated national parks, for a whole variety of reasons, and at considerable expense. Today those national heritages, integral parts of national identities, are being challenged by cities, localities and regions wishing to use heritage for their own purposes, by minority groups attempting to reclaim hidden heritages and by international organisations attempting to discover international similarities. Among these international organisations, UNESCO designates World Heritage Sites, some being of cultural significance, some natural and a few Cultural Landscapes which lie between. However, many international organisations, including UNESCO, largely operate on behalf of their constituent national members, who are the parties to the various conventions. In Europe there is similar pressure, with the Council of Europe taking a leading role in facilitating discussion and comparison between national heritage organisations, and the European Union beginning to understand that common identity will necessitate common heritage. Within that developing scene, there can be no surprise that a book concerning the planning and management of heritage in Europe should appear.

There are two further developments we need to note. Not only is the conservation and management of heritage a much enlarged business, but so is its academic study. The French Ecole Nationale du Patrimoine is one major centre, and there are several university courses in the United Kingdom. Some Spanish universities have course elements on heritage, especially within the autonomous regions, and the same is true of Scandinavia. In addition there are important centres of conservation technical knowledge for example at Leuven, at York and at Litomysl. This book acts as the core text of the first part of one such course devised and run jointly by universities in France, Spain, Italy, Portugal, the Netherlands and the United Kingdom. Other readers may notice an inevitable interest in the heritage problems of those countries, but will find that much of the material is relevant to Europe as a whole. Nor is there any reason to suppose that Europe is always unique in heritage matters.

The other major development is that people are recovering their own heritage. Traditionally governments, whether national, international, local or civic, have appropriated tax income to designate or collect heritage, ostensibly for the benefit of their citizens, though often for the benefit of only a small minority. This is now rapidly changing. Not only are families, perhaps under threat of dispersal, more self-consciously aware of their own history than ever before, but everywhere people from all walks of life are making collections, conserving gardens, protecting landscape features and buildings, preserving steam trains and forming folk music clubs amongst other activities. People are defending what they see as their own heritage, which sometimes equates to the ideas of academics and of governments, but frequently does not.

# Europe

The course material that follows does assume a general knowledge of the history and geography and societies of Europe. Modern historians and geographers rarely write broad introductions to an entire continent and some readers may find themselves searching for texts of quality sufficient for them to work through the book without constant reference to atlas, or encyclopaedia. The authors do expect to be able to mention the North European Plain, or the Apennines; the battle of Austerlitz or Verdi's *Aïda*; Chartres Cathedral or the Alhambra without having to explain them. Readers who feel less than confident in this area will find that time devoted to some background reading will be of real value. There is no need to do this in English although reading books written by foreigners, even in translation, is very valuable. Sometimes it is quite a shock to see how unimportant other people think that your national heritage is. An excellent work on the history of Europe in English is that by Norman Davies (1996). So many European history books are about western Europe since 1789. Davies is a scholar of east European history and he corrects some imbalances. He gives equal importance to all parts of the continent, not just the west, and he looks at the sweep of history over thousands of years. Some further suggestions are given at the end of this chapter.

# Heritage

If Europe is one difficult concept which needs some preparation before even the extent of the continent can be discussed, then heritage is a concept of equal universality and complexity. This text will spend a considerable number of pages discussing its meaning, but its importance needs to be stressed at this early stage. To many, especially many in government circles, heritage is usually associated with buildings, and certainly many buildings are officially classified as heritage, but if heritage is everything that anybody wants to save or conserve or collect, then it is a concept which can include almost anything. Certainly there is a considerable number of people engaged in conserving the 'natural heritage' and many more concerned with in museums. All those are largely public concerns, but many of the things which are precious to us, and which we want to conserve, are not public at all, but personal effects, for example, family photographs and belongings. Some have no real physical or material existence at all, and may be simply methods of behaviour.

A few hours studying both local and national newspapers will soon reveal the vast extent and the vital importance of heritage. At the time of writing Serbs and Kosovan Albanians are meeting to discuss whose heritage and traditions are to prevail in a small area of the Balkans. They meet in Rambouillet, a magnificent and carefully conserved palace outside Paris. In Northern Ireland there is still a stand-off at Drumcree where one group insists on exercising its traditional heritage of walking down a particular street with drums beating. The local paper is much involved with a proposal for new building in the city, which would mean replacing shops built in the 1950s, which some people have now decided are historically significant. In the parish magazine there is a report of the National Trust starting to restore the water pump in the village, which has long since been derelict.

A great deal of comment on heritage, both in academic texts and in the press, seems to start from the premise that heritage is a precious and strictly limited physical asset which has to be preserved, often in the sense of being protected from people. This book takes a contrary position. Heritage is regarded as in plentiful supply, various parts of it being designated heritage in various places at various times for the pleasure or other purposes of a whole variety of people. People and their needs lie at the very centre of heritage. So students of European heritage are strongly advised to prepare themselves not only by reading about Europe's history, geography and society, and not only by following heritage issues in the press and mapping their extent, but also, and perhaps most importantly, by observation. Heritage sites, whether nature trails, country houses or museums are places to visit, not only to admire the architecture, the exhibits or the animals, but also to watch and listen to the other visitors. Who are they? Where do they come from? What are they enjoying? How long do they spend with various items of heritage?

The ideas in this book may well seem quite strange to students who have spent years within disciplines which either define the heritage to a narrow range (nature or buildings or collections) or which presume that the need to conserve the raw material of that discipline's study is self-evident. Art historians, by and large, are opposed to destroying paintings; archaeologists don't like putting new buildings onto ancient sites; architectural historians do tend to assume that older buildings by famous architects are more valuable than newer more anonymous ones. A few weeks spent with the sort of reading suggested here, and making lots of visits to listen to people talking about what they think is their heritage (and what is someone else's) will soon make the ideas presented here seem less revolutionary.

## Planning and Management

The last part of the title involves two active verbs, to 'plan' and to 'manage' which at the very least suggests that this course moves from an analysis and explanation of what exists to some sort of action to maintain or create heritage, or to organise its use according to some pre-established goals. 'Who does this, for what reasons and with what instruments?' are central questions of the text. This has no specific, coherent political agenda but is ultimately political, in the sense that public heritage is created as an act of policy, maintained by political systems and decisions, and conveys political messages from those who created it to those who experience it. In particular it involves choices about what is to be designated and treated as heritage, who is to use it and in what ways, and who is to reap the benefits, whether economic, social, political or cultural, from its continued use. Every act of selection implies consideration. Each act of heritage creation disinherits someone, in some way. Thus policy, whether exercised by political bodies, private companies or concerned individuals is unavoidable.

The chapters that follow are composed of a main text supplemented by summaries, case studies, self-assessment discussion questions, conclusions and further reading. They were produced to accompany, with other materials, a course developed by an international consortium of university teachers. For further reading, consider the following:

- G.J. Ashworth & P.J. Larkham, eds., *Building a New Heritage: tourism, culture and identity in the New Europe*, London: Routledge, 1994.
- K. Cameron (ed) *The Nation: Myth or Reality*, Oxford: Intellect, 1996
- N. Davies, *Europe, a History*, Oxford: Oxford University Press, 1996.
- B. Graham, *Modern Europe: place, culture, identity*, London: Arnold, 1998.
- D. Pinder, (ed) *The New Europe: economy, society and environment*, Chichester: John Wiley, 1998.
- P. Wagstaff, (ed) *Regionalism in Europe*, Oxford: Intellect, 1997.

# 2. Dimensions and Scope of Heritage

## Summary

Europe is introduced as a problematic concept with no simple definition. Heritage is seen to be closely involved with people and their self-identity, as well as the places in which they live. Seven categories of heritage objects are offered: nature; landscape; monuments; artefacts; activities; people; and sites, and the importance of keeping all these in view is stressed. A market classification is introduced; the demands on heritage coming from owners, insiders, governments, visitors and academics. Heritage is best seen as a cycle, from creation through development to loss as heritage. This makes heritage a significantly different subject from history, cultural studies, art history and town planning. Finally there are a few terms with which the student needs to be familiar, and some notes on the people and organisations involved.

## The European Dimension

This course could deal with either the Heritage *of* Europe, or Heritage *in* Europe. In the second case we would deal with the planning and management of all those things which might be considered heritage within a geographical area which we shall call Europe. Some of those things would be of European continental significance, but many would be of national significance, and most would be of local significance only. Thus while we could easily agree that the battlefield of Austerlitz is of European significance, the battlefield of Bosworth Field (near Nuneaton in England) is probably of only English significance. However, if we take the first definition, the heritage *of* Europe, we would be concerned only with those items of heritage which somehow defined European-ness. Many such sites, monuments and buildings may actually lie outside any definition of the geographical limits of Europe, in America, Africa or Asia. The plan of Washington DC is surely an example. By no means all European heritage is within Europe—most European countries make some effort to prevent the export of their heritage overseas notably to America. 'Who owns what heritage?' is one of the most complex problems in heritage studies and this course will return to that question on many occasions.

One of the common inheritances of many European countries is the tendency to colonise overseas, so that there is real difficulty in finding a common European heritage that is not equally common to both North and South America, Australasia, most of Africa and much of Asia. European architects have worked all round the world. French, Spanish or Portuguese literature does not necessarily come from France or Spain or Portugal. The opposite is also true. Overseas cultures have been imported into Europe for several millenia. This could apply to Moorish remains in Spain, to the Notting Hill Carnival in London, to Indonesian restaurants in Amsterdam. The current disputes in Kosovo and in Bosnia are, in part, a reflection of such movements.

This course does not propose a single answer to the problem of a European Heritage.

Just as in most European countries there are some components of heritage which are of local significance and others which are national, so there are some themes in Europe which seem to be international and others which are not. Which elements of heritage would be lighted on by a politically unified Europe to strengthen a continental rather than a national identity, is an interesting question. Some readers will strongly resist such developments, others may support them. At this stage it is only important to note that all political units with a geographical extent attempt to develop a common identity, and that heritage of all kinds is a major component in that enterprise.

## *Exercise One*

European Heritage, as discussed in this course, is assumed to apply much more widely than the nations of the European Union. Which countries are in the EU? Which others have applied to join?

The Council of Europe has done a great deal of work in Heritage. Which countries are included in the Council of Europe but not in the EU? Should we include the three Caucasian Republics, Georgia, Armenia, Azerbaijan within Europe? Should we include Russia? All of it? If we include Vladivostok, why not include Washington? Turkey, like Russia, has territory within the formal limits of Europe. Should Turkey be included within the course? At the other extreme of debate, to what extent should we look at Canada or Brazil as European? Which countries within the formal limits of Europe, members of the Council of Europe, regard themselves as less than completely European? Why?

## The Russian Dolls Concept

Heritage is one of the components in people's identity. Perhaps ALL heritage is concerned with someone's identity. Certainly one of the most useful ways to debate heritage is to think of the numerous ways in which we use the word 'my' or 'mine'—ways in which we express ownership. If I talk about MY country or MY village I do not mean this in the same way as MY hat. I do not imply formal, legal ownership, merely sharing in some common identity. MY wife is different yet again, as is MY family or MY house (it belongs to US not to ME, indeed it probably really belongs to the finance company who loaned us the money!) I talk about MY view, but I do not own the fields across which I look.

The geographical identities which many of us feel are not the only identities we possess, of course. I am part of all sorts of groups, sporting, musical, academic, religious. Modern communications enable us to discuss ideas more easily with a colleague in another university, who speaks a different language, and lives on the other side of the world, than with our next-door neighbour. Even today, however, many people feel committed to several different geographic levels of identity. We may have a home, to remind us that Heritage and Inheritance are similar ideas, and we have a neighbourhood or community, or village which is 'where we belong'. Then there are various levels of regional identity, whether counties, or provinces, *departements* or *länder*. Sometimes the regions with which we feel identity exist on the map, delineated by governments; but sometimes they do not.

Most people feel some sort of national identity—though this may be quite complicated. In the UK or in Spain these national identities may be doubled, people feel both English and British, Catalan and Spanish. Others will feel considerable identity with a former nationality, perhaps of their birth. In some parts of Europe these identities are in brutal conflict, in parts of the Balkans, in Northern Ireland, in the Pais Vasco, in parts of the Baltic countries. Some people have considerable affinity with Europe, though this is far from universal among people on the continent, and may have very little to do with the official organisations of the European Union. Lastly there is surely some universal identity with all human beings everywhere.

The important thing is that these identities are not alternatives, like different hats; we do not often put one identity down and pick up another, we are all those things at once. Individual human beings resolve these conflicts within themselves, but they are not so easily resolved between groups. We are a complex of Russian dolls, each fitting inside the other. However, today we probably have more choice about which identity we want than people have ever had in the past. Identity can almost be purchased; certainly it can be selected. Now that there are some advantages to being Native American, the number of those claiming Native American ancestry has risen dramatically. These are not liars; they merely feel that now is the time to stress the origin of one great-grand-parent rather than another one.

## Landscape

One of the focal points of this course is Landscape. Heritage has many parts to it, but many of them come together within places. Landscape is a multifaceted concept and may itself be very largely a European, indeed a west European concept, which was then exported. Early travel literature, certainly up to 1700, for example the English works by Celia Fiennes or Daniel Defoe, contains virtually no comment on whether the country appeared attractive or not. Nearly all debate was about function, whether the land produced good wheat or good grass, that the roads were terrible or that the bridge was sound. Almost anything modern was praised. When a town is described as 'fair' it means little more than it was comparatively clean, did not smell too much, and had some modern buildings. The idea that a view of land could be considered attractive belonged to an emerging leisured and wealthy class who nevertheless owed their wealth to the land. Even since landscape became an understood concept, the notion of what constituted attractive landscape has varied dramatically over time. Heritage similarly changes. Any suggestion that a certain kind of landscape should be conserved for future generations is, therefore, likely to be frustrated. Future generations will want something different. Every generation discovers new landscapes and invents its own heritage.

Nevertheless there is some value in keeping Space and Place as fundamental elements in our thinking. Space we can understand to be an almost neutral extent of land—space can be defined by latitude and longitude, it is a geometric concept, and by the area in square kilometres. Space carries no additional connotations or meanings. Once meanings are invested in a space, then it slowly becomes a place, and some places are richer in meanings than others. Plus of course there are places within places within places—just like the Russian dolls of our identity.

## *Exercise Two*

Decide on a Place which is significant to you. What are the meanings which are invested in that place? Meanings for you? Meanings for others? What about this place is 'heritage', what is being preserved? how? what else should be conserved? The place might be as small as a building, but might be as large as a town or even a district. It probably is not as large as a country, because a country is an 'imagined community', is an idea which we carry in our heads, not a place with which we can be fully familiar—unless of course you come from Liechtenstein or Monaco! Two or three paragraphs should be plenty.

*Example: Dinder is a small village in the county of Somerset, with a population of about 150, only five km from the famous cathedral city of Wells. My parents moved there when I was 21 and had already left home for university - so I never lived in Dinder, though I stayed there frequently both on my own, with my wife and later with our two older children. At that time in my life we were moving around the country, in various jobs, living in the suburbs of one city and then another. Weekends and holidays at Dinder represented the 'real England' which we hoped to aspire to one day. Of the particular features of heritage, the church is a listed historic building; lovely little church though it is, the really important feature is my parents' grave in the churchyard. Their house, now a second home for an American visitor, is not protected. Although very old in parts it is too much altered. While the house was interesting, my memory is much more of the garden, and the sadness to see it now largely overgrown. To my children, the bit they remember most is a Pill Box, the name given to a Second World War defensive concrete bunker, up in the fields behind the village, which they used as their 'den' whenever they were in the village. They also remember the old lady who took them in to her house and gave them sweets and talked to them, when we did not have time. To them the fact that Dinder House, a big Palladian mansion, is preserved is much less important. There are at least two groups of people who think quite differently about Dinder's heritage. Archaeologists would note Maesbury Castle, an Iron Age hill-fort and a Scheduled Monument. I only went there once, and there were some mounds in the ground. The other major piece of heritage I never visited at all, and very few have. Underneath Dinder (where the geology is Carboniferous limestone) is one of the largest limestone caverns ever discovered, the largest in Britain. There must exist a very small group of people, probably none of them locals, for whom Dinder is a famous name, with a heritage entirely underground.*

As is shown by the above prose, places mean all sorts of different things to different people.

# Heritage

Such an exercise demonstrates that the definition of heritage is problematic. We certainly learn that it has much to do with people and with activities, that things are important to people, and that the meanings which people invest in things, often through the activities associated with them, are often meanings to do with other people. Hence things, whether buildings or smaller artefacts, are often all we can effectively conserve; they represent the heritage of people and activities, and remind us of them. A 50-year-old photograph of an old woman may well be collectable heritage, perhaps filed under the name of the photographer but if it is a photo of your grandmother, the set of meanings changes dramatically and is much strengthened. It ceases being an object and becomes a person. The simplest definition is possibly 'Heritage is whatever people want to conserve, preserve, protect or collect' usually with a view to passing it on to others. Heritage is very difficult to define by listing all the things which people do save, and is best considered either a process which happens to things or as a marketing device. Some things become heritage, but others do not, and the reasons and process are important studies. To define heritage in terms of objects is only useful in describing the enormous range of things which people think are worth preserving.

The seven-fold catalogue of heritage which follows is far from a complete list. Like every catalogue, there are lots of cross entries. Things listed under Nature might easily have come under Artefacts. The categories are:- nature, landscape, monuments, artefacts, activities, people and sites. None is watertight. By no means everything in the category is heritage, and many heritage items would come into several categories. Indeed it may be that a heritage concept which incorporates buildings, landscapes, collections and nature which has come about partly in the United Kingdom, may well be a result of the British, or at least English, tendency to define the aristocratic country house as one of the critical exemplars of the national patrimony. Perhaps each country has one particular kind of feature which is regarded above all others as indisputably heritage. If in England it is a country house with a landscape garden, it might be the small-town centre in Germany, the Gothic cathedrals of France and the town halls of Flanders.

'Nature' refers to plants, animals, ecosystems, geological and geomorphological features. There is a fixed idea in many countries that the natural heritage has little relationship with the cultural heritage. In most European countries nature conservation is not the responsibility of the same ministry as other heritage sectors, a situation often supported by the conservationists themselves, who regard themselves as scientists, and their judgements as objective ones. There is little justification for this position, and it may do positive harm. First, in much of Europe, there is almost nothing natural; the land has been intensively occupied for so long that natural habitats no longer exist—all nature is cultivated and cultural. Nature itself is simply a cultural concept, a concept invented by humans for their own purposes. Consequently species of animals and plants are not conserved equally. Large, woolly mammals get a particularly good deal; small poisonous spiders rank at the other extreme. Human beings seem to be more enthusiastic about preserving whales than in preserving krill. Should we conserve the AIDS virus or the cholera bacillus?

Of course, the techniques of conserving brown bears are different from the techniques of conserving frescoes. The techniques of conserving bears are different from the techniques of conserving tarantulas. A heritage text based on conservation techniques could never be holistic, and could only cover a very narrow range of objects; a course in paper conservation for example is typically specialised. Conservation techniques have to be left to the experts within other disciplines, whether architects, zoologists, ecologists or art historians. But if the 'how?' of conservation differs (though the legal and financial means may well be similar), the 'why?' the 'by whom?' and 'for whom?', the 'when?' and the 'where?' are all questions where the answers may well be similar across the board, or where the experience of one may be valuable to the other.

There are differences of course, not the least being that the natural heritage can be created anew, provided that the species are still extant, whereas the cultural heritage often cannot be recreated without losing authenticity—whatever that means! Nevertheless of all the millions of cultural artefacts which exist, only a small proportion are declared heritage—and much the same is true of natural things. The World Heritage Site designations insist on authenticity for cultural sites, but on cohesion for natural sites, with both concepts being highly contentious. Scientific conservators often believe that they are not conserving a species for the sake of human beings but for the sake of the species itself. Actually this is not very different from the position adopted by many archaeologists for example, who would feel that ancient structures have a right to be conserved, and that human visitors are not to be encouraged.

'Landscape' refers to areas conserved for their aesthetic appeal and their cultural evidence, rather than the species they contain, though overlap is inevitable. It includes gardens, Areas of Outstanding Natural Beauty, *Parcs Regionaux*, National Parks and even 'the Alps'. In some countries there is little distinction between places conserved for their natural content and those 'cultural landscapes' conserved largely for aesthetic reasons. Czech National Parks for example are predominantly involved with the conservation of nature. To the English, however, landscape has been a central concept for a long time. To the French, local food and wine give value to the *terroir* whose qualities are, in reality as in advertising, linked with the landscape as a whole: it is protected by the Commission Départementale des Sites, the 30 Parcs Naturels Régionaux, the Grands Sites Nationaux and lately by the 'loi sur la protection et la mise en valeur des paysages'.

Protection of landscape also raises questions concerning the tourism resource: are beaches heritage? Not to consider them so would seem snobbish. They are clearly worth preserving for future generations, but they have the misfortune to be genuinely popular, so get generally left out of heritage debates. However, in France, where there is strong demand for the coastal areas, the government tries to protect the 'natural landscape' with a 'Conservatoire de l'espace littoral et des rivages lacustres' (10 July 1975) and a law about 'l'aménagement, la protection et la mise en valeur du littoral' (3 January 1986). In Britain there are Heritage Coasts though even these tend to be more concerned with cliffs than beaches, as that of Purbeck does not include Weymouth.

David Lowenthal once remarked that 'the whole of Europe is a garden'—a useful reminder that this is an old and much-used continent. There is much more landscape than nature. So landscape tends to be defined as an aesthetic resource, a fine landscape is one which looks good, whereas other functions are perhaps of equal importance. Certainly there is research which shows that senses other than sight are of significant, and the potential of landscapes to provide pleasure is much wider than passive observation. Landscape is usually taken to mean a rural scene, but the concept of townscape is obviously closely related, so there is only a fine line between the ideas of townscape and the next category of monuments.

'Monuments' – While none could deny the importance of works of architecture and archaeology in any listing of the heritage, the 'built heritage' is often seen as the most important focus of debate. Actually much archaeological heritage is small enough to be collected and lies within museums, but the amount of funding devoted to the conservation of buildings has probably been greater than their importance in the construction of identities and more in keeping with their ability to attract visitors. In English the term 'monument' is sometimes used only to mean a memorial sculpture, but a valuable extension is to mean 'a building which has been selected as heritage'. The conservation of buildings can be at the expense of other heritages, as when rare lichens are scraped off buildings to reveal the stonework. Some features, such as canals have a problem of definition here. How can you define a ditch filled with water as an historic monument? (See Chapter Three). Most countries also accept that some whole areas of towns are worthy of conservation, despite the presence in them of buildings which, considered out of context, might not be. Questions of authenticity arise here in a way which is less common in the conservation of nature or landscape. Which period is the 'right' period for a building? Should interventions in the fabric be a last resort? Who should decide the final result—owner, architect, public? The reasons for the conservation of buildings often encapsulate the most important reasons for so many other parts of the heritage, for example buildings may be conserved because they are the most outstanding examples of their type and time; because they are absolutely typical of their type and time; because they are the first appearance of a style which later becomes widespread; because they are a major work by a recognised great architect; because they are just odd (such as several follies); or because they have been inhabited by someone famous.

'Artefacts' are the things made by human beings and collected by them, curated in collections and museums, public or private, in a stamp album at home or in the National Museum. There are inevitable problems of definition, 'Is a stuffed giraffe artefact or nature?' 'Is a building not also an artefact?' Such problems underline the necessity of holistic thinking. Some artefacts, such as ships, are very large, and have been referred to as 'in-between' heritage (Young, 1996). They occupy the middle ground between the architectural heritage and the museum curator's heritage. Indeed many buildings have been moved and there are several collections of such buildings, sometimes housed within other buildings. Buildings collected as artefacts tend to shed their other functions and become objects purely for heritage purposes. Other artefacts raise all the problems of authenticity and restoration—how much of a car has to be replaced before it ceases to be authentic? This is a very live issue in the restoration of works of art such as paintings, as with Leonardo's *Last Supper*. After how much restoration is a painting no longer an authentic work of art by the original artist? This is an area where there have been major social and scientific scandals.

There is a long and distinguished history of museological study which underpins the museum curator's craft, as well as a long history of collecting and connoisseurship. This is probably the oldest traditional part of the heritage business—collecting was already important in the Middle Ages with the cult of relics, though whether saints' relics are more properly regarded as the heritage of artefacts or the heritage of people is another nice argument.

'Activities' – For many people, the heritage of which they are most proud, the heritage they would wish to hand on to their children, comes under none of these headings. It may have a much less conservable physical form, but it is clearly regarded as critical to identity. Together these activities constitute our ways of life. The most obvious example is language, especially where this is under threat, for example, Welsh, Rhaeto-Romansch or Basque. There are many other fields of culture which are regarded as worthy of conservation. The UK parliament has debated which sporting events are more than merely sport, and therefore should be shown on terrestrial television, available to all, and not sold to cable channels. In many countries food and drink are critical to identity, and a great deal of French effort goes to conserving the 'traditional' quality of food, while both Czechs and Germans can be very defensive about the quality of their beer. Film, television and the arts are also obvious examples. There is an emphasis here on activity rather than artefact. England is famous for its gardens, but many people are more concerned with the techniques and practice of gardening than with the conservation of significant gardens. Then there are folk dances and local customs and music—the Catalan *sardanha* and the Portuguese *Fado* are not only tourist products but regularly performed parts of their shared identity. For many people the conservation of their religious practices would also be a matter of the greatest importance—possibly even at the expense of the church building. At present the introduction of the Euro is making many people consider their currency to be a part of their heritage, while the British cling to a distinctive system of measurement, or defend, as do the Spanish, the traditional timetable of their working day.

'People' – Some people are also heritage. Many countries, trades and professions have a patron saint, though sometimes the connection is an obscure one. There are also living people, who either in themselves or in the office they hold are living heritage. Certainly there are artists who might be considered such—and Japan designates such Living National Treasures. The most obvious case in Europe is probably our royal families. Presidents are, of course, keepers of a large amount of heritage, much of it ritual, but Kings, Queens and Grand Dukes, because of the blood line of succession, are themselves heritage objects. The Duke of Bedford, who was among the first of the British aristocracy to open his home to the public (Woburn Abbey) makes it clear that many visitors wanted not so much to see the house as to see him, and his wife, the Duchess (Bedford, 1971). It is difficult trying to match being heritage with trying to live in the last few years of the twentieth century, but they are not the only people who have to do it. Many European countries had, and some still have, systems of giving honours, sometimes hereditary ones. These can easily be regarded as heritage designations. Perhaps there is not a lot of difference between the *legion d'honneur* and the scheduled monument! Most city mayors will understand the burden of having to *be* heritage, as will the young men who ride the horses in Siena or even people who dress up for regular carnivals only to find themselves the subject of tourist cameras.

'Sites' – There is also another category of heritage which has no physical remains at all. There is certainly a mythical heritage, which may be connected to certain actual places but has no physical evidence. Glastonbury in southern England has a host of myths concerning King Arthur, and even the Holy Grail. Brad Castle in Transylvania is the 'site' of Dracula's castle. People visit the sites of Agatha Christie's mysteries and television and film have dramatically increased the significance of some places, not the 'site of the novel' but the 'place where the novel was filmed'. Loch Ness is alleged to have a monster in it—much the most valuable piece of heritage in the whole of the Highlands of Scotland! In addition to completely mythical characters there are the host of places associated with artists and writers, frequently  without any necessary physical remains. Battlefields too often lack phsical evidence but are carefully conserved places.

## A Comprehensive Study

Listing the separate resources available to be made into heritage inevitably brings forcibly to mind that anything can become heritage. Even more importantly, even nothing can be made into heritage, which does not have to have a physical form at all. Without a single holistic field of study, priorities are difficult to resolve. Very many parts of the heritage overlap with each other. National Parks contain all sorts of things other than scenery. Conservation areas in towns also contain animals and artefacts. From this point of view the small islands of Europe—and also the overseas islands with a European background—can be laboratories for holistic studies in heritage planning combining both local and intercontinental levels.

Also, only by looking at various resources can ideas and techniques be transferred from one to another. The question of heritage and national identity, which has recently become an issue in the landscape sector, has long been a problem, with a considerable literature, in the museum sector. Similarly, in Australia and Spain, the technique of listing, long considered appropriate when applied to immovable and expensive resources, such as buildings, is now being applied to portable artefacts. If paintings, documents or books are regarded as important for Spanish heritage, they are listed and included in an inventory, whether the owner is public or private, and called *Bien Inventariado*. The law  establishes what may be done with such objects.

In terms of Place-making, these categories are not entirely equal of course. While landscape, and buildings are integral to place, collections of artefacts are not,  or not necessarily. However, there is plenty of work by museologists which stresses the importance of the local, regional or national museum in underlining the identity of places (Uzzell, 1996). Similarly activities, including diets, dialects, games and religious practices may all be of great importance in making Places.

Already we can discern the beginnings of a most serious debate. Many sites fall into more than one category. Take the village church in Exercise Two. Many people, especially architects of course, will assume that the church is fundamentally a monument, and that its importance is for architectural historians to judge. But it could easily come within four other categories. Certainly there is a very considerable constituency who would start from a totally different perspective and would not accept that the church is a work of architecture. The Church, (with a capital C) is the congregation of the faithful, so the heritage within it is the heritage of the Christian faith; it is what people do and say and sing which is important, and the building is of very little consequence. The other three areas may not differ so much in principle, but they may well have significantly varied viewpoints. The church may well have an important colony of bats in the tower, or the stones may be covered with rare lichens. The landscape specialist may wish to retain the presence of the church in the view, but may well not care whether the tower is built of 15th-century stone or 20th-century plastic, so long as it displays the churchyard to best advantage. The local museum keeper may well covet the church's silver plate which will surely look better displayed in a glass case in her museum than be used for Mass. A course centred on Place, may tend to give its primary consideration to buildings, but such primacy is not automatic. If the care of the church is left in the hands of architects, then it is vital for them to recognise that they are custodians of much more than a building.

This grid of seven kinds of heritage can form the start of our theoretical structure, but we must now add to it several more sets of ideas, to complete a complex three- or even four-dimensional construct of heritage.

# Markets

The second part of the grid is in terms of the people and organisations who want heritage and are affected by it, the markets.

## Owners

Owners often get forgotten in the heritage debate, but almost all objects are owned by someone, though this may not apply to some of the more abstract activities that we wish to save. Does anyone own a folk-dance? The owner may acquire the object through inheritance (a literal heritage) or may purchase it, for a whole variety of reasons usually all mixed up together. Connoisseurship is certainly one of those reasons but there are a whole raft of others including as an investment for financial gain, to acquire status, out of intellectual curiosity, for sensual pleasure, or for purely functional reasons.

At the end of the 18th century there appeared a new idea of heritage. Until then, heritage was a question of power and authority (kings, nobility, bishops) but after the French Revolution heritage became a question of interest for everyone. Since then we have inherited this new concept, and all the debates between the owner and a bigger group of stakeholders. In Spain, cathedrals, churches and monasteries belong to the Catholic Church but for historical, artistic and religious reasons in fact play an important role in Spanish life. Some important private palaces are considered by Spanish legislation to be of public interest, despite having private owners. Here public interest has superiority over private ownership. In Britain there is a debate about the 'right to roam' with walkers claiming that the land of Britain is the heritage of all, and everyone should have the right to walk on it. Land-owners, not surprisingly, resist this claim.

There are also those who seek to 'own' heritage by other means. Some heritage is valuable, and its security is a matter of great concern, to prevent thieves who wish to re-allocate its ownership. Robbing graves is considered outrageous and illegal, but museums are full of goods from graves. Today there are many who use metal detectors to transfer heritage from one ownership to another. Not all the stakeholders in heritage have legitimate rights!

A great deal of heritage debate concerns the rights of owners, whether private citizens or public (Governments, companies, the Church) as against the rights of others. There are certainly occasions when one begins to suspect the beginnings of an Aesthetic Police Force enforcing Good Taste. This question of private property rights as opposed to public / national / human rights is a central issue in Chapter Three.

## Exercise Three

What heritage do you own? How did you acquire it? Who else should have rights over it? Why do you keep it? Would you be happy to accept that the public has a right of access to see it?

*Example. This writer is the owner of part of a listed historic building. Certainly my reasons for purchasing this particular property include the fact that it is historic, but it is also a convenient distance from my place of work, at the right price, with more or less the right number of bedrooms, and sufficient garden. My commitment to its conservation is very considerable, but probably does not equate very comfortably with what architectural or landscape historians think I ought to do with it. The difference is, of course, that I am almost certainly paying for it, and they, probably, are not.*

## Insiders

Individuals are not the only ones who hoard things. Communities do it all the time. At first unselfconsciously, and later knowingly, groups of people look after their past, and indeed their present. They don't want to see that wood chopped down, nor that field built on. They regard such things and places as part of their identity, and their roots—communities prefer stasis to change if only because it is easier to defend. The community's heritage has little to do with the values recognised by the heritage bureaucracy and the government agencies, aesthetic quality, monetary value or rarity. Insiders within communities usually wish to commemorate the past, but this is a past of events and of people (Griffiths, 1987). Houses are important because of who lived or lives in them, not because they are beautiful, or architecturally significant. Lanes may not be beautiful, but they may be where the local lovers always go. It is almost as though everything that exists has a right to continue to exist. The older the existence the stronger the right. Communities are also quite prepared to pay for their heritage. Small communities have collected huge sums of money to pay for something they value, the church, the pub, the post office. This is often to do with traditional function; the church is saved not because it is a splendid example of 15th-century architecture, not even because of its spiritual importance, but because it is where we were baptised, where dad is buried and where we hope our children will be married. Although this book is concerned primarily with the public heritage of wider societies, unless heritage managers understand that local people have a quite different view of their heritage from the professional, then they will be very surprised at local reactions.

## Governments

Governments at various levels 'buy' identity and recognition. By designating and conserving the heritage they legitimate themselves as organisations, and their boundaries. (This legitimation is considered later.) Governments fund museums, they put money into protecting the built environment, they fund courses. Inevitably they have a particular interest in those aspects of heritage which can be shown to be unique to their particular area, or to be particularly indicative of it, and also which are not divisive within the government area. This book is supported by the European Union presumably because the EU sees some advantage in it. There are of course many levels of government.

## Exercise Four

What are the various levels of government which have responsibility for elements of the heritage in your place?

*Example. Living in rural England those which affect me are:-*

*The Parish Council, responsible for maintaining the village green and our footpaths, also puts money aside to help support the church building, and gives a grant to the History Society.*

*East Devon District Council is responsible for the planning regulations, so largely funds the maintenance of the lists of historic buildings, and also is responsible for museums.*

*Devon County Council makes strategic policies which greatly affect which parts of the county are to be developed, and which are to be designated as Areas of Great Landscape Value, or as Conservation Areas (in built-up areas).*

*United Kingdom government sometimes acts on the advice of the Advisory Bodies it has set up, such as English Heritage, English Nature, the Countryside Commission. It designates National Parks and National Nature Reserves, Scheduled Monuments and Sites of Special Scientific Interest. It also funds the National Museums, and disperses funds from the National Lottery in many other heritage directions.*

*Various European governmental agencies, most notably the Council of Europe, take an active interest in the natural heritage (for example the Birds Directive, and Special Protection Areas) and have supported several significant charters intended to support heritage. (See Chapter Four)*

*At world level UNESCO maintains a list of World Heritage Sites, both natural and cultural, and also supports many conventions, as well as the list of World Heritage in Danger.*

In all these cases, in a democracy, there is a theoretical convergence between the heritage needs of the community being represented and the policies of the government, but modern research consistently demonstrates that the people-oriented interests of communities get lost as the formalities of government take over. Even at the parish level it cannot be assumed that the views of the people and the views of the Parish Council necessarily coincide. Governments, therefore, must be taken as a separate market for heritage, and often the one with the deepest pocket.

On occasions, governments are pressed by political needs and use heritage as an instrument to control national identity. This is not an innocent matter and can be direct and serious. The library in Sarajevo was destroyed during the recent war, because it acted as a symbol of the pacific coexistence of three separate cultures. Other examples show how heritage is used by different groups for political objectives. October 1997 saw the opening of the Museo Guggenheim in Bilbao, for which occasion the local authorities asked Madrid for the loan of one picture for the new gallery. This was Picasso's *Guernica*. Technicians and curators at the Museo Nacional de Arte Reina Sofia suggested it should not be moved, having serious problems of restoration and conservation. The discussion was not technical, however, but political, *Guernica* being seen by some as a symbol of the Pais Vasco. In fact the picture, painted in 1937 to report the bombing of a small Basque town by the Condor Legion was intended by Picasso as a statement against violence, concerning not only the Basques, not even only the Spanish, but all people.

## Visitors

In discussing the markets for heritage many people jump to the conclusion that the market is tourism. Tourism is certainly part of heritage—not least because tourists can be the best source of funding. There is a complex and frequently difficult relationship between those whose interest is largely in the conservation of the heritage and the tourists who come to see it. But there are many different kinds of tourist, and then there are many other kinds of visitors who cannot be classed as tourists at all. Different segments of the tourism market are concerned with different heritages. There will be tourists visiting the area purely to visit archaeological remains. There will be others solely interested in lying on the beach. Most, of course, will do a bit of both, according to the weather. There is a real danger of regarding the former as a 'heritage tourist' who is almost 'on our side', and really interested in conservation. The beach parties, however, cannot be accused of eroding the archaeological remains, but they are often very interested indeed in maintaining the cleanliness and quality of the beach.

Apart from the variety of tourists there are many other visitors. For most heritage sites there is a local trade, people who come to this site time after time, not any longer because they want to learn about it, but just for a picnic, or for a walk, or as the regular place to take visitors. The Duke of Bedford long ago realised that the main reason why people visited his country house was because they had a car, and they wanted somewhere to go in it (Bedford 1971). Then there are the pilgrims—those who visit a site for reasons which have more to do with the spiritual and aesthetic rather than simple sight-seeing. Whether tourists and pilgrims can mix is a major issue for some heritage managers, not only in cathedrals but also in art galleries. Motives for visiting are always difficult to disentangle and usually mixed. There is plenty of evidence that mediaeval pilgrims were not always deeply spiritual; nor were 18th-century gentry on the Grand Tour of Italy solely interested in their intellectual gratification. Today's heritage tourist is just as complex a person.

Other visitors are attending a conference, or arrive as educational parties, whose needs are quite different from tourists, but like them and like the governments, they will be outsiders, if not geographically then mentally. Educational parties cause a major problem for heritage managers, not only because they may not be there voluntarily, but also because there is a deep seated presumption in many countries, that education ought to be free.

## Academe

Heritage is clearly an arena of dispute and dissonance. Academics usually try to take a lofty view of such difficulties, and even in the heritage arena academics like to imagine themselves in the emperor's seat acting as arbiter and referee. This is quite the reverse of the truth. Academics are deeply involved in heritage—they are down in the arena with the other gladiators. Academics are often responsible for discovering new heritage (i.e. recognising the heritage value of something), and this is a proper purpose of research. Art and architectural historians do this as their daily task. Recently Judith Roberts discussed the English suburban garden of the 1930s (Roberts, 1996). That article is part of the process by which such gardens become heritage. Academics also are the ones who need to conserve the material artefacts of our culture, and indeed of nature. When we ask 'Who is heritage for?' the answer very often is that it is for scholars. The great collections in our museums, in our zoos, and the listed buildings in the streets are there, at least in part, to provide the relevant disciplines with things to study. Each gallery in a museum is looked after by a curator from the appropriate academic discipline. There is a danger that our landscape can also become divided into galleries—a few hectares for the archaeologists, a national park for the geographers, a nature reserve for the ecologists, and a few streets for the architectural historians—each discipline guarding its own outdoor gallery and keeping it safe from the depredations not only of tourists but also from other disciplines. Thus it is sensible to treat academics as just another market for heritage, except that, unlike all the other market segments for heritage, academics do not often expect to pay for the heritage, and sometimes even seem to take delight in despising anyone who does!

Conflicts both within and between all these categories of market are endemic to the nature of heritage. The question 'Whose heritage?' always receives multiple answers.

### Exercise Five

Select a major heritage site (perhaps a UNESCO-recognised World Heritage Site) and discuss the various stake-holders. Who regard the place as 'their' heritage, and how do their various views differ and conflict?

*Example. Stonehenge, in Wiltshire in southern England is without question a major prehistoric site. There is an enormous literature about Stonehenge, not only about why , when and how it was built (though there are many unanswered questions) but also about how it has been perceived throughout history by all sorts of different groups for their own purposes. Very often the functions attributed to the original Stonehenge builders tell us more about the people making the attributions than the original builders. The 19th century thought it a druid temple; the 20th century thinks it is a computer!*

*Archaeologists are the prominent academic stake holders, although it has now been so studied that it is difficult to imagine what else could be discovered from the actual site—we have archives of drawings, plans, radar plots. Any archaeologist working on Stonehenge really does not need to visit, not until there are completely new tools for excavation and measurement. Until then probably the best management for Stonehenge will be to protect it from the weather, from tourists and from everyone else. It might be best to bury it under a mound of inert sand, so that whenever we do have new tools we can dig it up again. Educational parties, however, do need to see it. Only so can the scale of the monument be imagined. Only so will children appreciate the technology of the peoples who erected it. Only by inspiring these children will there be any future archaeologists.*

*Then there are druids and others who feel that this is their temple. Being kept 100m away from the stones by a wire fence is, they would say, equivalent to Catholics not being allowed into St Peters. Every summer they set up camp as close as they can. Being very clean people they dig good deep trenches to act as latrines. This does not please the archaeologists!*

*Then there is the Highways Agency. Faced with a major tourist attraction within 500m of a major highway, and in clear view (the A303 from London to the South West), they have a problem. They claim there are accidents on this stretch of road because of people looking at the stones, and they cannot widen the single road into a dual carriageway because the whole area is a World Heritage Site and there is underground archaeology everywhere. They propose a tunnel.*

*Tourists visit the site in plenty. There is interpretation to help them imagine the site as it was completed. The interpretation does take scrupulous care to point out that everything is hypothesis, but it still offers all the legends as well. Perhaps many of the visitors would be happy to have it rebuilt!*

*Then there's me. I live 100km from Stonehenge and 200km from London. The sight of Stonehenge tells me I am half way, and those great stones rising up and brooding on the hill on the north of the road is important to me. I have never actually been, not since I was a child, and I do not contribute to its upkeep other than through my taxes, but it remains part of my life.*

## Heritage as Process

We have already suggested that Heritage is more a Process than a Product. Possible heritage is all around, and can come into the process given the right circumstances. A fundamental element of change is the development of self-consciousness. Recognition is essential - things are not heritage until recognised as such.

### Heritage Formation

How does something become heritage? There are several different routes to recognition, including:

#### Obsolescence

As technology progresses, so things become obsolescent. Many of these become heritage. A very obvious example which is occurring at the present time is the typewriter. Most of us these days use word processors, and my typewriter gathers dust under the desk. Milk stands, structures made of concrete blocks and railway sleepers that stood outside every farm yard, and on which the farmer placed the churns of milk for collection are, now that milk is collected in bulk by tanker, being recorded. This obsolescence is responsible for huge parts of our heritage, from thatched cottages to sailing ships. This leads to the interesting proposition that the faster technology progresses, the more heritage is produced!

**Survival and rarity value**

Many things have simply survived for a very long time. Unlike typewriters, stone age flint tools did not become obsolescent in recent years. They are simply hallowed by age—their sheer survival makes them important. Most mediaeval churches are still used as places of worship; they are not obsolescent, but they are of sufficient age to merit conservation. Ancient manuscripts are in the same category.

**Artistic Creativity**

Some things are created as heritage—they are made to be collected. One very obvious example is those wonderful coloured postage stamps once issued by Vatican City or Bhutan, but now by every country, and which are clearly intended not for posting letters, but for the albums of collectors. Works of art come into the same category. Today, paintings and sculpture are made to be collected either by private or public patrons. Some literature and music is also intended to be culture rather than simply to make money. There are now many shops which advertise 'collectables'. Sometimes these are antiques, or at least second-hand, but quite often they are newly made.

**Association**

Some things become heritage because of their association with people or events. Chopin's birthplace near Plock, in Poland, has many more visitors than its modest architecture would suggest. Sometimes the relationship between the place and the person is dubious or downright fanciful, as is the case with El Greco's house in Toledo. John Lennon's personal possessions fetch good prices in auction houses, as recently did the black hat worn by Yul Brynner in the film *The Magnificent Seven* and there are enough fragments of the True Cross still in churches throughout the continent to reconstruct Noah's Ark.

## *Recognition*

Whatever the reason for the object becoming latent heritage, waiting in the wings, there still has to be a recognition that this piece of heritage has significance. The latent heritage has to be called onto the centre stage to take its part. In order for this to happen the context has to be right. Not everything which is obsolescent has been recognised as heritage; indeed typewriters still await their call! This is where research is of great importance. Judith Robert's 1996 study of 1930's suburban gardens demonstrates that such things have a coherent and interesting history, and that they are distinctively English. That is perhaps enough to turn suburban gardens which survive from the 1930s, from the wings onto the stage. Scholars are for ever finding new examples. Commonly things may be 'rubbish' for about one and a half generations, before they become 'heritage' once the children are in their fifties.

Major shifts in politics may result in things which one administration has consigned to oblivion emerge once more. There have been plenty of examples in the recent history of eastern Europe. Indeed there are several large parks full of displaced statues of Marx, Engels and Stalin in east European cities. These now show signs of becoming tourist attractions in their own right. In Ireland by contrast there has been a more subtle shift so that the Anglo-Irish heritage can now, 70 years after Irish independence, be acknowledged. The same will surely happen in the former European colonies in Africa and Asia. Cecil Rhodes still lies in the Malopo Hills and the Trekker monument still broods over Pretoria. Queen Victoria still presides over 'palm and pine' in many a city of the former British Empire.

## Designation

The next stage for many heritage artefacts, including especially places and people, is designation, which is the stage at which the government sector usually gets involved. Most countries now have a large battery of various kinds of landscape and building designation. In Spain, since the Law of Spanish Historic Heritage in 1985, there are different levels of protection according to circumstances. There is a single designation for buildings, historical city centres and their surroundings, archaeological sites and natural sites, and historical gardens, which level gives  a major grade of protection; all these could be listed and and declared *Bien de Interés Cultural* if they have a great value for history, art, culture, nature.

The equivalent for the portable heritage is purchase. Listing, designation, scheduling of buildings is the best that can be done when purchase is not possible, or rather a fair price is beyond what the state would wish to pay. Of course, some buildings are indeed purchased by the state or local authority, or more frequently by a preservation trust, of which perhaps the most famous is the National Trust, though there are many others. As for mobile heritage, there are, in Reggio di Calabria, famous statues from a wreck offshore in the Strait of Messina. These were probably crafted by Greek sculptors in Alexandria and may have been *en route* for Marseille. Which nation's heritage is that? Even immobile heritage can have such difficulties. Fishbourne Roman Villa in southern England was built by Greek craftsmen for a Romano-Celtic chief. On which countries' lists of heritage should it appear—Greece, Ireland, Italy, United Kingdom?

There are also concerns, of course, of the extent of listing. The use of listing to impose conditions which are unreasonable and which the listing authority certainly is unwilling to carry out on its own buildings is often suspect. There are other problems with designation. As with design (the two words have the same root) the object is made self-conscious, a commodity. This may not be a problem when the object was always intended for show, such as a sculpture, a palace, a symphony, but when a folk-song, or a suburban garden, or a vernacular cottage is designated, and becomes a self-conscious show-piece, it may lose the very charm for which it was famous.

## Conservation

Designation will usually involve conservation or even preservation. The designation itself will usually lay down guidelines for the extent of repair, restoration and rebuilding which is acceptable. In the case of sites there is often some dispute over exactly which parts of the site, which buildings, are to be conserved. Where places were built over long periods, which period is to be the 'right' one? For many architect-designed buildings this causes no problems, but many buildings and all gardens developed over a long period of time. In the case of much industrial heritage, for example transport, almost every part of the vehicle will have been replaced. In the case of events, re-enactments will be organised; in the case of art, retrospective exhibitions; in the case of music a series of performances. Even people are routinely conserved, though by proxy, by inheritance, through portraits, through possessions (as with saints' relics) and through the giving of inherited titles.

## Interpretation

The place must now be interpreted, though which comes first, the interpretation or the visitors, is a difficult question. The inevitability of interpretation is quite a recent practice. Most old museums restricted themselves to labelling and would not necessarily regard visitors as an essential part of their job, which was to take care of the material remains of the culture. Nowadays most museums regard their primary task as an educative one. In many areas of the built heritage, however, interpretation is very rudimentary. Not many towns have easily available information on all the buildings which are listed. However, buildings which are open to the public are nearly always expensively presented—guides, possibly in costume, leaflets, panels, an Audio-Visual show, items to be touched and felt and, of course, a gift shop. It is entirely possible to consider that the interpretation actually becomes the heritage. More and more museums have only graphic displays, no real artefacts at all. Quite frequently the building itself is lost below the weight of interpretation. In any case as we move forward into an era of virtual reality, the place can be dispensed with, as anyone wanting to see the cathedral can be given the headset through the post. This will save a great deal of wear and tear on the real place.

## Loss

Virtual reality is certainly one way in which the circle may be completed. As the interpretation becomes what people want to see, then the original product can be quietly separated. This may mean that it can be returned to another use, or multi sold to another type of market, or simply abandoned. Certainly heritage is lost behind the façade of virtual heritage. Other times there is physical loss, either through human action, as with the destruction at Dubrovnik, or through erosion, which is a particular problem on some delicate nature reserves, on coastal sand-dunes for example or in Shakespeare's birthplace. Other heritage sites may be closed, as were the caves of Lascaux, to prevent further erosion by human breath.

Still other heritage is consigned to oblivion. All heritage organisations will stress certain aspects and suppress others. The French government largely ignores the Maginot line, (Smart, 1996) although local populations have found it and are restoring it despite government aloofness. Newly independent nations often sweep away their hated past, or reclaim it for themselves. The countries of eastern Europe are probably as busy eradicating the heritage of the last 50 years, as they are in rediscovering their older heritage. Human beings have always invented facts, changed dates and names and altered or invented heritage.

Can vulgarisation be another type of heritage loss? There are certainly places whose visitor numbers are so great that any real impact that they have had is lost. The gigantic works of nature seem to stand up to tourism and television better. Having seen Niagara many times in brochure and film, the real thing is still stupendous. Churches may be the most susceptible to the loss of the expected and intended experience through the weight of numbers.

## The Fourth Dimension - Time

Kevin Lynch wrote a book called *What Time is this Place?* (Lynch, 1972) and one cannot study Heritage Management without a clear concept of the role of time. Heritage exists in the present, of course, so that the ethical concerns are always those of the present. We may re-enact Dickensian London, but we don't accept the violence, the racism, the sexism or even the tobacco smoking! So the past is inevitably sanitised for the present. Which past is the right past? In the case of buildings it is often possible to decide that the 'right' past, the past to which conservation should seek to return the building, is the point when the building was completed. That may be so for major pieces of architecture, but things are much more difficult when it comes to smaller vernacular buildings, and yet more so when it comes to gardens and landscapes. In any case we appreciate them in the present. When discussing period music, music played on 'authentic' reconstructed 16th century instruments, in a manner as close to that of the 16th century as possible, a music professor said 'Yes, but you are listening with 20th-century ears'.

Then there is the problem of the preferred period. Each nation, and many smaller regions, seem to have a preferred time—a Golden Age. In England the two preferred are Elizabethan (16th century) and Victorian (19th century), for the Czechs it is the period between the two world wars, for the French the time of Louis XIV, and for the Dutch the 17th century. Tastes also change. There is clear evidence that preferred landscapes have changed dramatically over time, (Howard, 1991) and that there are numerous people trying to conserve beautiful landscapes ostensibly to pass them on to their descendants. All the evidence is that the descendants will want something completely different. It is highly likely that we are busy destroying, with little thought, many buildings and other types of heritage, which our grand-children will wish we had kept.

## Exercise Six

This is where we begin to investigate the role of heritage in supporting a place's identity. Would you prepare a three-day programme for a visitor to introduce them to 'your place'. This visitor is a person from a foreign country of about your own age and interests, and this is their first visit to your country. You have three days (Friday, Saturday and Sunday) to make them feel that they have begun to understand how your place 'works'.

*Example. Day One:- I would start in town—in Exeter, a city with a Roman street plan and mediaeval walls which my visitor might well recognise. The 1950's buildings and plan would tie up with World War Two, when Exeter was flattened, and a visit to the Gothic cathedral, perhaps to hear evensong being sung. Shopping would reveal some famous English names, such as Marks & Spencer. Lunch in a town pub. Afternoon spent in the suburb, perhaps visiting some friends in a semi-detached house who make wonderful afternoon tea and scones (though she is Dutch!). In the evening we might visit the Red Lion public house in the village and try the local cider.*

*Day Two :- After a cooked breakfast we might go further afield. If the visitor were from an inland country we would go to Sidmouth, a seaside resort of about 1780 with some wonderful cottages ornée, with croquet on the promenade and cricket on the green, as well as a splendidly old-fashioned department store, and fishing boats. The alternative (one could do both) would be Dartmoor, a high granite moorland with Bronze Age stone circles and many other archaeological remains. Ideal for Dutch visitors!*

*Day Three :- A local day, starting with Church of England service in the parish church, and Sunday Roast Dinner. Afternoon is the village cricket ground (or rugby if winter), including tea of course. Evening is the Bell-ringers annual dinner at the pub.*

*Of course this is England as I wish it was, and what I fondly imagine it might once have been. It does still exist today—but it is highly selective.*

## Heritage in Wider Perspectives

### *History*

Heritage, as a disciplined study, needs to be quite clear about its relationships with its cognate subjects. The most obvious of these is history, and other historical disciplines which use different methodologies such as archaeology. A great deal has been written on this distinction, and historians are often disparaging about heritage. Indeed historians show surprisingly little interest, if the journal literature is any guide, in how history is presented in museums and other heritage sites, or in any other area than in books. We need to be quite clear that heritage is concerned with the present-day, though a substantial part of heritage is concerned with how the past is dealt with in the present day. Of course, there is also a history of heritage, as is dealt with in Chapter Two. Such a student might examine how the Romans preserved artefacts from the past, or, as in this text, how the ideas evolved which have led to our current thinking.

Heritage therefore uses, quarries from, histories, from things, from nature, from culture, to create something new for today. The heritage student is interested in the past only in so far as it provides materials for the present. We have to trust that our historians do their job with scholarship and care and provide us with a usable product. So history is merely one of the disciplines which studies the raw materials of heritage; geography, archaeology, history of architecture, zoology are other such disciplines. Just because economists spend some of their time examining car production does not mean that economics equals engineering. By the same token heritage scholars make no claim to be historians.

Modern historians are very aware that there is never a single truthful history, that in most cases there are many truths, and that historians too always interpret the past in the light of the present. There are real dangers with this process. The history which is used by the heritage manager is already only one interpretation of many histories. We should be most careful how we transmit that history further, through our interpretive techniques, as we end with an interpretation of an interpretation of an interpretation. Nor must we allow our understanding of the relativity of historical accounts blind us to the fact that there are still lies. Some things are not true, and heritage scholars, like all scholars, surely have a duty to avoid lies.

## Cultural Studies

Most heritage, certainly most which appears within this book, is culture, i.e. it is part of the achievements of the species *Homo sapiens*, so heritage studies could easily be seen as part of cultural studies. Certainly a great many of the major insights within heritage studies have come from cultural studies, but heritage managers are much more practical. Cultural studies has usually been an intensely theoretical, and heavily politicised, analysis of cultural artefacts, usually with very close links with the study of language and literature. Heritage studies has been driven much more by the need to do something with this artefact, this building, to conserve it. The questions of what the things mean come later. So cultural studies theories are tools which heritage managers need to be able to use. Certainly we need to ask of an artefact 'Why should we conserve it?' 'What meanings does it carry?' 'For whom?' 'Are there alternative meanings?' '*Cui bono*' but we are asking these questions for good practical reasons—the answers will help us manage the artefact more effectively.

One of the most important areas of cultural studies is the relationship between the High Arts, the Vernacular (Folk) Arts and the Popular Arts. This relationship is similar whether one is discussing literature, architecture, gardens, music or the visual arts. We need to be very clear that with post-modernism, the traditional arrogance of the aesthetic elite has been severely dented. A great deal of the canon of artistic quality can now be seen to be the taste of the rich and powerful as distinct to the preferences of the poor and weak. So high art is the art of the rich, and popular art of the poor. If we are intending to preserve the musical heritage of Europe should we looking to Mozart (High Art), or Sea Shanties (Vernacular), or the Eurovision Song Contest (Popular)? In the case of architecture is it great palaces, or traditional old cottages, or 20th-century social housing?

## Art History

Art History, like heritage studies, sits alongside cultural studies, rather than being a part of it. Once again there is the necessary emphasis on the objects under study. Museology as a discipline has tended in many countries to occur within departments of art history, and this has undoubtedly led to a problem—though one of which modern art historians are well aware. Too often objects have been displayed in museums (and indeed buildings themselves have been presented) as if their significance were purely aesthetic. At its most objectionable this led to religious or totemic artefacts from other cultures being presented on plinths or on gallery walls as if they had no meaning other than to western artistic sensibilities. Items became decontextualised.

Art historians construct history. They explain the value of facts and objects. They argue how and why some pieces have interest and others not. So they are important in the construction of heritage, although their ideas may not agree with the perception of heritage that other groups have. Art historians have a major influence in the world of the restoration of masterpieces. They direct attention to some artist or artefact with their researches and this becomes restored and exhibited. When a restoration is carried out, it sometimes provokes the discovery of new dates or techniques, and these dates change the history of the age and the painter. Nothing is completely fixed; things change and art historians play an important role in this moving game.

## Ecology

In many countries a distinction is made between the natural and the cultural heritage. Often the two areas are divided at the very top level, with nature being the responsibility of the Minister of Environment, and man-made heritage being under the Minister of Culture, or some similar title. Even where there is only one organisation (as for example with the National Park Service in the USA) there is still a great divide in the educational field between Natural Resource Management and Cultural Resource Management. In terms of conservation practice, there is some reason to keep the two areas apart, but when it comes to the theories of heritage conservation, to interpretation, to visitor management there is little significant difference. Natural heritage experts are very loath to surrender their scientific status. Of course, they are very aware that the difficult decisions of what to conserve and when and where are political and social decisions, but they have used their scientific authority very successfully in the past. Cultural heritage specialists are also perhaps a little jealous of the naturalist's ability to create new habitats, in some ways as authentic as the previous ones.

## Town and country planning

In several European countries the concept of heritage conservation has been strongest in two fields. One is the museum, and the other is the built environment. Landscape, nature and the less easily conservable cultural areas have been later in being accepted. The discipline of architecture has been involved only to a limited, and late, extent, largely because architects traditionally image themselves as a creative art. Consequently the significance of building new buildings has always been stronger than that of conserving old ones. This has meant that schools of town and country planning have often been the centres of heritage thinking, as at Groningen. The historic parts of towns, whether these are individual buildings or whole quarters, are usually those parts where there are major conflicts of interest consequent upon functions. This has led heritage studies to have a very clear idea of heritage being a function and having markets. Conservation has been viewed as competing in a difficult market place (sometimes quite literally). However, the concentration on buildings has also led to a concentration on conservation rather than heritage interpretation. Conserving the building has been regarded generally as more significant than communicating the meanings of the conserved building to the public. In many countries and cities there is a comparative lack of interpretive material concerning towns and buildings, compared with that in museums. Some countries are trying to tackle this problem.

Rural heritage is also perceived as of immense importance. In many European countries the rural areas are perceived as being the repositories of the true heritage of the people, a national ideal of a rural idyll, nationality played out on a very localised level. Local field systems and names, vernacular housing, local songs and dances and regional varieties of apple or grape, are carefully recorded and conserved, most meticulously by the new rural people, the urban workers who have moved to the countryside in recent years. The apparent stability of the rural scene is used to give a depth and root to people who otherwise possess none. There is nothing new about this invented rural heritage. There are plenty of examples of villages being built by landlords not in the local vernacular, but according to patterns of vernacular which derive from some other part of the country or even abroad.

## Tourism Studies

Tourists are only one of the markets for heritage. Nevertheless they are a large and increasing market, and probably the one with most money to spend. Certainly heritage tourism, along with green tourism, the equivalent concerning the natural heritage, is a major interest of those academics who specialise in tourism, and to a lesser extent of the tourism industry itself. Heritage managers certainly need an understanding of the visitors to the places which they manage, and that understanding has got to reach beyond a general contempt. The development of quite new sociological groupings has been dramatic in the last few decades, and visitors to heritage are changing. There is a major danger in much of the literature of defining both heritage and tourist restrictedly in order to denigrate the latter. Some visitors to the Greek islands may be more interested in the archaeological heritage represented by monuments; others may by more concerned with the geomorphological heritage represented by superb beaches. To class one of these as superior to the other is a common danger. Visitors often come simply as a place to go for the day—Woburn Abbey or the seaside, or the zoo or a shopping trip. Heritage is in a very wide marketplace. Tourism Studies has been in the forefront of such market-oriented thinking, and in the techniques of Visitor Attaction Management. An understanding of such ideas is vital to the Heritage student, but tourists are only one of the groups of people who 'buy' heritage.

## Exercise Seven

Has your town got an historic city centre? Describe its characteristics, situation, problems. What political, administrative instruments are used to control and design urban planning in the city centre? What kind of instruments are developed to manage the heritage of the city centre?

*Example. Zaragoza is a middle-sized city in Spain with a population of about 700,000, and its charac- teristics could be used as a model for the rest of the country. It is situated in the northeast of the Spain, in the middle of the Ebro valley, the largest river of Spain, so the town controls the transport between the north and the south-east coast. Its privileged situation was the main reason to found a town in 18BC. Zaragoza is a Roman foundation and has a long history. Also it has an historic city centre, although the town lost important pieces of heritage from Napoleonic times (War of 1808-1809) until today. As the Spanish heritage law establishes, it is the local council which manages the planning of the city centre with a special legal instrument called Plan Especial. This is a document which includes the extension of the city centre, its history and characteristics and sets rules to live, build and change form and function in this historic area. It includes also a list of scheduled buildings and zones where little can be changed. But sometimes the same local council changes the rules in order to build more modern buildings, because of the stress of economic groups or even the same population that want to have the same facilities the modern suburbs have. This provokes great confrontation among the council, private interests and conser- vation groups, The same happens in other towns and villages throughout Spain.*

## Sectors of Involvement

In most countries those involved in conserving the heritage can be grouped into four major sectors - International, Public, Voluntary and Private. There are, of course, very significant differences between, and within, countries.

### International Sector

At a world level the chief player is UNESCO, based in Paris. UNESCO's World Heritage List accepts both natural and cultural sites (which include cultural landscapes) and mixed sites. Sites can only be recommended for inclusion by the states within whose boundaries they lie, and those states undertake to legislate for the protection of the sites. Inevitably this leads to patchy representation, which represents debate between nations rather than an international view. One state may be more interested in a certain kind of site than another state. Within states there are different regions to be satisfied; as the finest cathedral in one region is listed shouldn't we inscribe the finest in our region?

### Exercise Eight

List the WH sites in your country. Suggest others which appear to be equally important. Why do you think they were proposed and selected? Find the ICOMOS committee for your country.

At the European level there are two major organisations. The Council of Europe, based in Strasbourg, is geographically the more extensive and is much the more active in heritage terms, particularly in the nature and landscape sectors and with buildings and monuments. They have been busy producing conventions accepted by most European countries, both in the natural and built heritage. There is little contact, however, between the two areas. They have produced a series of publications on the cultural heritage of each country.

The European Union is geographically less extensive, and so far has been much less active in the heritage area. There are important EU designations in the field of nature conservation, such as the Special Protection Area and the Special Area for Conservation. Programmes run under the Raphael scheme have been largely concerned with sharing conservation technical expertise between the member countries.

### Public Sector

The most important features of any governmental involvement with heritage is that elected representatives will usually take the boundaries of their jurisdiction to be true reflections of identity and heritage. They normally act as if two facts were true:

a) that their state, region, district is significantly different from other neighbouring states, regions or districts.

b) that, despite local idiosyncrasies, all the territory within their boundaries is cohesive and united.

#### Central Governments

In detail there are, of course, as many systems of heritage protection as there are countries. The most common division is that between a Ministry of Culture where policies for the

Arts, and for Monuments, are usually housed, and a Ministry of Environment which is involved with the conservation of nature. Landscape conservation is often split between those two. The degree of centralisation within the nation state also varies within Europe. In some countries, such as Germany and Switzerland, there are very few policies held in common at the national level. Nearly all power rests with the *länder* or cantons. Others, especially the small countries, are much more centralised— although the situation is quite common also where policy is made nationally but administered locally. British policy is often of that kind; policy is made in London, but is administered in Edinburgh or Cardiff, or even at local level.

## Quangoes

Another common device is to set up Quasi-Autonomous Non-Governmental Organisations which are funded by the Government to act as the Government's official advisors in defined fields. Thus the UK has devolved advice on landscape matters to the Countryside Commission in England. In France, Monuments Historiques acts in a similar way. These organisations do occasionally criticise government policy, but in the end are official bodies. Indeed the patronage employed by the government in appointing people to these prestigious bodies is quite considerable. This technique is also practised at local government level. Members of these organisations are not a random selection of the public. They are chosen for their particular knowledge, expertise, interest and influence. Collectively they are a very powerful way in which the 'great and the good', including many academics, keep influencing policies and their implementation.

---

### *Exercise Nine*

Study the QUANGOES that exist in your region/area/country and that have got some relation to Heritage. Analyse their characteristics—size, members, objectives, strategy.

---

## Local Governments

The distinction between national and local government is not always easy. There are special cases, such as Catalonia, or Scotland, which probably consider themselves as nations, whatever is the view held in Madrid or in Westminster. Otherwise local governments, of which there may be many levels, act in ways analogous to those of central governments, within the powers allowed to them. Elected representatives will tend to support the boundaries of the place which elected them. An elected representative on East Devon District Council is almost certain to consider East Devon a unified region with common problems and solutions. It is very doubtful if many of the electors consider that to be the case, and most are probably very hazy as to the boundaries. Just as collectors impose order on their collections, so people in authority like to impose order on the areas they govern, if only for ease of understanding. For those holding power at the centre, it seems absolutely natural to attempt to make all the provinces, counties, *länder*, roughly the same. So Napoleonic France produced *departements*, and modern Britain has divided huge Yorkshire and merged little Rutland with another county. Historic identities, which may be perceived by the local inhabitants as of great importance can be lost either accidentally on account of administrative convenience or deliberately to prevent there being too powerful local identities.

## Voluntary Sector

The voluntary sector includes non-profit organisations which are specifically involved with heritage conservation and interpretation. There are thousands of them, and in every country, including some very powerful organisations indeed, such as the National Trust in Britain and Natuur-monumenten in the Netherlands. At the other extreme are the Local History Societies and similar bodies which exist in almost every village. The interconnecting network of these is one of the most powerful systems in many areas.

Many such societies have local, regional and national organisations. In examining any society, there is an important distinction between those which are national organisations which have regional offices and local branches, the Top Down organisations and the Bottom Up organisations where local organisations get together to provide themselves with a regional or national umbrella organisation which speaks for them, but where the real power still lies at local level. In examining a voluntary society also it is worth discovering the source of finances and to consider the tensions within organisations. Very commonly there are tensions between a comparatively small group of activists, those who do most of the work, but who have less interest in increasing the membership than in getting things done. They are often opposed by those who prefer to have a very wide membership even at the expense of being less radical in their demands and activities.

In the UK nationally there are the amenity societies, such as the Ancient Monuments Society, the Victorian Society and the Georgian Group. Although they are entirely voluntary organisations, they have rights enshrined in law to examine and comment on all proposals for listed buildings and scheduled monuments within their area of expertise. In practice these organisations are run by scholars and other experts. They may be regarded as an outstanding way in which to bring expert advice to bear on particular detailed issues, or as another way in which academic experts control the heritage business outside the democratic process and in their own interests.

### Exercise Ten

Examine a voluntary organisation in your home area. You will need to look at its name, its history, its purpose (what it tries to do). Is it a campaigning organisation, or an owning organisation, or both? Who are its members? Is it Top-down or Bottom-up? Does it publish a magazine? How is it financed and what does it spend its moeny on?

## Private Sector

Lastly there are the profit-making companies, organisations and individuals involved in the heritage business, who often are the owners, especially in the buildings sector or in landscapes. A few of these companies are actually making their profit from the conservation of the heritage itself, but conservation is usually a secondary purpose for them. They occupy a heritage building either by accidental inheritance, or because it gives some prestige. Even the churches fall into this category; their possession of many of the finest buildings in Europe is comparatively marginal to their interests, and indeed there are powerful lobbies within the church which would advise shedding the built heritage.

| Outsider | Insider |
|---|---|
| Professional | Amateur |
| High Art | Popular art |
| Design | Non-design |
| Self-conscious | Unselfconscious |
| Aesthetics | Meanings |
| Artefacts | People |

*Table 1.*

## *Professional and Amateur*

At several points in this discussion there has arisen the potential conflict of interests between the notion of their heritage as understood by ordinary people (the insiders) and a rather different notion purveyed by governments and experts (the outsiders). This might be a useful point to refer to Table 1 where we can distinguish between two emerging attitudes to heritage.

The left hand column suggests the dominant ideas of heritage conservation. Expert professionals, probably with university training, decide on a range of objects to be conserved. They employ equally professional conservators to do so, and then professional designers, and marketeers, to decide on the target audiences to whom this heritage ought to be interpreted, and to produce an interpretive package so to do. The final product is inevitably a self-conscious piece of showmanship, a commodified package. This is exactly the difference between a group of farm workers singing their local folk songs, learnt from their fathers, over a glass of beer with no other audience than their neighbours, who would often join in, and the packaged folk group (possibly the same farm workers!) paid to stand on a stage and perform in front of paying audience. Many would find that the professional, concert hall approach which is entirely proper for Mozart or Verdi, is much less suitable for the folk song. The main charm of the folk song, its unselfconscious homeliness, gets lost in the context of the classical concert hall. Exactly the same is true of art. The gallery context for looking at great paintings does not work so well for children's drawings. In conserving a great palace or a cathedral, or a landscape garden, it is entirely proper to create a designed image, a corporate identity, to assist in packaging such a self-conscious piece of high art. Whether the same techniques work when the building is a small vernacular house, or a cottage garden, is quite another matter.

The two columns suggested above are not absolutes, of course. It is certainly possible for meanings to be considered by professionals, and locals are interested in collections of things as well as people. Nevertheless the duality is a useful one, and should be considered at many levels. The amateur approach is an entirely creditable one, and one which is frequently to be preferred to the professional. Where the purpose is to provide local people with an involvement with their local heritage, the amateur approach is much to be preferred. Make the exhibition about people of the village; to them the interest of a village house is who lived there, rather than its architectural glories. Use oral history and the local signwriter, not professionally designed boards. Host events where people do things rather than preserve artefacts. Commemorate events and local names.

## *Essay Project*

Inevitably this chapter has thrown at you a huge amount of material, much of it probably new to you. Many of the points made here in outline will be given much more depth later on in the course, and not all of the reading needs to be done before you proceed any further. This first major essay requires you to go and talk with people rather than do masses of reading.

Look at a defined place—one where you are an insider. This could be a rural area or a small town, or part of a city. Try and define what is the heritage there:-

*    Seven areas of heritage :- Nature: Landscape: Buildings: Artefacts: Activities; People: Sites

*    Five markets for heritage :- Owners; Locals: Governments: Visitors: Academics

*    Levels of Identity:- Local, regional, national, European,

This will certainly require you to talk to the local museum curator, tourists, owners, the representatives of local government, and of course local people, of many ages.

The essay should explain the variety of heritage available in your place and should not be more than 3000 words. You may use diagrams, maps and pictures of course.

# What you should know

You should now be aware that heritage is everything that people want to save, and that almost anything can become heritage. There are many different heritage sectors, and these relate to each other, and most heritage items carry a multiplicity of meanings to very many people. There are many different people who have a stake in the heritage, and while the national governmental, professional interest is often the most powerful, it is by no means the most meaningful to many people. Above all, heritage is vitally important and almost always divisive. Wars are fought over heritage.

# 3. The Evolution of Concern for the Past

## Summary

This chapter is about change through time. In particular it will describe when and with whom an interest in aspects of the past originated in Europe. It thus raises the question 'why' as the justifications for preservation are made both implicitly and explicitly and shows how answers to this question changed and are still changing. Subsequently, the question 'how' is posed. The narrative begins with the enthusiasms of an eccentric but influential minority and ends with national legislative and organisational frameworks operated by politicians, government officials and professionals on behalf of a broad popular consensus. This juxtaposition of social and political cause and official reaction is a continuing theme worked out with varying time-lags and national variation throughout the different states of the continent.

## The amateur crusade

The questions we will be answering in this section are when, historically, did we begin to be concerned about the conservation of heritage as we understand it at the present time and, related to this question, who initiated this concern and why did it occur. These are historical questions and can be answered by looking back into the past. The division of the past into eras or periods is, of course, itself a device imposed by the present as an instrument for simplification and understanding.

### From antiquity to the 17th century

This stage is characterised by an irreverent attitude to heritage; there is little historical consciousness of the past, as demonstrated by more importance being given to contemporary architecture and buildings than to their forerunners, leading to the dismantling of numerous buildings in order to put up new ones—the original St Peter's church in the Vatican was raised with stones from the Coliseum, and Hagia Sophia, Constantinople, was also built with pieces from numerous Roman temples. Throughout this period, however, certain differences in attitude are evident, at least amongst the groups we know about from documentary evidence—the powerful (institutions such as the Crown, the Church and the nobility). There was also the birth of the incipient collection of works of art (paintings, sculptures, royal collections) which are the starting point of a future collective consciousness aimed at safeguarding its heritage. At this point, the prevailing criteria for the selection of objects to be included in this legacy are pieces considered special for their unusualness, their value as curiosities and art from classical antiquity. The highest value, especially from the Renaissance onwards, is placed on the chronological criterion; up to, but not including, the Middle Ages.

## *The intermediate stage – the 17th and 18th centuries*

This period witnesses the appearance of an appreciation of the value of city and urban spaces, at least in the eyes of the state, which recognised that buildings and works of art lent prestige to a city and, by extension, to the prevailing powers and that they also attract travellers. Here begins the indirect and subconscious economic appreciation of heritage. This increase in awareness would be translated into the important Baroque interventions in European cities for example the renovation projects of the Place Royale or Place des Vosges in Paris, the Wren rebuilding of parts of London after the fire of 1666, or the many German cities reconstructed to reflect the prestige of their rulers.

The royal collections are perfected at about the same time, with the criterion of ordered collections of works of art (the idea of artistic value appears; its artistic or aesthetic quality) and reflect the taste of their patron and the times. Connected to the conservation of these pieces, the first steps are taken in the restoration of works of art. Simultaneously, the first guidelines for the protection of heritage appear and, in the 18th century, the first purpose-built museums are created to house these pieces (or to isolate them from daily life), as the idea materialises that they are bound by different rules from the rest of human and natural objects. Preservation presupposes listing and cataloguing, imposing an external taxonomic structure of logical order. This period witnessed the birth of antiquarianism for historical artefacts, in parallel with similar movements in archaeology, anthropology, geology and botany, (Linnaeus published his *Species Plantarum* in 1753). It is noteworthy that the most recent tendencies in museums lean precisely in the opposite direction, returning the pieces to life, and their original place context, such as for example the call to return the Lindisfarne Gospels to north-eastern England.

The era ends with a profoundly important historical phenomenon which serves as the transition to the modern world—the Enlightenment, with a redefinition of the concept of culture and a new interest in the past and, consequently, in its material remains—monuments—which, for two centuries would give a concrete meaning to the concept of heritage. From the Enlightenment onwards, throughout the next century, scientific histories begin (the history of art and archaeology amongst them, often promoted by the State, Charles III of Spain promoted the archaeological excavations in Pompeii and Herculano) and as a result of study—the systematic cataloguing of works of art from the past and the definition of the styles and periods in art, there appears, for the very first time, the awareness that all historical periods have a beginning and an end, and leave behind a material witness to their past. Of course not all historical periods merited the same interest, and the division into periods helped to separate what were regarded as important (mainly the Classical) from the unimportant (the Dark Ages) and thus which art or building was to be regarded as worth preserving.

Also in the 18th century there developed an incipient awareness of the value of nature, a love of the countryside which would be deepened by Romanticism and which is the forerunner of the concept of natural heritage and of landscapes. On the other hand, historical phenomena such as the religious and dynastic wars on the continent, the French Revolution and Napoleonic wars and the beginnings of the first Industrial Revolution all involved very serious destruction of material heritage, but at the same time generated a reaction in which heritage became valued as a collective good, owned by society to be enjoyed by all. The idea of a national heritage which belongs to all citizens and which should therefore be protected on their behalf by the State, was born with the French Revolution. The collapse of Europe's absolutist Ancien Regimes involved episodes of vandalism and destruction of symbolic monarchical or ecclesiastical property as one past was firmly rejected. The new concept of state and citizen, however, itself required a past for its legitimation and the modern concept of heritage was formulated. Jean Baptiste Mathieu defined the essence of heritage in a speech to the French House of Deputies of the First Republic in September 1793, referring to everything which gives 'a sort of existence to the past'. In the following year Father Gregory defined the opposite concept, that of vandalism, declaring that, 'the barbarians and slaves detest the sciences and destroy artistic monuments; free men love and conserve them'. From this point onwards, Republican virtue is allied to an interest in the arts and the freedom to destroy, which had reigned during the most violent period of the Revolution, gave way to the freedom to conserve as a demonstration of equality between citizens because all of them would now be able to enjoy the national heritage on equal terms. Without doubt, the French Revolution marks a turning point in the understanding of heritage.

## The 19th century

There have been two centuries of work on monuments, with a systematic, institutional, legislative and cultural effort to build a concept of heritage through the practice of restoration, reflected in documents of intent called International Charters to which states and professional organisations become signatories. The 19th century reaffirmed and spread the idea that heritage was the footprint of the different peoples conveying a sense of ethnic, social or national identity. The monument was seen as an historical document of the society it belonged to: it was a symbol of collective identity and buildings are therefore restored for their particular importance to each society.

The Monuments Commissions created in France after 1790 were quite rapidly copied in Spain resulting in national protective legislation and the restoration by the state of many medieval cathedrals, such as San Juan de la Peña in Huesca, birthplace of the Aragonese Kingdom and Santa María de Ripoll in Catalunya.

An additional circumstance which would decisively affect heritage, as every other aspect life in Europe, was rapid industrialisation and its associated urbanisation. The age of revolutions, whether economic, social, or political had an impact upon heritage which was equally revolutionary. Very rapid change in almost all aspects of life led to both considerable destruction of the monuments, buildings, landscapes and urban patterns of the past but also in reaction a perceived need to maintain some link with the past as an anchor during a period of fundamental instability. The combination of artistic romanticism and political nationalism led, among other changes, to the creation of the great European national museums and art collections in which objects are kept as isolated symbols of historical memory. The first effective national laws for the conservation of natural heritage appeared. In addition, the concept of 'work of art', and therefore heritage, was widened to include the applied arts and artistic manifestations of non-western art (resulting from the large colonial empires). The consideration of periods in art, restricted until the neo-classical period to Ancient Greece and Rome, was broadened to the other stages and especially to the Middle Ages, thereby sparking a special interest in the conservation and restoration of the remains from that period.

The increasing valuation of the heritage of the Middle Ages, which was derisively called the 'Gothic' by supporters of classicism, was in part a response to classical architectural forms but was also strongly linked to many other ideas, These include Catholicism (the 'ages of faith') in opposition to neo-Palladian styles which were self-consciously Protestant, aesthetic romanticism, burgeoning nationalism and even the antithesis of rural virtue against urban vice. The development of these varied and complex ideas are often associated with particular influential individuals among whom the most well known are the trio of Viollet-le-Duc, John Ruskin and William Morris. In particular two basic, and ideologically contrasting tendencies developed, which were personified by these individuals. These were restoration *á la mode*, associated with Viollet-le-Duc and the Anti-restoration movement, associated with Ruskin and Morris. Although there were other ideas and individuals, a closer investigation of these three provides some simplified answers to how the previous century saw the relationship of people with history and its material manifestations and, interestingly enough, the controversies raised then rage still in many of today's heritage conservation decisions.

## Viollet-le-Duc

Eugene Etienne Viollet-le-Duc (1814 - 1879) was an extraordinarily cultivated man, restorer, architect, archaeologist and historian of French art and is one of the fundamental figures not only of the France of his time but also of Europe, owing to the importance of his ideas as represented in such famous texts as the *Entretiens sur architecture* or the *Dictionnaire raisonné de l'architecture française medieval*. In addition his many restoration projects, such as Notre Dame in Paris in 1857, or his most famous spectacular work on the reconstruction of the medieval town of Carcassonne in 1844, stand as monuments to his work and ideas.

Viollet-le-Duc began what was subsequently called restoration 'a la mode', developing existing ideas in the world of art at a time which thought that a building should consist of only one style (Louis Vitet, France's first monuments inspector, was the first to spell out these concepts), that restoration should consist of reintegrating the 'lost' parts in a search for the original style and that the criterion was the copy and reproduction of analogous elements (Prospero Merimée, France's second inspector of monuments, and great friend of Viollet, was the author of texts explaining this idea). This context helps us to appreciate better the well-known lines by Viollet in his 'Restoration' article published in the *Dictionaire raisonné de l'architecture française medieval* (Paris 1854):

> 'Restoration', both the word and the thing are modern. To restore an edifice means neither to maintain it, nor to repair it, nor to rebuild it; it means to re-establish it in a finished state, which may in fact never have actually existed at any given time.

The basic idea, therefore, of mimetic or 'a la mode' restoration is that the architect can and should complete the building to leave it in its original state and style, returning its purity, which implied the possibility of removing the additions of other epochs and filling in the lost parts with pieces copied from the same building or others of the same period. This was not, however, the product of an architect's whim; it was style, not matter which was important for 19th-century society and so the criticism of false and pastiche which have been directed at the movement's interventions should be seen in the light of the antagonistic confrontation with the conservation tendency or viewed relatively from our own, contemporary, perspective, when we have already accepted Cesare Brandi's principle that the work of art, the cultural object such as it is conceived today has a threefold value—historical or documentary, artistic or aesthetic, and material; each should be respected in all its integrity.

The difficulty of course lay in determining what was the 'pure' or 'proper' style. Consequently many buildings restored in the 19th century in the Violettian manner, such as those by Gilbert Scott in Britain, or Cuypers in the Netherlands, have been re-restored a century later as interpretations, or just artistic fashions, have changed.

## John Ruskin

Confronting Viollet were John Ruskin and William Morris, both moving spirits behind the Anti-restoration movement, a precursor to a more scientific and respectful way of conserving heritage, an almost ecological school, one might say. For the English Romantic writer and propagandist John Ruskin (1819 - 1900) restoration meant the greatest danger to a building which, from the perspective of the Romantic concept of the ruin, are like living beings; they are born, grow and die, and should be allowed to complete their biological cycle.

> 'Restoration' means the most total destruction which a building can suffer: a destruction out of which no remnants can be gathered: a destruction accompanied with false description of the thing destroyed. It is impossible, as impossible as to raise the dead, to restore anything that has ever been great or beautiful in architecture. ('The Lamp of Memory' chap. 6, in *The Seven Lamps of Architecture*, London, 1849).

Ruskin would only admit maintenance and conservation, an idea which is considered a priority nowadays in the conservation of heritage 'Take proper care of your monuments, and you will not need to restore them.' Amongst other values, Ruskin underlined the value of the patina, of the quality of atmosphere and the surroundings of the object and his final posture was, in the face of decisive activity in 'a la mode' restoration, to be that of non-intervention.

## William Morris

Ruskin's ideas were enlarged upon, defended and adapted to some degree by William Morris (1834 - 1896), famous politician, philosopher, critic of English art and artist himself who stood out in the defence of heritage and denounced the stripping out of buildings and excessive interventions (in the manner of Viollet) through the Society for the Protection of Ancient Buildings which he founded in 1877. The manifesto for this organisation contained the proposal, already discussed by Ruskin, that heritage belongs to society, it is a collective possession for which we are doubly responsible; we preserve it for ourselves and also for future generations. Morris also reaffirmed in the text the need to maintain monuments instead of restoring them and the possibility of intervening in them only to make them safe and thus always differentiating the new from the old materials. Some of these new ideas, not well understood at a time when Europe was dominated by 'a la mode' restorations, were taken up at the end of the century by the Italian architect Camillo Boito (1836 - 1934) who started a new way of dealing with restoration, more scientific and respectful to all the building's values, in turn, the forerunner of contemporary restoration which builds its principles and content basing itself on the international charters.

More than a century later we can to an extent objectively evaluate the contributions of these pioneers. The questions that they raised have never been definitively answered. Restoration 'a la mode' often meant heavy alterations to important monuments but the patina of age has, to some extent, made these interventions more acceptable. In fact the 19th-century restorations have sometimes themselves become valued monuments to their own period. We should also remember that many notable architectural sites would have been lost had they not been restored. On the other hand Ruskin and Morris are responsible for the insistence on the importance of daily maintenance in the preservation of heritage as well as the concept of minimal intervention in restoration, key concepts in the present-day management by many official heritage management institutions.

### Exercise Eleven

The Violletian school had followers all over Europe; there is hardly a medieval cathedral or castle that remained untouched. There were undoubtedly 'a la mode' restorations of historic buildings in your country. Who carried them out and did they give rise to comments or criticism at the time? Have they been subsequently re-restored? Should buildings be preserved 'as found' even if they are only ruins? Is the ruin itself a monument, a *memento mori*, more evocative than the original (some romantics went so far as to actually build ruins)? Or, conversely should ruins be restored to give a more accurate idea of how they used to look, how the artist intended they should appear (or how we think or hope they used to look)? Shall we replace the fallen sarsens of Stonehenge and straighten out the leaning tower of Pisa?

## The development of national frameworks

The essence of the following argument is that countries created national organisations, legislative frameworks and working practices to identify, preserve and interpret national heritage. Logically therefore each country could be considered separately in these respects. However as this would be repetitive and tedious, the following discussion will focus upon the general trends and policy reactions to them which applied to a greater or lesser degree throughout Europe. The detailed application of these in specific laws, structures and practices in individual countries is sketched in Appendix 1.

### A reluctant but inevitable intervention.

The success of the amateur prophets described above in mobilising sufficient popular support to provoke official reaction can be viewed in the context of urban history as a whole as something of an aberration. There are instances in the distant past where sacred spaces or buildings have been deliberately preserved as a result of their perceived symbolic values to later societies but these are exceptional cases and neglect, demolition and replacement was the normal fate of structures that had outlived their function until quite recently in most countries.

The assumptions in Europe about the physical conservation of buildings are not universally held. In Japan they have no qualms about constantly rebuilding significant temples and palaces so that the term 'historic monument' is likely to mean that it has been totally rebuilt every 50 – 100 years. These differences may be connected with the main building material and even the prevalence of earthquakes. A culture using stone or brick may be more intrinsically conservationist than one based on timber. It is the space itself that has been sacralised rather than any particular structure, it thus remains 'the ancient palace/temple etc.' however new the structure is.

The rapid industrialisation and urbanisation of the last 200 years may have created a novel situation as a result of the acceleration of the pace of change which fostered the unease articulated by the prophets of preservation, but the direct involvement of the machinery of state is explicable largely through the needs of the state itself, especially in terms of its own legitimation. Whether the European state created the idea of nation, or the nation shaped for itself a state, can be argued in detail but clearly it is in the interest of the nation-state to discover and propagate the idea of a nation and thus a national heritage whether expressed through national museums, galleries, official histories or monuments.

The paradox in this argument is that the liberal nation-state may have needed a national heritage but its dominant political philosophy presented a number of inherent obstacles to intervention for its creation. Some of these obstacles which existed and to an extent still exist, can be briefly introduced.

### The idea of private property

A central principle enshrined in the constitutional legislation and practice of the liberal state is the defence of individual property rights and the prohibition of sequestration by the state. The simple notion that owners can do whatever they wish with their property, including its neglect or destruction, placed a brake upon preservational intervention and indeed is still a major difficulty. An early solution to this obstacle, which is still largely dominant in North America, was for the state itself to assume ownership of properties it wished to preserve through free market negotiation. More subtly, property rights became more complexly defined to separate rights of ownership and use from those of disposal and change; and the concept of a public interest alongside the various private interests was introduced. These ideas made intervention legally possible allowing the state to place restrictions on change, impose responsibilities for maintenance and even confiscate buildings in the name of a national interest. However, only after the Second World War did most Western European countries have a climate of opinion favouring radical reform in a number of areas of social policy, including the introduction of much town and country planning legislation. For very similar reasons nature conservators found it comparatively easy to get legislation to protect wild species of animal, but much more difficult to legislate for their habitats.

### The reluctance and inability to divert public resources to preservation

Even if intervention had been legally possible it would still have been financially difficult for the liberal state to devote its resources of personnel and finance to this task; the maintenance of cultural property was seen as a private function.

### The reluctance to include the management of cultural activities within the responsibility of government

The strict segregation of the functions of government from those of private endeavour left most areas of culture, together with science and even education, to private charitable or profit-seeking agencies. The present situation where European governments, and their populations, assume that the state has a major role to play in subsidising and encouraging many aspects of culture is very recent and still tenuous.

Thus by the end of the 19th century although there was a considerable and influential support for the protection of heritage buildings and landscapes, this was manifested in private bodies such as the British National Trust (1895) or William Morris's Society for the Protection of Ancient Monuments (1882). Government action through legislation was either non-existent or, in the case of such occasional pieces of protective legislation such as those of the Napoleonic regimes in Belgium (1809) and the Netherlands (1814), ineffective.

## Exercise Twelve

Do you think art is the business of government? If so, how should governments decide which art, and which artists, should be supported? Do you think governments should decide what is taught, or commemorated, as 'history'? If not, who should? Which aspects of culture are the responsibilities of governments in your country and which are not? How is this distinction made? Does cultural policy favour a particular section of society? Why is opera subsidised by the state whereas darts is not? To what extent is national cultural policy overtly fostering the existence of a national culture?

## *The first phase—the establishment of inventories*

The first phase of intervention in most countries was the establishment of national inventories, that is simply drawing up a list of those buildings, landscapes or sites deemed worthy of preservation by virtue of their national significance. This seems ostensibly a simple, clear and necessary task. It also had the advantage of appearing to involve very limited costs with no direct long term financial commitments and few legal or political complications. In most countries very small government departments were established, usually within Ministries of Culture or Education with the commission to survey and then list structures which by this designation became 'listed' [Fr. 'inscrits'] monuments, a title which in itself carried no further implications. Revolutionary France had such a Commission for Art and Monuments as early as 1790, although consistent inventorisation did not begin until 1889. Belgium had a Committee for Arts and Monuments in 1835 and the Netherlands formed a department for the care of monuments (later Rijksdienst voor Monumentenzorg) in 1875.

Of course such a task immediately raised two questions, both of which it was then assumed were readily answerable, namely who was to perform this task and how was a building suitable for inclusion to be recognised. The answer to the first was the professional 'expert' and to the second was through recognisable criteria, of which the three most important were age and beauty, both intrinsic to the building, and historical significance, which was less so.

### Age

This is usually the paramount criterion. Survival through the centuries is in itself an attribute, probably indicates a degree of rarity and is some possible indication of enduring worth. Although buildings may be built, enhanced, repaired and restructured at various periods, age also remains a relatively easily determinable condition. Almost all countries incorporate age criteria into the legislation in the form of a minimum, usually 100 or 50 years. Therefore the chance of a building being listed in practice correlates strongly with its age.

In the UK, for example, buildings built before 1600 are almost always automatically listed regardless of their condition; those dating from 1600 to 1800 are usually listed, so long as they are substantially intact; 19th-century buildings may be listed if they are in good condition, largely unchanged and are especially interesting for some reason; more recent structures are only exceptionally listed if a special argument can be made for their significance.

## Beauty

This is of course much harder to determine objectively. Although in the Age of Reason there were thought to be clear rules of aesthetics, beauty has for many years been thought to be 'in the eye of the beholder'. In practice there may well be a general consensus at least among the group of taste leaders in a given society at a given time. The problem is that widely different societies may have quite different ideas about what is beautiful which will have consequences for the designation of international heritage. Even within a society the views of the professionals may not correspond to those of the ordinary people. Also taste varies over time. For example in the 18th century the consensus in Europe was that classical architecture was civilised and proper whereas the medieval world was 'gothick' and barbaric. It is worth remembering that wild mountain scenery was similarly seen as useless threatening wastes, and travellers to the classical cities of Italy would draw their carriage blinds so as to avoid seeing 'ugly' Switzerland. The 19th-century's 'dismal swamp' is today's 'precious wetland'. The most common way of avoiding the difficulty of debate was to erect a canon of 'great' artists or architects, and use such authorship as a shortcut to an aesthetic decision. Post-modernism has, to a considerable extent, undermined the entire concept of aesthetics and replaced it with semiotics, the study of meanings. Hence cultural theorists today may well not accept the aesthetic precedence of St Peters, Rome over a vernacular cottage.

## Historical significance

Finally the significance of the building or site raises different problems. This value lies not in the structure or space itself but is an ascribed value that someone, for some reason, attributes to it. As the reasons change, with shifts in the social, political or demographic context, so also will the value ascribed to the monument. This raises both difficulties and possibilities. On the one hand the management of heritage must contend with a continually shifting definition of what is heritage. On the other hand heritage can be created even when nothing remains except the abstract qualities of location. The significance of '... on this spot...' / 'Here x lived/died/slept...' does not depend on the attributes of the physical survivals. Places where intense human dramas have occurred seem to endow the sites themselves with evocative emotions. Sites of murders, battles, atrocities and the like may look unexceptional but once we mark them they become particularly sacred. Such designations privilege the past over the present. The building 'ought' to be kept just as it was when x lived there.

## *Exercise Thirteen*

If what we value as age, beauty and even significance can change through time, then which of our present heritage will later generations regard as not worth preserving and which aspects of the present that we now regard as worthless will future generations preserve as significant? Which buildings or sites in your area have become 'heritage' recently? Which have ceased to be so regarded?

However, with all these criteria the idea of the authenticity of the object itself is clearly critical. The fierce controversy discussed earlier between the 'restorers'' and the 'anti-restorers', and also today between those who focus on museum artefacts and those who produce theme park interpretations, all ultimately revolved around the question of which is the most authentic. Age, artistic provenance and historical significance can all be subject to two separate tests of authenticity for inclusion on the list.
1) The authenticity of the object itself. (Is it actually 'of the period', 'of the artist', 'the actual place where it happened'?)
2) The authenticity of the complete historical record. This is an answer to the question, 'does a new addition to the total collection of heritage increase its representative nature?'
Although in principle authenticity of these sorts being intrinsic to the building or site is determinable by anyone ('All who look can see'), in practice it confers power of decision upon the expert authenticator, who declares that 'this building is genuinely of the historical period', '... is by the specific architect', or '... is where this event actually occurred'. They thereby in a sense create heritage by this process of authentication.

## *Exercise Fourteen*

A little thought or investigation of the actual history of a building will reveal that authenticity is much more difficult to determine than might be expected. The very act of designating something as a monument can be seen as altering its status but also how we view it and thus such preservation subtly alters that which it is preserving. How important to your appreciation of a building, work of art or historic site is the idea of it being authentic? If the painting you thought was by Rembrandt or the building by Brunelleschi, and you discover it was not, does it matter? Why? If a building is declared to be a 'monument', do you view it differently from before?

It is also worth noting here that although these definitions of authenticity are dominant in the selection of preservable buildings and sites, there are other dimensions (see Figure 1). For example there is functional authenticity ('Is a church or a castle now used as a museum still authentic?'), contextual authenticity ('Is an authentic artefact or building that has been moved to a museum or a new location still authentic?') and, most important in the discussion of users later, experiential authenticity ('Does the user enjoy an authentic experience?'). The importance to management is that if there are a range of different types of authenticity, then there must be different policies for the preservation of different authenticities (Figure 2). Even the absolute converse of authenticity for many, Eurodisney, is a perfectly authentic, even archetypical, Theme Park, while visiting heritage sites, and fighting battles in period costume is an authentic part of late 20th century society.

A major assumption behind the task of creating national inventories was that the resulting list was finite and probably quite short. In other words the number of buildings deemed worthy of listing was easily and incontrovertibly recognisable as a fixed quantity of

| The authenticity of ... | | | | | | |
|---|---|---|---|---|---|---|
| Creator | Material | Function | Concept | History | Ensemble | Context |
| 'The hand of the master' | 'The original material' | 'The original purpose' | 'The idea of the creator' | 'The history of the artefact' | 'The integrity of the whole' | 'The integrity of the location' |

*Figure 1. Meanings of Authenticity*

national heritage, and that the task would be completed swiftly with little controversy and presumably the departments concerned then disbanded. That this proved to be wildly inaccurate is obvious from the ever-lengthening lists and continued operation of listing procedures; indeed most of the inventories begun more than a century ago are still in progress with no end in sight. Apart from updating the meagre information on many buildings, English Heritage have now decided to record types of site in succession; they are shortly to start work listing canals and other water-side features. In Canada the objects included in national heritage lists has been extended from buildings and artworks, to canals, rivers, and species of fauna and flora regarded as 'indigenous'.

Clearly we can conclude that heritage does not exist in finite measurable quantities waiting for someone to recognise it but is, in fact, created by the need for it, as much in natural as in cultural heritage, a theme developed at length later. If this be so then such lists will never be completed and countries will never run out of possible heritage. One advantage of this is that it is not correct to think of heritage as being, at least in general and in the longer term, in

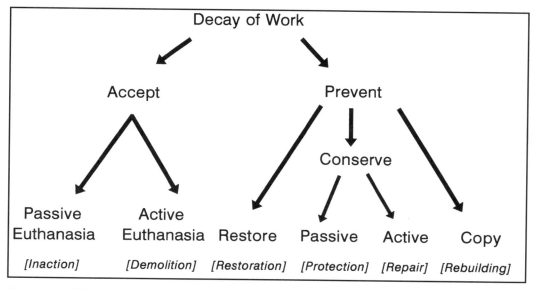

*Figure 2. Possible reactions to decay.*

limited supply. If we are creating heritage in response to demand then heritage planning is in essence a 'sustainable' activity, to use a currently fashionable test of political acceptability.

## Exercise Fifteen

Do you agree with the last paragraph? If so, then no list of monuments can ever be complete and we can never run out of heritage. How will you know when we have listed enough? If not, then how do you know when all heritage is listed? What buildings are still being listed in your area? Are there campaigns for places, whether natural or man-made, to be inventoried?

## The second phase - the conferring of protection

The step from creating inventories to conferring protection is so self-evidently obvious that it is remarkable that it took so long, as much as a generation in many countries. If monuments are to be listed and monumental status awarded then presumably it has some implications, moral if not legal, for the protection of the building; otherwise what was the point of listing? Officials dedicated to discovering and designating the national heritage will be motivated to press for protective legislation if only to justify their efforts.

The strength of legal protection offered varied between countries, from the absolute legal prevention of demolition or damage, through requirements for special consideration before development consent is granted, to, at its weakest, no more than delay allowing consultation, exhortation or public protest to occur. Similarly protection may extend to entire structures, to only their façades or appearance or even to the surrounding areas and vistas. A *champs de visibilité* of 100m was recognised for the highest class of monuments in the French national legislation of 1913, extended to 500m in 1962. British listing automatically includes the entire property including all outbuildings whether they are in themselves worthy or not.

The dating of the various national acts is described in Appendix 1. However, many of the early acts were extremely limited in their scope (such as Britain's 1882 Ancient Monuments Act or the 1913 French Law on Historic Monuments). Equally legislation, however strictly protective, depends for its effectiveness upon adequate inspection systems, the willingness of authorities to prosecute and the imposition of realistic sanctions. Much of the early well-meaning legislation was never in practice enforced and even the most diligently enforced regulations can do little if the profits from the redevelopment of a preserved site far outweigh the levels of punitive fines. Many countries failed to produce effective legislation at all. In the Netherlands attempts at passing a comprehensive Monument Act failed in 1910, 1921 and 1955. Many countries also have regulations to allow the demolition of structures which are unsafe or dangerous. Such regulations have frequently been abused by unscrupulous owners or developers determined to get rid of listed buildings.

## The third phase - the development of professional practice

The establishment of official national inventories, monument designation and statutory protection from arbitrary harm led to a growing intervention by public agencies. In the generation since the end of the Second World War in Europe three main trends have occurred in this field.

## The inflation of lists and the widening of criteria
- *From the old to the not-so-old.*

There is a tendency in most countries for 'forward creep' in the qualifying period for monument status. The first legislation was often for the ancient monuments of pre-history; then especially in the first half of the 19th century there was a growing interest in the monuments from the classical Mediterranean world; by the middle and late 19th century interest had been generated, largely by the European romantic movement, in medieval (gothic) architecture especially cathedrals. Only quite late in the 20th century was interest extended into the post-renaissance, Baroque, Palladian, and Victorian periods. Today the pre-1914 (Art Nouveau/Jugendstijl), interwar (the German Bauhaus or the Dutch Delftse School) and even post-1945 (International school) are receiving growing attention.

## *Exercise Sixteen*

The interest and enthusiasm of a minority usually runs well ahead of the official and popular consensus about what is preserved. In Britain for example, the 1882 Act preserved only pre-historic structures: this was extended in 1900 to the arbitrary date of 1714. However private pressure groups of an influential minority founded the Georgian Society in 1937 and much later the Victorian Society (1958) to raise the awareness of governments and public opinion. More recently the Thirties Society has renamed itself the Twentieth Century Society to allow for post-Second World War properties. What private societies and interest groups exist in your country to campaign for the recognition of particular periods of architecture and design?

In many countries a category of 'new monuments' (i.e. buildings too young for legal inclusion) but nevertheless worthy of preservation, has been created. There is even a Modern Architecture Movement that argues that at least a representative sample of buildings erected since the 1950s and 1960s should be preserved, whether or not we now regard them as beautiful, for their historical interest to later generations. DOCOMOMO is an international organisation attempting to protect buildings of the Modern Movement in architecture.

## *Exercise Seventeen*

One of the youngest buildings to be included as a national historic monument is the Economist Building London of 1986. Do you know a younger monument? Can you think of a recent building that should be protected now because it may be of value to later generations? More controversially do you think that we should only preserve the best of the past? Or should some ugly, poorly functioning modern buildings also be preserved as an illustration of our mistakes, so that the future may learn what not to build? If so, have you any candidates for such 'monuments to error'. The Czechs have retained a small section of the Iron Curtain as a reminder of the Cold War.

- *From the large and spectacular to the smaller and more mundane.*

As the lists grew they included more smaller, less obviously artistically meritorious, domestic structures. As such buildings account for a growing proportion of national lists a number of problems are exacerbated such as the financing of maintenance, the discovery of new uses, and the planning of extensive land areas.

---

## *Exercise Eighteen*

The inclusion of such buildings raises difficult problems of management policy. Frequently the fascination of such buildings is their constant and unself-conscious adaption to change. Is that continuous process of change now to be frozen? Are the techniques of interpretation and presentation, designed for large and grandiose structures equally applicable to more humble buildings?

---

- *From the monumental building to a broader definition of monument.*

The original definition of monument was confined to major buildings (especially cathedrals, castles and palaces). It slowly expanded its meaning to include many other types of building but also landscapes, machinery, utilities, vehicles etc.

One example of this extension of meaning was the invention of the topic, known in Britain by the curious term Industrial Archaeology (other countries use different terms not necessarily related to archaeology which it rarely is, such as Monuments of Industry and Technology in the Netherlands). Fifty years ago few people, apart from some eccentric enthusiasts, would have found industrial plant worth preserving. In Britain, however, in the course of the early 1960s the topic became increasingly of interest to a wider public. The country of the first industrial revolution focused upon this period at just the moment when de-industrialisation was first evident. It soon spread to the USA and in the 1970s to Western Europe. This led to a designation of, not only factories but mills, public utilities, machinery of various sorts as well as transport vehicles (ships, planes, trains etc). The initial focus upon technology was itself extended to the workers with such technology and to the whole way of life. The idea of Industrial Archaeology was seized upon by those who wished to present a sort of counter-heritage to the existing monuments which stressed the lives and actions of the rich, powerful and famous in society reflected in the cathedrals, palaces and stately homes. A sort of 'heritage of the common man', often stressing the hardships of working class life in industrial times became a theme of the interpretation of monuments, museums, theme parks and even whole towns. Not only did such industrial heritage offer an ideological alternative, it also offered an alternative economic development strategy for many 19th century industrial towns that were suffering from a decline in their previously important industries. The places that first experienced de-industrialisation where also the first to realise the heritage potential of their industrial past. The leaders in this now world-wide phenomenon were the textile towns of Northern England (such as Halifax or Bradford) or of New England (Lowell, Massachussetts).

- *There was also a recognition of historic landscapes and townscapes as monuments in their totality.*

This raises obvious difficulties, or at least a different type of preservation and maintenance.

People have clear ideas of what a landscape ought to look like. Landscape perception is strongly individual, influenced by class, nationality and culture. People may hold clear ideas, but there is rarely a shared view, except within small, if hegemonic, groups. Many assume that a particular set of landscape features is somehow 'natural' or correct for a particular region. A difficulty is that such landscapes have usually been produced by the actions of farmers and others over time. Changes in agricultural practice or in landscape management may lead to changes in such landscapes. Wetlands are especially prone to this problem: consider for example the Fenlands or Somerset Levels in Britain whose current, recently much valued, appearance stems from their drainage for agriculture in the 16th to 19th centuries or the grass-covered chalk 'downlands' of Southern England whose present open appearance was largely created by past sheep and rabbit husbandry. The maintenance of such historic landscapes may involve active intervention in natural processes in order to sustain what people regard as natural to the area.

Conversely delisting (removal of structures from lists) or de-designating (removal of protection from monuments or conservation areas) is extremely rare and tends to meet with severe political difficulties. Retrospective changes in the listing criteria to meet changes in contemporary opinions or values rarely happen. Major ideological shifts, as in the former Communist countries of Eastern Europe, may lead to some removal of memorials, re-dedication or reinterpretation of sites and even de-listing of monuments, but this is exceptional. Thus inclusion tends to be permanent which again encourages inflation.

**The introduction of categories of monument and levels of protection**

The increase in the lists led to a need for categories of status and thus different levels of protection. These may be in terms of intrinsic worth (grade 1– 3) or spatial scale of significance (unique at international / national  / local levels) or amount of protection / subsidy offered.

Figure 3 compares the monuments in various quality categories in four countries. The two important points are that although almost all countries do classify monuments, each country does this in different ways. Secondly there are enormous differences in generosity in such classifications; the Netherlands for example is much more generous is its level of award than the United Kingdom, where grants are not only small but unevenly available.

**Monument and setting**

There is an increasing awareness of the monument in its physical setting and in groupings of monuments. This focus on setting has various important implications:

- In the designation of structures for their significance to landscape, streetscape or roofscape, contributing to the 'cityscape' or literally 'picture determining' (in Dutch, Beeldbepalend) rather than their intrinsic value as structures in themselves. There is also a shift in focus from the building to the cadastral plan (i.e. to the actual patterns of buildings, streets and spaces) as the unit of preservation.
- In the necessary inclusion of large quantities of lower value structures. The growth of the lists and the focus on collections and settings almost inevitably extended some sort of protection to buildings whose intrinsic worth was low or whose state of repair was poor. For many buildings the location in relation to other buildings was the factor determining preservation rather than the intrinsic quality. There is a converse to this argument about the preservation of low value structures because they are in high value areas, namely the non-preservation of high value structures that by chance are in otherwise low value areas. Many would now argue that preserving an 'incongruous monument' (i.e. a carefully preserved monument which stands in the middle of a contrasting cityscape) is

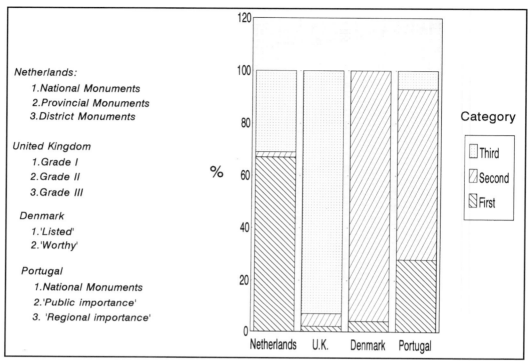

Netherlands:
  1.National Monuments
  2.Provincial Monuments
  3.District Monuments

United Kingdom
  1.Grade I
  2.Grade II
  3.Grade III

Denmark
  1.'Listed'
  2.'Worthy'

Portugal
  1.National Monuments
  2.'Public importance'
  3. 'Regional importance'

*Figure 3. Categories of protected monument.*

pointless and such structures should be either demolished or relocated. Sometimes, however, incongruity is deliberately intended as a means of underlining the significance of the monument. Think of Berlin's ruined, Kaiser Wilhelm Gedächtniskirche or Plymouth's church ruin, deliberately retained as a memorial to the bombardment in 1942 and now located on a traffic roundabout.

## Exercise Nineteen

Think of a case of an 'incongruous monument'. There are many examples of a small medieval church towered over by high rise buildings, a single preserved old house in the middle of a modern housing development, or even a monumental building now marooned in the middle of a busy traffic system. Would you argue to save it regardless of its setting, move it or demolish it?

•   In the possible demolition of non-conforming structures and/or replacement of missing elements. If structures are to be preserved because they add to the total urban or street scene, the converse of this is that structures, or parts of structures, that intrude into such scenes should be removed or demolished. This leads to the seeming paradox that effective preservation may almost inevitably lead to selective demolition.

## *Exercise Twenty*

This problem can lead in extreme cases to the preservation of an individual building being dependent upon the extent to which it fits the wider chosen period or theme of the area or town. A fine example of particular architecture may be cherished in one town for its rarity while being demolished in another as non-conforming. Can you find examples of, for example, good quality nineteenth century structures being demolished as non-conforming in a baroque or medieval town?

---

- In the necessary attention to the function of areas as a whole in addition to their physical form. When only a few notable buildings were protected little attention was given to their present and future function or to their effect upon the functioning of the wider areas in which they were set. But the expansion of areas obviously raises the question of use and function otherwise preservation will lead to empty buildings, which may be tolerable, and even empty quarters or inner cities, which is not.

These trends within the professional practice of monument preservation, together with an increasing popular awareness of the value of heritage, shaped a new political climate that led to a reassessment of organisations and objectives and ultimately new national legislation, in most countries of Europe, in the period 1960 – 1975. The degree of congruence is marked between for example the Dutch 'Monumentenwet' 1961, the French 'Loi Malraux' 1962, British 'Civic Amenities Act' 1967, Italian 'Urban Planning Act', 1967 and even Turkish 'Monument and Historic Buildings Act' of 1973.

The common features of this legislation were:
- the recognition of the value of 'ensemble' and setting.
- the consequent creation of the idea of conservation areas (whether *secteur sauvegarde* (France), Conservation Area (UK), *Beschermde stadsgezicht* (NL).
- the consideration of the implications for types of building and wider spaces.
- the consideration of the implications for the present and future functioning of buildings and areas.
- the switch in emphasis from architecture to planning and thus from architects as the key actors to town planners. *Denkmalschutz* (D) or *Monumentenzorg* (NL) was extended to *Stadtsbewahrung* or *Stadsbescherming*.
- the switch in emphasis to local area management in which form and function both receive attention in the same plans and policies.

## *The fourth phase - the balance of interests*

The experience of about 30 years of operation of the basic legislation in most countries can be summarised as the attainment and maintenance of a number of balances.

**The balance between law and practice**

The 1960 – 1970 legislation has proved in most countries to be extremely robust. Most subsequent Acts only extended or modified original laws. The accent is thus mainly on the operation and application of the laws rather than substantial new legislation. There has been a detectable move away from judicial approaches towards a more flexible management approach. There is little demand for new legal instruments. This shift has been encouraged by the development of conservation planning practice (and of a growing group of practitioners with working experience) and by an increasing integration of conservation with other planning matters at local level. For example the conservation of areas and the finding of suitable functions to occupy conserved premises almost automatically raises important issues of wider environmental, traffic and economic management.

## The balance between preservation and change

The early phases of the preservation movement were dominated by 'fire brigade' actions, reacting to the threats of others by *ad hoc* campaigns to 'save this building/area'. When the threats are many and there is much to be saved, then any preservation can be seen as meritorious. As more monuments and areas have been preserved a new balance was required between the preservation of existing structures and the preservation of the possibility for change. This is expressed either by the posing of the question, 'how much / how many?' or by appreciating the counter argument that preservation leads to fossilisation and eventually the prevention of new developments. Some would now argue that the capacity to change is now threatened and should itself be preserved.

## Balance of public and private interests

There has been a recognition of the roles of private investment and the importance of non-governmental interests alongside, or supplementary to, the public interest as articulated by governments described above. This is noticeable in many ways and for many reasons. The more conservation, the greater is the strain on public finances; the wider the scope of conservation areas then the more non-governmental interests are involved. This simple point has many implications for the role of property markets, and social changes resulting from the conservation process which will be considered in detail later.

It is perhaps worth remembering in this long account of government action that most preservation is performed and financed by individuals. The extension of conservation interest to areas containing dominantly small domestic buildings has placed the stress upon the private investment of, or for, owner-occupiers in the renovation and maintenance of the housing stock. Private individuals each investing small amounts in the maintenance of their own property for, amongst other reasons, their own capital maintenance is actually larger in total than all government expenditure for these purposes. Also much heritage can be profitably sold as a commercial product (and not only within the tourism industry). Therefore private firms can and do manage large sections of the heritage market. Finally the importance of the so-called 'third sector' i.e. voluntary/ charitable agencies, should not be underestimated. In most countries these agencies operate as land and property owners, as information and stimulation providers and as political and social pressure groups.

Thus a major task in the last few years has been to delineate the roles of each of these sectors and to attempt to establish partnerships, cooperation agreements, understandings or just local coalitions of interests combining official agencies at various levels, private owners and individuals, commercial interests and voluntary bodies. Attaining the correct balance in such a coalition of interests is clearly a difficult and politically sensitive problem that will arise in various guises later.

**Balance between designated heritage and other places**

There has been an increasing realisation that the conservation of specified buildings, areas and even landscapes has consequences for those not so designated. Resources of money and the attention of managers is always finite and thus it is not fanciful to assume that the preservation of the select will imply a lack of care or financing everywhere else. On the local scale increased attention and investment on the favoured side of the designation line may lead to less on the other side. Legislation or policy that treats all places as in some sense different but significant would be very difficult to devise.

**Balance between official jurisdictions**

As heritage exists at various spatial scales, as was discussed in Chapter One and will be examined further in Chapter Three, so its management is likely also to reflect the interests and values of multiple jurisdictional spatial scales. The question, 'who should do what', receives changing answers. There has been, however, a broad European trend towards devolution from national agencies to regional/ provincial and local especially city-scale authorities. Different countries, however, have arrived at different answers to the question of the appropriate scale for designation, financing and management of heritage, whether in the built environment or expressed through cultural activities. This spatial division of labour has implications not only for management practice but also for the sort of heritage selected and interpreted.

Although for various reasons the trends mentioned above are apparent throughout Europe, there is nevertheless a recognisable spectrum from the most nationally centralised to the most locally devolved. France has a post-revolutionary tradition of centralised government whereas the Federal German system devolves almost all heritage matters to the *länder* as does the more recent Spanish system of autonomous regions. In countries such as Belgium or Switzerland with distinct regional cultural differences, heritage is normally a responsibility of the sub-national unit (*Cultuurgemeenschap* or *Canton*). In most countries responsibility is shared between government levels. In Britain national legislation is generally locally implemented but the new sub-national governments in Scotland, Wales and Northern Ireland will almost certainly assume responsibility for most heritage matters. Equally some devolution of responsibilities for listing and consequently financing designated monuments and areas occurs principally as an economy measure as in the Netherlands since 1988.

## *The current phase*

It would be tempting to portray the final and present phase as a successful end-state. In fact this would be one type of 'progress thesis' interpretation that is itself commonly encountered in heritage, namely that the past, as related above, has led inexorably to the best of all possible presents. This is not true and the situation existing now is in all likelihood itself only a transition phase to something else. Interest in conservation has ebbed and flowed in response to changes in social, economic and political environments (Figure 4).

It is certainly not correct to argue that all threats to the survival of heritage buildings and artefacts have now been removed. Indeed about 5 per cent on average of all designated, and thus protected monuments are destroyed annually; many more buildings that are not yet designated but could, or should, be designated are demolished. Even more important is the damage caused to heritage areas by nearby developments or by aspects of modern life-styles. Landscape areas have been even more stressed with pressures on agriculture and on habitats.

All the legislation and working practices described above have not eliminated such factors as:

- the natural processes of decay. Atmospheric weathering, chemical decomposition, structural failure are all impossible to stop and can only be slowed down. Indeed modern life-styles have actually accelerated many of these processes substantially. (Cleopatra's Needle in London or the Parthenon in Athens has suffered more decay from atmospheric pollution in the past 50 years than in the preceding 1000).
- accidents, such as fire (Lisbon, Barrio Alto 1995), flood (Florence, Venice, 1966), earthquake (Central Italy, 1997). Some of these 'natural accidents' may be exacerbated by human actions which makes them more likely to occur or more serious when they do.
- the deliberate action of people whether for commercial profit or in pursuit of political goals.

If, as we have argued here, one of the main functions of heritage is that of identity, allowing people to identify with places, then the destruction of heritage may be seen as an important way to displace people; to break the link binding an ethnic group with a particular place. There is nothing new in the destruction of cultural features and historic monuments for political purposes; it is one of the oldest traditions in Europe. In modern times Göring ordered the German Luftwaffe to destroy every monument in the tourist guide book to Britain (the Baedecker raids). More recently in Europe we have witnessed attempts at 'cultural cleansing' as part of 'ethnic cleansing' in Yugoslavia (1992 – 1999). The deliberate shelling of the old town of Dubrovnik, the destruction of the Bosnia national library in Sarajevo, the destruction of the famous Mostar bridge are the best known examples but countless churches and mosques, and even their graveyards were deliberately destroyed by one group or another in order to remove the link of identity with another group.

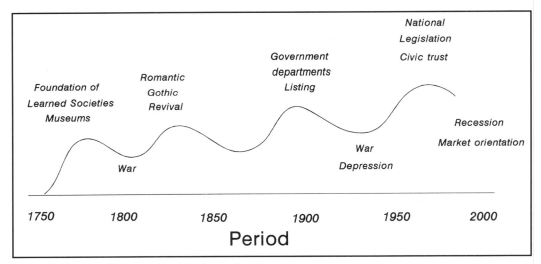

*Figure 4. The ebb and flow of interest in historical conservation.*

It must also not be assumed that all the rest of our world has the same concerns and protective management as Europe. Heritage planning as we have described it here is largely an invention and preoccupation of Europe and those other continents peopled by Europeans, or strongly influenced by European ideas. However we must constantly be reminded that this course focuses upon a small, and in many relevant respects, eccentric continent. Much of the rest of the world has cultural and historical artefacts, buildings and landscapes as worthy of preservation as the cherished heritage jewels of Europe. That they are not preserved is often a result of different economic or social priorities of such societies rather than any difference in intrinsic worth.

There are also enormous differences remaining within the countries of Europe and even within individual countries. There is a danger that because this chapter constantly generalises across Europe that the impression might be created that all countries have similar policies with similar results. This is no more correct in this sphere than in other aspects of social or cultural life. Some countries are just more 'conservation-minded' than others; they place a higher priority on the conservation of the built environment than upon other aspects of government expenditure. Figure 5, for example shows the total number of legally protected monuments and the average population per monument. Such a measure, crude though it is, with no indication of what is meant by the term monument or what such a designation actually implies, does show considerable differences even between otherwise similar countries such as Denmark and the Netherlands. Even within the built environment, there are marked differences between the types of preferred monument. While the British put an unusual emphasis on the country house, the Germans are particularly concerned about their market town centres.

Finally although we have been successful, however incomplete such success may be, in preserving buildings, areas and landscapes, we have failed to preserve the people that used them. To return to the form / function dilemma with which we began, we now have quite sophisticated management policies for structures and spaces, we have been much less successful in devising policies for conserving the activities, behaviours and ways of life that produced and inhabited them. This is almost certainly inevitable but raises sets of serious problems which will be discussed in Chapter Four.

However, all this having been said, in most European countries the problems now being faced by conservation planners are the consequences of a spectacular success. We have been, in many ways too successful and now face the problems of this success. These include:

**Increasing costs**

Although legal protection, or area designation, imposes few direct costs, in practice many costs are unavoidable. There seems little logic in giving legal protection without at least some grants for the maintenance and possibly repair of preserved structures. Also the design and maintenance of the public spaces and street furniture in conservation areas is likely to be a public cost. At a further remove, restoration and rehabilitation are a logical step. The problem with such cost commitments are that they are open-ended and long-term. It is deceptively easy for a government to accept the responsibility legally to protect a building or area but the costs of doing this are almost certainly an unknown and limitless burden upon the budgets of future governments. We may be passing on a valuable heritage to future generations but we are also endowing them with a less welcome inherited debt.

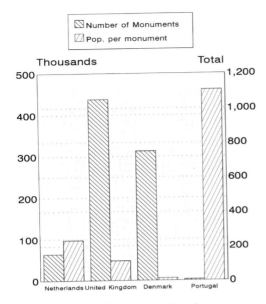

*Figure 5. Numbers of monuments in various countries.*

Solutions to these financial pressures on public budgets are sought in;

•    decentralisation i.e. shifting responsibilities to lower levels in the jurisdictional hierarchy, thus expecting local councils to fund costs from extra local taxes.

•    partnership/sponsorship. Public agencies enter into cooperative agreements of various sorts with owners or commercial interests who contribute to the costs out of private self-interest or altruism in the public interest.

•    privatisation. The disposal of public responsibilities to other non-governmental agencies who presumably will meet the costs from the profits earned. This includes voluntary and charitable bodies as well as private companies.

Heritage, of course, produces very large benefits as well as large costs. One of the problems is that the costs are often specific and public (for example the maintenance of large public monuments) while the profits can be either vague and general (the public good) or accrue to private enterprises, such as in the tourism industry, or to owners of property when it is sold. Perhaps the most important economic problem relating to heritage is how to devise means whereby costs and benefits can be balanced.

In the UK public expenditure, through the agency of English Heritage, is very commonly linked to providing public access. Commonly the owners of large old properties (often already wealthy) receive state subventions in return for providing public access which is frequently difficult to enforce.

## Exercise Twenty-one

Think about the most important historic buildings in your town or region. Who pays for their maintenance? Are they free to look at, go inside? How do tourists pay for the maintenance of what they want to see? Is there, or should there be, a special tourist tax or other means of subsidy?

### The increasing quantity of protected buildings and areas

This leads not only to increased direct costs but, even more important, the indirect costs of fossilisation or sterilisation. The growing danger is that space for new developments is increasingly limited and burdens and restrictions are imposed by conservation upon the functioning of areas. They may be just less efficient in their exercise of modern housing, shopping, commercial or transport functions. The ultimate danger is vacancy. The preservation of large areas of cities may in fact leave these areas empty, non-urban places and thus little more than open-air museums. Thus heritage may itself be a force helping to empty the central cities and reinforce edge-city developments with shopping malls and employment on the urban periphery. In an exact parallel, heritage landscapes are progressively more out of date in economic terms, and need increasing subvention to sustain them.

This situation may be no more than a bearable local inconvenience but attention has been drawn by some commentators to what can be termed the conservation 'time bomb'. The current age of building stock determines that a larger pool of potential preservable buildings will shortly exist. If preservation operates with a time-lag of about a century then the results of the European building boom in the period 1890 – 1914 will shortly become preservable. Using current criteria this implies an increase in conservational designations over the next 50 years by a factor of around five.

When monuments were rare and threatened phenomena then preservation was 'emergency rescue' and each structure saved was an advance. But now it becomes valid and necessary to pose the new questions of 'how many?' and 'how much?'. How many buildings, areas, towns etc. do we require for current and future needs? The answers imply a non-selection of some potential monuments / areas and are thus difficult to make as they involve choices that are not only politically tendentious but require a prediction of future tastes. Indeed the whole basis of heritage requires an attempt to predict the future; this is always difficult and in this case involves a prediction of future artistic taste as well as life-style. We can be reasonably certain that society in the year 2100 will almost certainly still value the older parts of Bruges or Venice, although how they will actually express this valuation is not so clear, but it may also value such 20th-century creations as Britain's Milton Keynes, Paris's Sarcelles or Amsterdam's Bijlmer. But if these, or a sample of them, are to be preserved then the difficult question is, 'which presently valued structures should be demolished to make way for the new additions?' The evidence from studies of landscape preference is not so much that some categories become unpopular, but that more and more are included among the popular. Seventy years ago few thought that farmyards were attractive; today they frequently figure on picture postcards.

Solutions are generally sought by focusing on use and adaption to re-use. Potential future uses become a criterion for designation, the idea of 'preserving purposefully', rather than a consequence of designation for intrinsic reasons. Equally it may be increasingly necessary to relax over-rigid restrictions of changes in the physical fabric to permit or encourage the continued profitable use of preserved structures. Where potential re-use is not a criterion of designation there can be real problems for owners. In the UK very large blocks of flats built in the 1960s are now being considered for listing, but the search for tenants is a cause for concern.

### Love them to death

The eccentric preoccupations of a small minority are now the conventional wisdom of a majority. The success of the prophets in teaching the general public to appreciate their pasts has led to the mass demands of people to experience their heritages. This is after all what was intended, but Ruskin or Viollett-le-Duc scarcely foresaw the results of their advocacy in the visitor numbers to the buildings and sites they propagated. People, their physical presence, breath and body warmth and also their modern means of transport, accommodation and sustenance are more destructive of the heritage they have come to appreciate than any other variable. The demonstrable proof that many centuries of neglect may cause less damage than a few decades of popular appreciation can be seen whether on Hadrian's Wall in Northern England or in the Cathedral of St Iago in Compostella in Spain. The major historic cities of central Europe, abruptly opened to mass tourism in 1990, are now struggling with the consequences of their new found interest, which may be more damaging than the previous neglect. We can now arrive at the paradox that the continued preservation of the most-loved monuments and cities, may depend upon keeping people away from the objects of their affection. This is of course a basic problem of heritage management, for which there are fortunately many solutions, and it will occupy much of the later discussion. Nor is this situation only evident in comparatively small cities. In many conserved landscapes, including national parks, the main threat to the habitats now comes from people coming to observe wildlife. When the British National Parks were set up in the 1940s few appreciated that the twin objects of 'preserving natural beauty' and 'encouraging access' would prove to be antithetical.

## *Exercise Twenty-two*

Do you know monuments or sites that are being 'loved to death'? Are visitors damaging the physical structures or the atmosphere by their presence, or by their supporting facilities? If so, would you try to restrict the numbers of visitors? How would you do that? The prehistoric cave painting at Lascaux in France have been closed to the general public because of their deterioration. Some more recently discovered paintings in Bulgaria have been hermetically sealed. What is the point of a heritage that we cannot experience? Can it be called 'heritage' at all?

### The dangers of a heritage mindedness

Finally and more broadly there are increasing misgivings about what has been termed the 'heritage mentality'. The new prophets of doom (of which Hewison, 1987 is one of the most read) argue that the success of the heritage movement has led to societies becoming trapped in their pasts. A backward-looking romantic nostalgia is seen as a symptom of an inability to face futures. Some have claimed to notice a link between conservation success and such trends as poor current economic or political performance. We should, it is argued, be less concerned with our remembered pasts and more with the promise of our futures. He further argued that Heritage was largely concerned with persuading the comparatively poor to pay for the pleasures (and even the very homes) of the comparatively wealthy. This notion of an elitist heritage, has, however, been forcefully denied by Samuel's (1995) demonstration of the enormous commitment of all kinds of people to their pasts, and the considerable and widespread economic benefits which stem from this. Wright wrote a book on Britain in 1985 entitled *On Living in an Old Country* which examined the modern social and economic consequences of an obsession with the past. The present book could be subtitled, 'on living in an old continent' in that a distinguishing characteristic of Europe is not just that it is old (so are other continents) but that we are constantly aware of our antiquity. If heritage is 'back to the future' then these arguments need serious consideration alongside the argument that there is no future that is not rooted in an appreciation of the past.

# What you should know

When, and why, did the idea of preserving aspects of the past for the present and the future arise in Europe? Who were the prophets of preservation? How did the enthusiasms of a small but influential group of people eventually became reflected in laws and official organisations? How did the operation of government-sponsored preservation slowly extend to become an important part of area management and planning? How did the various countries of Europe, for various reasons, lead or follow these trends? How has the very success of the urban conservation movement raised difficulties that now create many dilemmas in management?

# Further Reading

Accounts of changing tastes and the effect upon how places and buildings are viewed;

D. Lowenthal (1985) *The past is a foreign country*, Cambridge: Cambridge University Press.

S. Schama (1997) *Memory and imagination*

The way the past has been used to create a sense of national identity, country by country, in;

D. Horne, (1984) *The great museum: the re-presentation of history* London:Pluto Press.

and for Britain in particular,

J.A. Wright (1985) *On living in an old country: the national past in contemporary Britain*, London: Verso.

The way museums have altered their approach to the past is argued in;

N. Merriman (1991) *Beyond the glass case: the past, the heritage and the public in Britain*, Leicester: Leicester University Press.

An argument for a 'paradigm shift' from preservation through conservation to heritage as fundamentally different approaches to policy is made in;

G.J. Ashworth (1997) 'Conservation as preservation or as heritage: two paradigms and two answers', *Built Environment*, Vol.23, no.2, pp.92-102.

Among the uses of the past in urban planning, is the importance of a sense of time in identity;

K. Lynch (1972) *What time is this place?* Cambridge (Mass): Massachussetts Institute of Technology,

and the difficulties of reconciling old forms and new functions;

G. Burke (1976) *Townscapes*, Harmondsworth: Penguin.

The development and operation of preservation legislation is usually described on a national basis. Such as;

For the UK, P.J. Larkham (1996) *The conservation of cities*, London: Routledge.

One of the few attempts at a European comparison is;

D. Dobby, (1978) European conservation planning, London: Hutchinson.

Typical of the misgivings about too much heritage is the polemic account of,

R. Hewison, R. (1987) *The heritage industry: Britain in a climate of decline* London: Methuen.

This is to an extent countered by:

R. Samuel (1995) *Theatres of Memory*, London: Routledge

# 4. Heritage and Identity at Different Spatial Scales

## Summary

The previous chapter looked at the way heritage has been created, mostly quite recently and often for quite specific purposes. Implicit throughout is the idea of place. People, heritage and places become linked together in a complicated and sometimes bewildering variety of ways. The cement binding these three elements together is identification i.e. most people wish to identify with places because these places have a unique character, or identity, and a major contributor to this is heritage. It became evident in the account in the last two chapters that heritage can exist at various different spatial scales from the international to the very local. This chapter will examine the different levels in such a spatial hierarchy and explore how places acquire identities and how people identify with places through their heritage.

Different people, at different times, for different reasons have emphasised different levels in a scale hierarchy of places. It is not enough just to recognise that different scales exist and make distinctive contributions to the identification of individuals with areas because heritage developed at different levels, often for functions quite specific to that scale, may be complementary or competing. An individual may quite happily identify with the heritage of a whole nesting hierarchy of areas (the 'Russian doll model') and regard these as non-competing and even contributing to each other.

Reread the personal account in Chapter Two of the author's identification with 'his' village, region, nation, multinational state, continent and, ultimately world; the heritage of each of these was incorporated into his personal heritage without seeming conflict. He would be the first to argue, however, that the harmony is far from complete. Like many others he is often not sure whether to take a local, national, European or even global view. Identity, like love, may not be a finite product, and having one identity does not necessarily diminish another.

However, the situation is not always so harmonious and heritage at one scale can, deliberately or not, undermine other levels. The identification of an individual with other individuals results in many, often overlapping, 'imagined communities'; these, in turn, may or may not coincide with identifiable spatial entities nor with jurisdictional boundaries. It is also worth remembering that defining an inclusive group ('we are "us"') through the use of heritage ('because we have always been "us"') inevitably excludes others ('we are therefore different from "them"'). This may not matter much if both 'we' and 'they' are defined in terms of positive non-conflicting characteristics but if 'we' are defined only in terms of difference from 'them' the past all too easily becomes a disputed heritage of claim, grievance, and resentment. Not all heritage has spatial significance. Some communities, like the family, or

'Manchester United supporters' or 'Catholics' have identities, and heritages, but little identifiable, contiguous, territory. Such communities' heritage can easily conflict with territorial identities.

Thus as heritage is a major contributor to these identities it is understandable that it is often differently defined, interpreted, claimed and even violently fought over. The relatively recent idea of nationalism is by no means the only political ideology that contains these intrinsic heritage conflicts. It does, however, particularly encourage them because it asserts the supremacy of one such imagined community, the nation, over communities at other spatial scales and then goes further to claim that such imagined nations should correspond to politically sovereign entities called states. As nations are essentially subjective imagined communities they are unlikely to be delimitable in a way that excludes no nationals and includes no non-nationals, to be stable over time, or to correspond to specified spatial areas. The result has been Europe's internecine conflicts between and within nation-states which generated the need for national heritage to encourage national identification at the cost of both sub-national and continental identities as well of course as other such nations. Very often nations, and other spatial groups, define themselves as different from another, usually neighbouring, group. Irish nationhood was defined as being 'not English' but also Canadians are 'not American'.

Regional or local heritage, as well as heritage at the supra-national scale may thus be seen as either a potential competitor and thus dangerous threat to the integrity of the state leading to disintegration and separatism, or alternatively, in the case of local heritage, only a variant of a wider national heritage and even a source of strength in 'unity in diversity' and in the case of international heritage, just an aggregation of national heritages.

As there is no 'correct' spatial scale of heritage, this chapter will examine the various ways heritage and spatial scale interact in Europe.

---

### *Exercise Twenty-three*

Do you identify with a European nation? Is that nation the same as the state on your passport? On what do you base your feelings of national identity (language, customs, culture, history)? To what extent is your identity defined in terms of not being something else?

---

# Some theory

Three theoretical notions underpin much of the following discussion and are useful in providing a structure for thinking about these matters.

## *Legitimation*

This idea is simply that governments of any sort or scale need a right to govern, a justification for their exercise of authority over a particular area, which may or may not be the one which they *de facto* control. Most governments use the past to legitimate themselves; to give themselves the right to rule. This 'legitimation theory' (usually associated with the German sociologist Habermas) is most obvious in 'national' museums or even in the teaching in schools of national histories. A very common method of presenting the past can be labelled the 'inevitable progress' technique. Here the past, its objects, events and ideas are presented linearly, beginning with the oldest and culminating at the present time. Often a clear narrative of progress is implicit from 'primitive' to 'advanced' which of course automatically justifies the present as being both an inevitable outcome of the past and also a highly desirable point in time. Present society, its institutions and ideas are thus legitimated and opposition is implicitly presented as flying in the face of historical logic. This use of the past is most easily recognised in the propaganda of totalitarian regimes but is certainly not confined to them. Pluralist, liberal democracies also legitimate themselves through the idea of progress and it is not only national governments that have the need to legitimate themselves as will become clear in the cases below. At this point, remember that organisations from the United Nations and the European Union to local city councils have their flags, coats of arms, anthems and the like; all declaring the identity and legitimacy of governments.

## Exercise Twenty-four

How does your city or region legitimate itself by using selected aspects of the past? If there is a local museum does it select, order and interpret the exhibits so as to present an idea of progress to the present? Does it also establish a 'difference' between the artefacts of this nation/region/city and those of others?

## Culture capital

The French sociologist, Bourdieu took the economic idea of capital and proposed the addition of 'cultural capital'. In the same way that rational individuals accumulate economic capital, they also find it advantageous to gather another form of personal capital from culture. This can be objects (paintings or books), experiences (concerts) or, most significant, standards of taste and cultural judgement. Cultural capital like economic capital is very unevenly distributed through society and the ruling elites capture most such cultural capital. In particular they become the taste leaders who determine what is regarded as valuable capital. Although there may be a significant distinction between the cultural elite and the wealthiest part of society, there are usually many interconnections. The situation is, of course, never static as this cultural capital is contested (in the same way as is economic capital). New groups or ideas will continually arise and attempt to compete for possession with the present owners which explains why art and culture are always a struggle between the traditional (i.e. the present 'owners') and the *avant garde* (i.e. the would-be future 'owners').

## Exercise Twenty-five

Think of a case reported in the local or national news where there has been a dispute between the 'traditional' and the 'avant garde' for control of cultural taste? How were the arguments presented on each side?

## *Dominant ideology*

If the ideas of legitimation and cultural capital are taken together then a much wider theory called the 'dominant ideology thesis' emerges. The assumption here is that society is divided into dominant and subordinate groups; the ideas and values of the former are presented as the dominant ideology to the latter who are passive recipients accepting their subordination. Heritage generally occupies an important place in such an ideology; the cultural capital of the past is captured and used to legitimate a governing group which seizes power and maintains it through the use of a dominant ideology. George Orwell's novel, *1984*, described a future world in which the past was constantly altered on the principles, 'he who controls the present controls the past; he who controls the past, controls the future'. Again this is easy to recognise when presented as crude propaganda but less easy to recognise when presented as more implicit assumptions.

The dominant ideology thesis is far more subtle than appears in the short explanation above, which you may dismiss as self-evidently obvious. There are many complications, especially in mature pluralist societies. There may be many such dominant ideas that are quite different but yet co-exist. Subordinate groups may not passively accept the heritage they are given and thus accept their subordination. The most usual reaction of such groups is actually to ignore completely such dominant ideas. It is well known that museums, galleries, concert halls, theatres and even libraries and universities in most countries are overwhelmingly used by a small minority drawn from the educated controllers of the cultural capital. The dominant group is in fact talking to itself, not to the subordinate group, and is thus legitimating itself to itself. Even when subordinate groups visit museums, theme parks, historic monuments or heritage centres, the message they receive may be quite different from the one intended by the presenters. Finally some observers claim to recognise the existence of an unofficial, almost underground, counter-culture which is a sort of ideological resistance movement of a subordinate ideology. This may be expressed through popular music, sporting events or youth fashions or even the idea of folk crafts and cultures which may exist outside the official cultural agencies. The popular heritage of Robin Hood, Til Eulenspiegel, trolls and leprechauns could be viewed in this way.

There have been many attempts to overcome some of these problems. However honestly meant, such attempts to bring subordinate groups into the museum, just like the similar attempts at taking culture into the community, usually leave the definition of culture firmly in the hands of the dominant group, who thus can be perceived as seeking further recognition of their dominance.

Each of these concepts stresses the political uses of heritage both in the sense of legitimating a government or governing idea but also legitimating a group which constitutes itself as an entity. Although heritage has since acquired other purposes, not least the economic, these, however profitable, remain incidental and do not determine what, where or how official heritage is created. In nearly every case if the 'heritage industry' ceased to operate then most of our museums and monuments would remain because it is the political motives that dominate. These roles of heritage and these issues of people, places and identity will now be considered in their spatial contexts.

*Exercise Twenty-six*

What would happen in your town or region if suddenly there were no tourists. Would the museums, monuments etc. be closed or differently interpreted? Would the local heritage, and the way local people use it, be different in any respects?

## The dominance of the national scale

To start the discussion of particular scales in the middle might seem perverse but there is a good historical argument, implicit in much of the account in Chapter Three, that the national scale has nearly always been dominant, in official heritage. Of course, as individuals we each have our own constructed heritage, which justifies each of us to ourselves, and supports our identification with the family, which can be extended to include 'clan' and, historically in Europe, 'tribe'. This usually takes precedence over identification with the state. However as our concern is mostly with public rather than private history (the latter typified perhaps by family inheritance and the photograph album), then the dominance of national heritage is clear. The story of this dominance has already been told and does not have to be repeated here but the point should be strongly made that heritage became 'nationalised', largely in the course of the 19th century. Answers to the question, why this happened, why the national level became so dominant, have also been already given in the historical accounts of how national governments became progressively more and more involved, despite their initial reluctance, in the designation, maintenance and presentation of heritage. The difficulty now is that this dominance is now so all pervasive that it is difficult to question it and thus imagine heritage without national museums, archives and theatres, without national monuments, historical narratives, heroes and villains, without national ministries, agencies, laws, policies and financial subsidies. Yet it was not inevitable and other scales could have been so dominant if we had so chosen. Indeed increasingly this dominance of national heritage is being challenged from below and from above. The regional challenge is the more longstanding and the continental or even global, the more tentative and recent.

The countries occupying the British Isles (the sovereign states now known as the United Kingdom, the republic of Ireland and less clearly the Isle of Man and the separate Channel Island sovereignties) present numerous variations upon these themes, if only because it is one of the oldest extant political entities in Europe and developed through numerous historical political compromises between the palimpsest of cultural groups over many centuries. So complex is the relationship between the patterns of identity that no attempt to describe them would meet with a consensus of approval. We cannot even identify a national scale to correspond with a state entity because identification with nation varies enormously between individuals. There are overlapping and nesting identities among English, Scots, Welsh, Irish, let alone Cornish, Ulster, Channel Islanders, Manx, Norse Shetlanders, and more recent immigrants, any of which could be subdivided or re-classified in almost any combination. Cultural identification does not always, or indeed mostly, correspond to particular spatial locations nor is always related to existing governmental structures. The relevance to our discussion of heritage and place identification is that the 'whose heritage?' question becomes almost impossible to answer in terms of geographical areas or in terms of legitimating dominant political entities. Who, or what, or where is politically legitimated by for example, 13th century Norman castles in Wales, Scottish Highland dress and music, Dublin's Georgian architecture of the protestant ascendancy, Hindu temples in Leicester, Mosques in Bradford, the Norwich School of Landscape painters and many more? In some instances regional heritages competed successfully and replaced a previous national heritage and thereby supported political separatism. Most notable was the creation of the Irish republic on the basis of a Celtic, Catholic, rural heritage that replaced for some but not all of the inhabitants of an area, the previous idea of Irishness as a variant of British heritage. At the other extreme, few inhabitants of the now extinct political entities of Mercia or Northumbria would see their heritage as other than a regional variant of a British or English heritage. These material heritages are also often supported by perceived heritages of blood, or race or residence. In a country which has long had a very mobile society, the ability to prove one's origins remains powerful, to the extent that there was recently very vocal opposition to the closure of a maternity home in east Cornwall, because women would have to travel to Devon to give birth, thus threatening their children's 'nationality'.

# The international scale—European heritage

The first word in the title is 'European' and this spatial focus should presumably be present in every aspect of it but we need at this point to consider the idea explicitly at some length. But what do we mean by European heritage? When we use the term in this course do we always mean the same thing and do we, and you, actually have the same understanding? I will first argue the need for a heritage at this scale, which is not self-evident but quite a recent idea. Then the argument will consider various ways of defining European heritage before trying to determine what should, or should not, be included.

### Heritage—does Europe need it?

In one way this question seems almost naive as Europe is in many ways the heritage continent *par excellence*. The ubiquitous economic commodification of the past as a central element within the tourism industry ensures that heritage is a vital consumer product throughout Europe's increasingly free-market dominated economies. Analysing the contents of the photographs in holiday brochures reveals that Africa means 'wildlife', Asia means 'exotic culture', America means 'fun', and Europe means 'heritage'. However, the concern here rests more narrowly with the issues of identification and legitimation discussed earlier. There is a discordance between the political-economic integration and potential appeal of a unified Europe and the ambiguity of legitimation accorded such a construct, because it lacks the validation of cultural consciousness vested in place. There might once have been a concept of Christendom, which was largely coterminous with Europe, a concept that survived even the division into Catholic, Orthodox and Protestant parts, but this concept scarcely survived 19th-century nationalism and today seems both out-of-date and seriously divisive. The concept 'Europe' exists as a bureaucratic entity of regulation and intergovernmental agreement which does not inspire popular identification with the same commitment as does the nation or even region. Most Europeans are still more likely to die for their country than for the European Union. This is the current situation, though there is nothing pre-ordained about it. Three hundred years ago people were more likely to die for their religion. It can be argued, therefore, that the successful integration of Europe, as other than an organisational convenience, requires an iconography of identity that would transcend national and regional identities. This would involve the management of heritage so as to superimpose additional layers of meaning to built environments and landscapes that are already fundamental symbols within national iconographies and narratives.

## *Exercise Twenty-seven*

Are you a European? When? How do you know? Which aspects of your heritage contribute to your national identity and which to your European identity? Does the one identity include the other or compete with it?

## *What could we mean by European heritage?*

At the simplest and most uncontroversial sense we live in countries that perceive themselves to be in Europe and therefore anything and everything relating to us is by that fact 'European'. However that does not help us at all to answer the two key questions namely:
- what is distinctly European as opposed to being for example American or African?
- what is heritage at the European scale as opposed to heritage that is French or Greek, let alone Breton or Ionian, Parisian or Athenian, or even of that of Montmartre or Plaka.

Even the definition that European heritage is heritage that occurs in Europe, or relates to Europeans, presupposes, as Chapter One argued, a prior definition of Europe and Europeans.

**Heritage by Europeans**

There is a simple and obvious definition that in practice denies the importance of the word European other than as mere geographical chance. The geographical adjective can be taken to apply to those doing the study rather than the object of study. Thus any heritage studied by us, wherever located, would in this sense be relevantly European.

**Heritage of Europeans**

Logically heritage 'belongs' to those that created it or those for whom it is currently relevant. These are, by our definition of heritage, the same, as all heritage is ultimately consumer-created. It seems reasonable therefore to consider the heritage of Europeans as including heritage of whatever sort, and wherever now located, which was created by, or can be considered relevant to, Europeans. This has much to recommend it as European peoples have, over the past 500 years, demonstrated a remarkable capacity for global involvement of various sorts. The settlement of Europeans overseas has not only transplanted European languages, cultures and economic systems to very extensive portions of other continents, it has shaped links between heritage artefacts, such as architectural styles, urban designs and the like, that would make it illogical and artificial to include Novara but not Louisbourg, Bath but not Boston, Seville but not Santo Domingo. Equally as a result of this global interaction, so much of the remembered and memorialised symbolic past of Europeans occurred outside of Europe that our heritage is truly world-wide.

There are two main difficulties with this definition. First, like the previous definition it presents an extremely wide selection of possibilities and does little to limit an already wide field. Secondly it raises the major difficulty of the treatment of the reverse case, namely heritage that can be classified as non-European heritage although located in European locations. Logically, for example, Islamic heritage in Europe whether a relic of previous occupation, as in Spain or of more recent immigration as in industrial cities such as Bradford, would have to be excluded, as would substantial parts of the collections in the museums of Europe. This would remove one of the most important and interesting aspects of the use of heritage to support the shaping of new multi-cultural identities.

**Heritage in Europe**

This, simply defined, is heritage occurring in what can be recognised as the continent of Europe. Of course the definition of that continent (or western extension of the Eurasian landmass) is highly tendentious and based upon few universally accepted applicable delimitation criteria.

The link between people and places through heritage is more complicated than it sometimes seems, if only because people are mobile and places may 'belong' to different peoples at different times or even at the same time. Poland even has a Minister for Polish Cultural Heritage Abroad. But once Europe and Europeans have been identified then two questions remain:

- What would be the content of a European heritage? Do specifically European heritage themes exist?
- Which organisations, with what powers, undertake, or could undertake, the task of recognising, protecting and presenting a European heritage in the same way that national agencies are responsible for national heritages?

# Content of a European heritage

## *The heritage of the pan-European idea*

This defines European heritage narrowly as relating to the origins, evolution and achievements of what could be termed the pan-European idea. This quite clearly opposes, or at the very least is an alternative to, the idea of national heritage described above which thus provides a clearly comprehensible justification, goal and answer to the problems of selection and interpretation. Its purpose is the legitimation through heritage of European unity and of a European organisation and ultimately state in opposition to the nation-state legitimated through national heritage.

Presumably there could be a focus on 'European cities', here defined as cities with designated supra-national, European functions, such as Brussels, Strasbourg and Luxembourg within which are such sacralised space as the Berlaymont or the European Parliament. The need of the existing European Union for just such a popular identity as a counter to the otherwise all pervading national heritage of the European nation-state is obvious; the chances of success of such a policy are however limited if only as a result of the dominance of the national level in heritage provision. In addition there are two practical and almost unsurmountable difficulties. First there are very few resources to be found in buildings, events and personalities from the European past that can in practice be used in the creation of such a European heritage. However, the people, events, the buildings created to house them and indeed the cities in which they are located, are generally uninspiring at best, and quite unable to compete successfully in popular imaginations with the personalities, events and structures which underlie national, or even regional, heritage narratives.

Secondly the selection of artefacts and events to shape a specifically European Union heritage poses the question of how to treat heritage that does not support this ideology which in practice of course is overwhelmingly quantitatively dominant. Orwellian rewriting of the past and the physical destruction of its relics we can assume is beyond the current power, although maybe not ambitions, of the European Commission. Therefore the choice would be between policies of conscious ignorance and acceptance, the latter presumably attempting to reinterpret national heritages as either primitive precursors to the European idea or as warnings of the consequences of nationalisms. None of these policies has much chance of success.

## *The heritage of pan-European ideas*

A less drastic approach but equally less focused would be to develop a pan-European heritage based upon those ideas, aesthetic creations and activities that of their nature were continental rather than nation-bound. Many general artistic, philosophical, political, economic, social and religious themes suggest themselves as being intrinsically international although not necessarily specifically European. Architectural themes from the Gothic to the Post-modern, philosophical ideas from Classicism to Romanticism, political movements from the Crusades to Marxism, economic and social trends from liberal capitalism to lifestyle choices provide an almost infinite quarry of resource possibilities for the selection of heritage that disregards national boundaries. The advantages of these heritage themes is that they are mostly safe (i.e. they create little dissonance), self-congratulatory (i.e. the consumer shares the achievement with the 'greats'), some are inclusive, (i.e. they disinherit few excluded groups) and many may even surmount the barriers of cultural and linguistic communication. In this respect conserved built environments are in many ways ideal, being composed of internationally legible forms, which are both an element in, and a stage for, wider cultural expressions, while acting as a primary resource for the international heritage tourism industry. Natural heritage also has much to recommend it in this respect.

There are two difficulties. First, and as applies also to other definitions, there is little guidance here about selection from such a myriad of possibilities. Secondly, much of the interaction between Europeans which could form the basic themes is dissonant in some way or another. The proverbial visitor from Mars would, I have no doubt, summarise the memorable heritage of us Europeans as pogrom, persecution and prejudice manifesting itself as near continuous internecine oppression, war and genocide. Therefore the search for a distinctly European heritage will be depressing indeed, however instructive the possible lessons that might be learned from it.

At a more prosaic level, a structuring of European heritage through the concept of dissonance (Tunbridge & Ashworth, 1996) recognises that the past is a resource in conflict but is itself seriously dissonant with the currently dominant interpretations of most of what could be termed the heritage industry, who are strongly wedded to what in Britain has long been called the Merrie England approach to history. Much of the contemporary market for heritage is quite simply seeking entertainment and much heritage is maintained in existence principally to supply fun experiences for this leisure market.

## The heritage of European conflict

Both of the above ideas for structuring a content of a European heritage founder on the dissonant nature of the European historical narrative. Simply, much of the interaction between Europeans that could form the basis for such themes is dissonant in some way or other to some Europeans. The past is a contested resource and thus the recognition of any one claim upon it disinherits others, sometimes with serious results. This is manifested in several ways in Europe. The nation-state is generally perceived to be forged through a 'freedom struggle' for existence. Further the region-states, or even less overt expressions of separatist identity within the nation-states, are equally defined by histories of subjugation and rebellion. Conflict is essential to these narratives and war, atrocity, repression and revolt are needed to produce the folk-heroes and martyrs, as well as the folk-villains and oppressors that differentiate the national character and virtues from the others.

The importance of these elements in existing national heritages may seem so self-evident as to be not worth arguing. The point here, however, is that it is so important that it can be neither ignored nor opposed. If that is so, then the only alternative is to accept its existence and to use conflict itself as the structuring theme for a European heritage.

However, the example of the battle-field at Waterloo (1815), ostensibly an ideal candidate for a heritage complex capable of European interpretation, demonstrates the practical limitations of reconciliation through the shared horrors of the past. In pragmatic terms this was one of the last battles fought on a site small enough to be capable of being visually appreciated and understood on the ground; it involved troops from many countries and regions in what is now the EU; it was fought close to the present European 'capital' of Brussels, and the cause for which it was fought has now very little meaning for most visitors. It is thus a potentially ideal demonstration of the folly of warring nations and the wisdom of unity. In practice, however, this opportunity has so far been squandered. Official interpretation is military-technical, treating the battle as a strategic and tactical game while most of the many museums and monuments are blatantly nationalist (commemorating for example the élan of Ney and the Old Guard or the steadfast British infantry at Hougemont). The dominating mound and lion actually commemorates the undistinguished role of the Prince of Orange and was erected to legitimate the short-lived Dutch annexation of Belgium. Most interpretation, however, is in the hands of private enterprises for whom Napoleonic imperial glories or the military skills of Wellington make better marketable products for visitors than do casualty lists or sermons on the value of European political integration. Yet if Waterloo, its horrors muted by time, cannot be used as quintessential European heritage, then what chance is there of exorcising the more recent and bloody traumas of warring European nationalisms?

The question is, should the content of European heritage embrace the distasteful, Srebrenica and Auschwitz as well as Chartres cathedral and the Sistine Chapel? Clearly, the Jewish Holocaust of 1933 – 1945 remains pre-eminent, archetypically European heritage and arguably the most serious challenge facing contemporary European society in managing its past. European Jews, the principal European people not nationally defined, were deported and murdered by Europeans in Europe in pursuit of a European ideology. The physical relics of *stetls* and camps remain throughout the continent, as do the memories of the victims, the perpetrators and the passive observers to haunt this and future generations of Europeans.

How would, or even could, a European heritage manage such a past? (Tunbridge & Ashworth, 1997). The camps themselves have become part of Europe's contested heritage, even Auschwitz being the subject of a 'steady Catholicising process' in which it increasingly stands as a 'symbol for Poland's role in Catholicising Europe'. It is perhaps more comfortable to believe that a European heritage, which includes war and atrocity, commemorates only former divisions. But the past, no matter how awful, can still be seen as constructive if one of the functions of European unity is to prevent its re-occurrence. Thus, Europe's camps, graves, battlefields and memorials must constitute part of its heritage alongside the more acceptable and commodious icons that support our ethnocentric notions of European cultural hegemony and civilisation.

## The European organisations

If there is a European heritage, however we define it, then the next question must be who is responsible for creating and promoting such a heritage. The underlying questions are also, 'why do they do this and what is their implicit or explicit agenda?'

At first glance, it might appear that many supra-national organisations might potentially be involved in European heritage; not only does much heritage obviously possess an international dimension but, despite the inhumanity of the continent's past, it is often seen as an easy and non-controversial manner of expressing internationalism, particularly if constructed as narratives of progressive perfectible humanity that gloss over the heritage of atrocity. Even then, however, closer examination does not suggest that this attention actually contributes over-much to a specifically European policy for a distinctively European heritage.

The European institution with the longest involvement in the heritage of the built environment in particular is the Council of Europe. This continent-wide intergovernmental forum has long regarded culture in general, and the urban built environment in particular, as a major focus of its work. From the 1970s onwards, for example, it has publicised best-practice examples of planning historic cities in various countries with the implied intent not so much of comparing European national practices, as using successful examples to stimulate the less active members. Equally promotional in its objective was the naming of years. European Conservation Year (1970) was followed by arguably the most successful, European Architectural Heritage Year (1975), and subsequently by European Campaign for an Urban Renaissance (1981) and European Year of the Environment (1989). These did provide national governments and agencies with an excuse and stimulant for increased heritage expenditure and raised the public profile of these topics. More recently the European City of Culture (not it should be noted City of European Culture) designation has proved a similarly efficacious means of obtaining funds for cultural and tourism initiatives at the local city scale, although the meaning of the 'European' in the title remains undefined and usually unexpressed. In the latest initiative a very mixed bag of cities (Avignon, Bergen, Bologna, Brussels, Krakow, Helsinki, Prague, Reykjavik and Santiago de Compostela) have been designated European Capitals of Culture. Again, the European dimension is largely unexpressed as the various cities attempt to capitalise upon their self-promotion as cultural products. Although its activities have been predominantly urban, the Council of Europe has also been involved in other heritage initiatives. In 1987, for example, it launched a cultural routes programme designed to celebrate the unity and diversity of European identity of which the first was the pilgrim route (Camino) to Santiago de Compostela, selected as a 'deeply felt commitment to the European experience' (Council of Europe, 1989). A different department has also been most assiduous in bringing together policies relating to the protection of the natural heritage, via a series of designations and conventions.

By contrast, the European Union has taken only sporadic interest in the heritage of the built environment and even the few initiatives that can be discerned make no particular use of a distinctively European dimension. One difficulty is that the topic does not fit comfortably into the present structure of EU administration or decision-making. Responsibility for urban policy, for example, is split between DGXVI (Regional Policy) and DGXI (Environment); the former allocates subsidies supporting programmes at the urban and regional scales, while the latter struggles to include the urban human environment within a natural environmental management brief. Other directorates, including DGXXIII (responsible for tourism), DGX (Culture) and DGXXII (Education) also cover various important uses of European heritage. Political responsibility is also divided between at least four of the 21 Commissioners' portfolios. This fragmented responsibility accounts in part, for example, for the failure of the arguments, put forward by DGXI, to have specific references to the historical role of European cities in nurturing a European civilisation included in the Maastricht agreement. In reality, European Commission concern with heritage amounts to no more than general exhortations that can be implemented only at the local scale through national conservation and physical planning systems. Thus, the vision of European spatial patterns and policies published as 'Europe 2000+' includes among its eleven focus topics, 'heritage preservation and conservation of historic areas'; such platitudes hardly amount to a distinctive European heritage policy in either content or method.

This discussion of the relative ineffectuality of official interventions into heritage at the European scale combines with two further important constraints on the development of a specifically European dimension to heritage. First, the dominant sphere of public sector intervention in the definition, preservation and presentation of heritage remains the national governments and their agencies, operating in pursuit of notions of national heritage. Secondly, private commercial enterprises, which can loosely be bundled together as 'the heritage industry', play a major role in the presentation and use of the commodified past, including the use of heritage resources preserved and maintained by the public sector. Much of this heritage is part of a leisure industry that provides fun experiences in response to a growing contemporary demand for the past as entertainment. The point is not that this somehow constitutes a less valid or less authentic use of the past, these terms being quite meaningless when applied to heritage, but more simply that this is an alternative and competing economic use of the past to the political uses discussed here. Inescapably, however, what can be termed 'official public history' exists within this context of a history exploited as commercial entertainment.

## *Exercise Twenty-eight*

What are your images of Europe? Suppose you are designing a book cover for a European Heritage course, what would you depict? What part would the built environment play in such depictions?

## The International Scale—global heritage

There is a strongly felt need to believe in the existence of a world heritage as the common property of all mankind. All political frontiers have proved to be highly permeable to aesthetic ideas and cultural movements and much of the conserved built environment in particular is on free, permanent display, needs no translation and is thus directly accessible to all. It would be desirable indeed, to regard the wealth of the centuries of human artistic productivity as both the responsibility of the whole human community and freely available for the enrichment of all. In a sense not only are Socrates, da Vinci and Shakespeare, my heritage but so also are Gautama Buddha, Mohammed, and Confucius. The implication is that the pyramids of Geza or the temples of Borobodur or Anghor Wat are thus to an extent, my responsibility in the same way as is York Minster or Hadrians Wall, namely that as I profit from their existence (or would feel the poorer if they ceased to exist) I thus should contribute to their protection and support. Every international heritage tourist is surely asserting both the existence of a world heritage and the right of accessibility to it, as well as more mundanely selecting what that heritage shall be and contributing directly or indirectly to its support.

### Is there a world heritage?

The close symbiosis between heritage and tourism is not new. From the first the desire to conserve and the desire to visit were mutually stimulating. The 18th-century Grand Tour 'discovered' and thus preserved the heritage of the classical Mediterranean world; today the global village is merely claiming its global heritage (Boniface & Fowler, 1993). The reality, however, is that the past is a contested resource and the global is in competition with other scales; a competition that it has in practice lost. In particular the national and the local scales have been far more successful in colonising the past for their purposes.

Although some spectacular modern events have demonstrated the strength of global concern and the readiness of people to translate this concern into international action in response to crises, they have also made its limits abundantly clear. International sympathy, expertise and money may be largely powerless to do more than renovate a few buildings in the face of both quite different local economic priorities and the procrastination of governmental structures. The temples of Abu Simbel were saved but the Aswan High dam was built. Ultimately the sovereignty of the nation-state over 'its heritage' determines that national priorities take precedence over global concern. Quite commonly even international charitable economic priorities are different. In the face of starvation and disease, calls for donations to save buildings can appear distasteful.

Similarly, but usually less stridently, at the local scale, there has been an assertion of the role of heritage in local identities. This is reflected in a view of tourism that takes primacy of local ownership of heritage as axiomatic. If tourists are in search of 'their' heritage (i.e. those past associations that relate to them) not 'your' heritage (i.e. the pasts required by local identity needs, which to tourists are irrelevant) then it is assumed that local authenticity and local identity should take precedence over global identity. This localisation of heritage has become a conventional wisdom of many museums who attempt to replace the colonisation of local cultures by policies of local empowerment. Heritage should thus not only be returned to local people but it should be housed, interpreted and presumably, if they so wish, disposed of, by them as being again 'theirs' not 'ours'.

A concept of 'Mundus Noster' as a global parallel to Europa Nostra (1963) will not just come into existence; it must be created and there should be no illusions about the difficulty of that task. If all heritage, by being someone's, must disinherit someone else (Tunbridge & Ashworth, 1996) then a world heritage is not a happy summation of local and national heritages but a denial of them. If the sour comment of Turner & Ash (1976) that 'tourism is everywhere the enemy of authenticity and cultural identity' is correct, or at least believed, then tourism is part of a heritage problem and not an instrument for asserting the existence of a global heritage. Heritage is simply an assertion of ownership of the past and until that ownership can be collectivised on a world scale, rather than nationalised or localised, then heritage will be more usually a cause of national and local conflict than of global reconciliation.

Art is often perceived as being a significant international heritage, whether art of the past or of the present. Certainly the market for portable artistic products is international as are many peripatetic artists and musicians. However, many art institutions act as part of national cultural policies. Sydney Opera House may not confine itself to Australian works or performers, but it nevertheless competes culturally and economically, with other national opera houses, in New York, London, Milan or Paris. Much the same is true of art galleries where the art may be international, but the presentation is strongly influenced by national goals and identities.

## The international organisations

There are of course international fora and organisations that attempt to articulate the idea of world heritage. Concerned experts have been issuing declarations on behalf of us all from the Charter of Athens (1931) to the Charter of Venice (1964); ICOMOS has delivered codes of practice, UNESCO numerous conventions on cultural property. Action, however, is beyond their competence. It is true that World Heritage Sites have been designated by UNESCO. While these are no doubt useful political encouragement and economic stimulus to national actions, these designations and awards are in practice little more than the results of political compromises between national governments, jockeying for financial support directly or indirectly through tourism as well as national prestige, and national legitimation, (and of compromises between regions within countries) rather than the beginnings of the recognition, designation and support of a distinctive world heritage.

None of this is very remarkable if it is remembered that the idea of a national heritage was synchronous with the idea of a nation-state. National museums, collections, histories, conservational legislative frameworks and practices were both created by, and instrumental in the creation of, the nation-state and intended to project national messages legitimating that structure.

# Who owns the past?

Ownership can mean quite different things. A medieval cathedral, such as York Minster, is owned in one sense by an organisation, the Church Commissioners in London and managed by the local diocese of the Church of England (who it might be argued by Catholics, acquired it by seizure from its previous owners in the 16th century, an early case of heritage nationalisation). In other senses, however, the people of York, whether or not they are Anglicans and use it for worship, the people of Yorkshire, England, Britain, Europe and the world, all own it. This is not just a vague sentiment but has many practical implications. The Church of England would find it difficult, actually impossible, to demolish or even change the building however much it might wish to do so and despite its legal rights to dispose of its own property. If they attempted, for example, to sell it to the Americans (as old London Bridge was successfully sold to an Arizona theme park) then the British state would almost certainly intervene, prompted by an outraged public opinion composed largely of non-Anglicans, refusing an export licence on the grounds that it was 'British', despite the historical fact that no such British state existed when it was built and the builders would have not recognised any such allegiance. Similarly however, if the wider owners of the heritage feel such a personal concern and also maintain a moral right of access then they presumably also have a moral responsibility to contribute towards its support whether through taxation or donation.

## Exercise Twenty-nine

Are you prepared to contribute financially to the support of historic buildings that you do not own, are not located in your country and which you will probably never visit? Should 'heritage-rich' countries sell their surplus heritage to 'heritage-poor' ones? Portable heritage, such as works of art, accumulate in rich countries who buy them. Why should the built environmental heritage not be treated similarly in this respect? As in a zoo, threatened buildings could be transported to a safer environment in a country with more resources to devote to care.

Severe flooding in the Adriatic in 1966 seemed to threaten the continued existence of the lagoon city of Venice. (At the same time the river Arno in Florence destroyed or damaged a high proportion of the renaissance art of the Uffizi gallery.) The world-wide response was quite remarkable. Concern about the future of 'their' heritage was marked throughout the world, even among people who had themselves not visited the city. Money, technical assistance, and volunteers streamed into the city to 'Save Venice'. Thirty years on, it is possible to evaluate the effect of this outpouring of global concern and to conclude that it had very little impact. The problem has been that the protection of the heritage city requires such control of the water in the lagoon that other functions of the region, especially navigation and industrial development would suffer. Local economic concerns were accorded primacy over international heritage by the responsible national and regional governments. In practice 'world heritage' is not protected by any world government but by sovereign national governments. This European case is magnified in many other parts of the world where international sentiment may prove all but powerless in the face of quite different local concerns.

These arguments can become much more contentious and complicated. The question, 'Who owns the past?' may resolve itself into further questions, such as 'What is meant by "own" in such a question?' and 'What as a consequence are the rights and responsibilities of such ownership?' A particularly widespread and controversial aspect of this question is the attempt to link heritage objects with specific places, on the grounds that a specific place is the correct location. The widespread nature of this problem stems from the inherent mobility of both people and much of their heritage so that they become separated and heritage thus finds itself in the 'wrong' place. Artistic property can be bought and sold, and thus tends to be located in the hands of rich individuals, museums or countries, or expropriated by governments and thus located in capital 'show case' cities—or just seized.

Shipwrecks provide some of the most complicated of these heritage ownership cases. The south Italian city of Reggio Calabria has a world-renowned museum of Hellenistic Greek statues which were quite recently recovered from a shipwreck in what is now legally Italian waters. They were enroute from a manufacturer in Alexandria, Egypt to a purchaser in Marseille, France. The legal owners of ship or cargo are now untraceable but the moral ownership could rest with any or all of four countries, none of which existed when the ship sank. If this case sounds too distant consider what would happen if (or maybe, given recent spectacular advances in submarine archaeology, when) the Titanic was raised and exhibited as a major tourism attraction. Who would own (and thus exhibit) a ship built in Northern Ireland, that was owned by White Star line of British registry, later incorporated in Cunard and now part of the multinational Trafalgar House Group, but salvaged from the high seas by a commercial company, full of the property, let alone bodies, of many nationalities whose heirs may or not be traceable, and sinking closest to what was then the Dominion of Newfoundland but which is now part of Canada? Or would it go, in effect, to the highest bidder?

The distinctly peripatetic nature of much heritage can lead to quite bizarre cases of conflicts of ownership and bodies are especially potent symbols and of course very movable. Empires in particular tend to collect the heritage of their far flung domains but there is nothing new in this. Alexander the Great's body was kidnapped by his general Ptolemy and taken to Alexandria in Egypt to legitimate a new kingdom. The Venetians stole the bones of St Mark from Alexandria and the bronze horses from Constantinople so that these could legitimate La Serenissima. The body of Columbus (or bits of it) are claimed to be buried in four different cities in two continents. The body of a prehistoric Ice Man was recently discovered in an Alpine glacier; both Austria, where he was found and Italy where the glacier originated, claim him as 'theirs'. The idea that 'wrongly' located heritage can be returned or repatriated to the rightful owner in the 'correct' location sounds convincing, as only natural justice but of course depends upon the capacity to determine ownership (Greenfield, 1996).

## *Exercise Thirty*

Who, in your opinion, is the 'owner' in this case? The German archaeologist Schliemann took what he believed to be the 'treasures of Troy' that he had unearthed in 1873 to his native Berlin, having first paid the Turkish government the money they required and having been refused permission by the Greek government to locate them in Athens. They were subsequently looted by the Russians in 1945 and recently revealed to be in the possession of the Russian state. Germany claims that 'their' property should be returned; Russia argues they belong to humanity; and both Turkey, where they were found, and Greece which claims to represent the Trojans could make counter claims. Where should these treasures be housed?

The Schliemann case is typical of many where looting and relooting leaves national governments arguing their respective rights over properties created long before any of them existed. A rather more complex and well publicised cases is that of the Elgin Marbles and the world-wide assembly of artefacts in Imperial capitals has been called 'Elginism'. The Parthenon frieze from the acropolis in Athens was collected in a discarded and ruinous state by Lord Elgin between 1803 and 1812 and brought from what was then Turkish territory to the British Museum, London for conservation and display in 1816. It has been vociferously claimed by the Greek government for more than 100 years on the grounds that it is Greek heritage—a claim firmly rejected by Britain. The curious point here is that 'classical Greece' was an interest of mainly Western European romantics in the nineteenth century. It was the countries of Western Europe (specifically Britain, Germany and France) that used their idea and invention of classical Greece to legitimate their political ideologies, especially democracy and liberal humanism. It was therefore 'their' heritage and this feeling, stimulated no doubt by the presence in London (or in Berlin) of classical artefacts, led to their crucial support of the revolt of the Greeks in the 1830s and the creation of the modern Greek state. The nationalism of Modern Greece however was rooted in medieval Christian Byzantium not heathen Hellenism but once created, it adopted the largely Western vision of Hellenism to legitimate not only the government in mainland Greece but claims upon large parts of the Aegean, Anatolia, Macedonia and Cyprus.

The 'Elgin' dispute is replicated throughout the world and is echoed in the well meaning attempts of UNESCO to establish some sort of international code of ethics on the national 'ownership' of national heritage, the international trade in art works, and where possible the idea of heritage repatriation. It does however raise the objection that a focus on the national automatically excludes the global. For example, if we accept that Rembrandt and Vermeer, because they lived in what is now the Kingdom of the Netherlands (which was created 300 years after their death) are Dutch national heritage then all their work should be relocated from around the world to the Netherlands and presumably, in return Dutch galleries will eject all foreign works and in future exhibit only Dutch painters. The access of world citizens to their global heritage would be severely constrained. Indeed if the parthenon frieze and all the classical artworks in the Louvre, Prado, and the like, belongs to us all, (not least as the heritage of European democracy) then, to return to the Elgin dispute, its location in a free museum, in a highly accessible European world city is presumably ideal. 'Elginism' was global, whatever else it was, and 'de-Elginisation' would result in a global disinheritance in terms of both practical accessibility and psychic identification.

Finally, and even more sensitive in many respects, is the growing concern and controversy over the ownership of heritage between ethnic or cultural groups within countries. Artefacts treated as historically or scientifically interesting by the present exhibitors may have deeply felt religious or personal significance for others who object to the treatment, interpretation or even exhibition in itself. This is especially the case when the cultural artefacts and even bodies of 'primitive' peoples were collected and displayed by European institutions. The arguments of, for example, many North American Indian or Inuit peoples has been that their cultures have been expropriated, misinterpreted and misused by others. Many museums now attempt to empower such groups by involving them in the presentation of their cultures or even handing them over completely.

One of many recent cases was the handing over to representatives of the Lhakota Sioux a shirt worn at the Battle of Wounded Knee which found its way to a museum in Glasgow. Such cases are likely to increase in number as museums become more sensitive to the ethnic symbolisms of the objects they have accumulated and which have often lain in store for many years, and as ethnic groups around the world become more aware of their 'lost' artefacts.

On a wider scale there has recently been a suggestion by representatives of one group of people, who have inhabited many different parts of Europe for many centuries, and thus could be regarded as archetypical Europeans, namely Gypsies (Romanies) that there should be a museum of their heritage. As a non-national minority they claim to have been either ignored in national heritage collections, misunderstood or just treated as colourful, if primitive, folk artists. Apart from the practical problems of the location and financing of such an intrinsically non-place bound heritage, there has also been resistance from other gypsy representatives who argue that the traditional forms of heritage presentation would be unsuitable for what is essentially a family-based, orally transmitted society, and even possibly dangerous given the hostility they have frequently encountered from settled society.

## Between hope and despair

It may appear from the above account of all the problems and disputes that the questions about the 'correct' spatial scale or even 'who owns what?' are unanswerable. Logically this is indeed often the case but it should be stressed that heritage is not only mobile it is also highly flexible, reproducible and malleable in that it can be interpreted in many different ways for many, even conflicting, purposes, sequentially or even simultaneously. There is usually no difficulty about the same building, for example, fulfilling the identification needs of different people or different scales. Globalism, nationalism, ethnocentrism and localism can in most cases be reconciled once the problems are recognised and mutual claims respected. The Benin bronzes, the Venetian horses and countless archival documents have been duplicated and redistributed. Venetian palazzi have been re-erected in North America and Australia, the temples of Abu Simbel raised above the water of the Aswan Lake. The technologies of conservation, reproduction and interpretation can bring objects and artefacts closer to those who wish to experience them so that the distinction between reality and virtual reality is becoming less discernible. The questions raised above may therefore become less relevant if a global heritage for the global village is our future.

## What you should know

There is strong link between heritage and identification with places. This identification is frequently deliberately created for various reasons. People can, and do, identify with places at many different spatial scales simultaneously and often without causing conflicts between these scales. Government interests in heritage coincided with the rise of the nation-state and is generally used to generate and sustain national sentiment. However heritage can and does exist at sub-national scales and two supra-national scales that are of increasing interest and discussion are the continental scale and the world scale.

As the countries of Europe extend their cooperation in many economic, cultural and political fields, they have an increasing need for popular identification with the idea of Europe. Heritage plays an important but not simple role in this identification. The idea of world heritage is powerful, growing and receiving increasing institutional recognition. If a world heritage exists, it can conflict with national claims on the past in various ways.

# Further Reading

The classic sociological texts which have examined political legitimation and culture capital are:

J. Habermas(1973) *Legitimationenprobleme im spätkapitalismus* Frankfurt am Main: Suhrkamp.

P. Bourdieu (1990) *Distinction*, Cambridge: Cambridge University Press.

Many of these ideas are explained and exemplified in;

B. Graham (1998) *Modern Europe: place, culture and identity*, London: Arnold.

The reports and studies of the official intergovernmental agencies are usually full of case details but, perhaps understandably, rarely clear about their approaches and philosophies. Try to find the publications and websites of;

Council of Europe

ICOMOS [International Council for Monuments and Sites]

UNESCO

The European dimension is considered in many of its different aspects and from different political visions, in;

G.J. Ashworth & P.J. Larkham (1994) *Building a new heritage: tourism, culture and identity in the new Europe*, London: Routledge.

G.J. Ashworth & B. Graham (1997) 'Heritage identity and Europe' *Tijdschrift voor Economische en Sociale geografie* 88(4) 381-88

Problems of conflict over heritage, including many similar cases to those discussed here about onwership are described in;

J.E. Tunbridge & G.J.Ashworth (1997) *Dissonant Heritage: the management of the past as a resource in conflict*, London: Wiley.

J. Greenfield, *The Return of Cultural Property*, Cambridge: CUP, 1996

# 5. The Uses and Users of Heritage

## Summary

The simple question of how old buildings, districts and cities are used relates, of course, to the earlier question of why they have been preserved in the first place. However, the two questions may receive different answers when heritage has been preserved for its own intrinsic values and uses of the resulting structure are only sought subsequently. The philosophy of preservation, described earlier, often results in vacant or underused buildings and areas combined with an often fruitless search by preservation agencies for appropriate users in order both to finance and to justify the preservation. Conservation on the other hand, following the famous definition of Gerald Burke as 'preserving purposefully' should include the criterion of contemporary use in the decision to conserve. Heritage is at least in theory demand-driven and thus is created by the uses for it.

This chapter considers the main uses we actually make of historic artefacts, buildings, areas, cities and landscapes. The many possible uses have been divided into three main, but often overlapping, categories. These are heritage as a cultural resource and thus base for collections of various sorts; heritage as a political resource in support of ideologies and jurisdictions; and heritage as an economic resource in the support, directly or indirectly of economic activities.

## The uses of the past

In practice there is frequently some tension between the answers to the two questions, 'Why preserve?' and 'How do we, should we or could we, use the preserved past?' This chapter will not repeat the list of motives that powered the heritage crusade described in chapter three and continue to be used to justify the increasing designation and maintenance of heritage. It will, however, describe the main ways in which heritage is currently used in Europe and answer not only the question 'how is it used?' but the related questions of 'by whom?' and 'in what way?'

These sets of uses overlap considerably, and frequently it is the same historical relics and associations that are being used in all these uses of heritage often in the same places. However, each relates to a separate area of policy, each of which is in practice pursued by separate agencies of government involving separate individual producers or resource managers. Furthermore, partly as a consequence of this, the motives, background and working methods of those involved tend to be quite different in each case. Finally, and this is usually less easy to distinguish, the consumers of each have different expectations and requirements of the resource and are using it in different ways.

## The use of heritage as a socio-psychological resource

Heritage is important to the individual in various ways. The brevity of this discussion is not because these uses are in themselves unimportant but only that they are very difficult to investigate and in any event beyond the scope of this book which focuses upon society. We need however to be aware that heritage appears to be important to the well being of individuals. The paradox in investigating this is that, although widely expressed, it is difficult to make explicit and next to impossible to demonstrate. Pearce (1998) has begun to investigate these meanings on a familial level.

It is often argued that, 'Our cities should provide visible clues to where we have been and where we are going' (Ford, 1978). Familiarity with places is claimed to be valuable in maintaining an individual's psychological stability and too rapid environmental change may upset this stability, therefore 'the excitement of the future should be anchored in the security of the past' (Lynch, 1960). Rapid change in the environment causes disorientation similar to that experienced by individuals as a result of clinical amnesia. The psychiatric analogy is a powerful and much used argument for which there is, unfortunately, no clear clinical evidence from a society without a consciousness of a past. The inhabitants of cities newly destroyed by bombardment or those settled in planned New Towns can be shown to have had many social problems but these are rarely related to the absence of conserved old buildings; nor has it been shown that the citizens of Bath or Heidelberg are intrinsically more psychologically stable than those of Brasilia or Milton Keynes as a result of their conserved environment. If a collective memory exists, other than as the aggregate of individual memories, then the important questions would seem to be what is its content and who determines this, as well as what are the public mental health roles of conservation policy in this respect. Ultimately the argument thus far seems only to conclude that too much change, including in the built environment, is disturbing regardless of whether that change is for the better or the worse.

### Exercise Thirty-one

Does a collective memory exist? If so, who decides what to remember and how is this memory transmitted through the generations? If a collective memory exists, does also collective amnesia?

Our concern, some might say obsession, with the heritage of the built environment does not blind us to the possibility that the heritages that matter most deeply to people and which are important to their mental well-being are usually about people and activities rather than places or buildings, and the latter are usually important only as reflections or memories of the former. Similarly while there is well attested work on the importance of good landscapes and environments to mental well-being, (notice the care taken about decor and landscaping in and around hospitals) there is no evidence that a heritage landscape is better in this respect than a modern one.

# The use of heritage as a cultural resource

## Heritage as cultural collection

Heritage becomes part of a broader idea of culture either because the artistic productivity of the past is included alongside that from the present in what is identified as culture, or more comprehensively because culture more broadly defined as the 'mentifacts' as well as artefacts of a social group, whenever it was produced is viewed as heritage in the sense that it is regarded as suitable for assembly, preservation and transmission to future generations as an inheritance. In either situation deliberate collection is a central activity, although clearly not all such heritage has been, or even physically could be, accommodated in museum buildings and physical memorials, buildings as monuments and even which historic cities are 'collected'. However the museum occupies an important and visible role in such collecting and thus can stand as an archetype for many other such institutions.

There are two main types of justification for collecting, and subsequently preserving and displaying heritage. The first is based upon the allegedly intrinsic qualities of the objects themselves and was the motive behind many of the world's oldest collections (see for example Hudson's (1987) account of the history of the museum, and thus of their underlying motivations, over the last 500 years). Such motives may include:

- the assembly of artefacts, divorced from their physical locations, made their comparative scientific study easier and was an important motive for many archaeological and anthropological collections, as well as collections of natural history, both flora and fauna, alive in zoos and reserves, or stuffed in museums;
- a desire to protect endangered objects, buildings and even methods of expression and ways of life threatened with extinction lay behind many folk and craft museums. Museums, once collections for scientific study or amusement, now justify themselves, in terms of conservation;
- similarly objects may be collected because they are seen as aesthetically beautiful, as art objects in themselves, or just as unusual curiosities;
- objects may just be in themselves collectable and fulfil some need, or even obsession, of people to collect for collection's sake. Commercial firms and governments often take advantage of this need by producing items such as limited-edition souvenirs or postage stamps specifically for collection.

These reasons are the most used justifications for museums as places where artefacts are assembled, protected from further harm, reconstituted, classified alongside others of their kind and recorded for their own sake, and not in furtherance of any other contemporary objective, by individuals and organisations uninterested in all save the values emanating from the objects themselves or the historic or aesthetic truths that they are believed to reveal.

The second broad category of justifications for collecting argue that museums, and cultural policy more generally, possess a role in creating and disseminating values which are ascribed to the objects extrinsically because they are conceived as being important for contemporary and future societies. Such values may be social, often expressed through an educational function, or ideological and political.

The term the 'new museology' (Vergo, 1989) has been coined, to contrast with the 'old', as a means of describing the differences between these two types of justification as well as attitudes towards consumers and methods of interpretation. The more traditional view of museums is focused upon objects, their acquisition, their conservation or restoration, their securing in safety, and their registration and documenting. The newer approaches focus more upon the wider contemporary roles of museums and collections and thus more upon actual or potential visitors and the methods of communicating with them. It has been argued that four questions are now central in museum practice (Hooper-Greenhill, 1992), which either were not asked previously or were assumed to be answered by a consensus which now no longer exists. These are, 'why are collections assembled?' 'what is considered collectable?' 'how is a collection to be classified?' and 'how are collections to be used?' The answers to each of these questions determines the active role of museums and other heritage resource collectors in shaping the heritage product.

## The housing of heritage collections

Museums impose their own visions of reality upon the objects they accommodate from the moment a decision is made to collect them and long before any presentation to visitors is considered. The selection of items, their separation from their original context of use and place, and their arrangement, all impose a particular vision of reality that is acquired outside the museum and varies over time. There is thus no one form of reality for museums which operate and reflect their own social, economic and political contexts. In particular, classification imposes a rationality upon objects that will reflect wider epistemologies. Thus the unavoidable structuring arrangement of exhibits, or of buildings as monuments, is a reflection of how the dominant group views and structures knowledge as well as an influence shaping those views.

Especially relevant to the main argument of this book is the question 'what is a museum?' Traditionally it was a room or a building in which items were stored and displayed; now there is a much wider range of possibilities. Museums may include sites, whether covered or outdoor, that are artefacts in themselves, collections of buildings, vehicles, mines, quarries and the like which are themselves the objects on display. The idea of a museum begins to merge with entire settlements. There are villages or towns which, in whole or in part, have been dedicated as museums but which remain in use for other residential and commercial purposes; they are literally inhabited museums. From this point the idea of a museum extends in two different directions. It merges first with the historic theme park often composed of reassembled buildings as St Fagan's, Wales, Gamle By in Aarhus, or Skansen, Stockholm. This may be of reconstructed buildings temporarily re-peopled by animators, or even merge with fantasy constructions it is imagined might have been, as Turin's Citta Vecchia. Secondly, it becomes increasingly indistinguishable from the conserved and interpreted tourist-historic city reconstituted by urban conservation planners as the 'heritage gem cities' such as Eger, Hungary, Heidelberg, Germany, or Bourtange, the Netherlands, or heritage districts in more multifunctional towns (Bottscherstrasse, Bremen; Elm Street, Norwich; Bergkwartier, Deventer and the like). An extreme manifestation of the inhabited museum is the ecomuseum, an idea developed in 1971 at Le Creusot and subsequently applied elsewhere (see Chapter Six). Here an entire region presents its distinctive geographical characteristics (physical as well as cultural) as a unique and indivisible heritage synthesis in which the daily lives of the inhabitants, past and present, constitute an essential integral component. The collection of landscapes by governments, by means of various designations, can be regarded as a very similar collecting activity writ very large at national, even occasionally at international scale. In the UK about 30 per cent of the land area has been 'collected' in this way, in National Parks, Nature Reserves, Sites of Special Scientific Interest or Conservation Areas.

## The interpretation of heritage collections

Many museums originally made no or heavily restricted provision for visitors (Hudson, 1987) and interpretation of the artefacts was often regarded as unnecessary. Either the object 'spoke for itself' or even 'if you did not know what an object was then you had no right to be viewing it'. Today however a dramatically different situation has been reached in which display and interpretation is considered to be the central function of museums. The museum has become an instrument for communicating with society and the artefact is subordinate to the interpretive story. Indeed the artefact is often barely relevant and sometimes not even physically present, in a narrative without objects. The focus has shifted from the object, its intrinsic values and authenticity, to the experience. The boundary between the museum and the heritage centre is now very difficult to draw (but see p. 123).

The use of the museum as an instrument of education, 'a classroom without desks' (Graburn, 1977, p.14) is not new but developed in the course of the 19th century when the democratic nation state felt the need to educate its population through public schools, libraries and museums. The museum was thus merely one instrument, among many in society, charged with the task of being the channel along which heritage is transmitted from past to present and from present to future. This public education function assumes that there are communicable truths, that these should be communicated to a general public for its own good, whether individually or collectively and that this public was waiting eagerly to receive them.

An important question here must be, 'Who decides whose heritage shall be transmitted to whom?' Museums currently have two main answers. The more traditional answer is that 'authority' generally the state, transmits the dominant values and ideas to its citizens. This is most easy to demonstrate in Europe where the national museum and the nation-state have enjoyed a close relationship in terms of finance, governing bodies and policy formulation. Horne (1984) has reviewed, country by country, the national museums' presentation of the national heritage of the European nation state. However this idea can be much wider and heterodox in that different levels of jurisdiction, different versions of the past and visions of society, and indeed different interest groups can all be represented in various ways in various museums in European pluralist, multicultural societies. While broad policies and approved histories were handed down by government organisations, the policies are largely implemented by academic curators, in discipline-based galleries, and with their own expert agenda, from a desire to maintain the material for the purposes of analysis and study by future generations of historians and scientists. They are therefore not immune to the creation of an atmosphere of mystique, scholarship, erudition and esoteric knowledge designed to legitimate their own, and their discipline's existence.

An alternative reaction within museums has been to challenge this top-down idea of a one-way communication between authority (however constituted) and passive recipients and replace it by versions of a bottom-up approach. This may be an attempt to represent the unrepresented. This is not a recent idea; it has constantly reappeared over the past hundred years and is often recognisable through the use of two key words, namely 'folk' and 'everyday'. The idea of the folk museum, pioneered in 1891 in Skansen in Sweden and throughout Europe, was based on the idea of 'folk' or 'people' being the unrepresented submerged masses whose life-styles and material culture were threatened with passing unnoticed and unpreserved into extinction, overwhelmed by mass-produced consumer capitalism. It was powered by an ideology that saw moral values in vernacular building and more broadly in ways of life illustrated by crafts and orally transmitted customs. Similarly the museums of 'everyday life' whether rural, as in Reading or urban-industrial, as at Beamish or most spectacularly encompassing a large part of the town as at Lowell, Massachusetts, were established with a clear intention of representing either a rural peasantry or an urban proletariat as a counter to what was seen as the official collections which represented social, cultural or political elites. These presentations, however well-intentioned, cannot always escape the paradigms imposed by the dominant cultural group, which was often quite prepared to perceive the rural poor, and later the urban poor, as charming and picturesque, and thereby unfitted for anything other than a subordinate role. Travel guides from the 18th century invite the 'civilised' traveller to explore backward peasantry, their crafts and customs, unsullied by modern progress. Rousseau's idea of the Noble Savage lives on in many museum interpretations as well as in holiday packages to visit the 'real' people.

The representation of the heritage of subordinate classes can more fundamentally result in museum and archive authorities viewing their role as one of empowerment. Here the unrepresented are not only represented by the museum authorities but are encouraged to interpret their own heritage rather than be educated as a largely passive clientele in a particular preconceived way. This may be little more than a presentation technique, for example encouraging interactive display, where visitors are encouraged to incorporate their own personal experiences in some way into the exhibits. It may also influence the choice of content, stressing the commonplace over the rare, the lives of ordinary people expressed perhaps in oral history over documentation of the 'great and good'. Alternatively it may mean no more than employing or consulting 'natives' about the display of their culture. More fundamentally it can lead to influence or control of the institutions themselves, through community involvement of various sorts and the return of artefacts to 'native' control.

## Exercise Thirty-two

There is a large and growing profession called 'interpretation' staffed by Interpreters who arrange exhibitions and displays. They are increasingly interested in the relationship between the exhibit and the observer. Check out an historical exhibition and ask, 'what is the role of interpretation and is the observer being treated as a passive recipient or an active empowered partner in the process? Watch other visitors, and notice what interests them, how long their attention is held by particular objects or explanations and what they pass by.

## The user of heritage collections

Most of the discussion about museums assumes a largely passive role for the customer. Even the attempts to represent the under-represented or to empower the powerless have occurred from the standpoint, and use the professional methods, of the current suppliers of the museum service. The two main characteristics of museum visiting are that it is increasing, albeit quite slowly, but that it remains the pursuit of a comparatively wealthy minority. Museum charges seem to make little overall difference.

The increase is similar to that for historic buildings, theme parks and even antique shops, all of which have participated in the heritage boom, an easily related story of successful, and often dramatic, growth. Britain, for example has increased the number of its museums tenfold over a century (from 217 in 1887 to 2,131 in 1987) with a new museum opening every two weeks, in the 1980s, according to Hewison (1987). The number of visits is also increasing (57 million in 1977 to 72 million in 1989). Similar figures exist in most Western European countries. The two contradictory explanations for this growth are the 'embourgeoisement thesis' i.e. museum visiting is a middle class activity and the middle class has grown in size, and the 'retreat into the past' thesis i.e. museums, like heritage in general are a symptom of a myopic escapist nostalgia which both contributes towards, and is an expression of, relative economic decline. The growth in museum visiting is thus either a consequence of absolute economic growth or relative economic decline or even possibly of both.

It must also be remembered that active and regular museum visiting is the pursuit of a minority in almost all societies. A majority of citizens never visit museums and many more visit only when they have to, for example in school groups. There are many reasons why museums are ineffective in attracting visitors, which include barriers of language, education, social convention and even physical aspects of the architecture itself. It is not surprising therefore that voluntary visitors to museums are disproportionately drawn from the middle-aged middle class. Visitors to museums, like consumers of many other heritage products and activities and cultural events in general have above average incomes and levels of educational attainment. This pattern is repeated for a wide range of visits to heritage and cultural sites and performances and also to natural landscapes. The only notable exception appears to be zoos which attract a wider social group.

Little really is known about the reasons why people visit museums, what they are expecting and what they are experiencing, although this is clearly important for heritage as a whole. The more traditional view of museums largely ignored this question regarding visitors as more or less passive recipients of whatever museums cared to display. However it has been argued that museum visitors are not passive recipients but active participants in the heritage process and that visitors bring preconceived expectations and experiences that structure their understanding. If this is so then the effectiveness of the reception of the messages relates to the individual's attitudes towards the past which are themselves shaped by attitudes towards the present and visions for the future. The impact on the visitor of the simple communication process of encoding, transmitting and decoding messages is only dimly understood. Evaluation studies that attempt to measure increases in knowledge as a result of a heritage visit generally produce results that show a disappointing increase. However, visitors may gain much in terms of a general appreciation of the past or acquire quite different increases in knowledge than those intended by the presenters. In general, it can be argued that people tend to take away from a museum visit what they want to take, and not necessarily what is offered.

Finally quite a large proportion of those who actually visit museums are infrequent visitors and a similarly high proportion have neutral or negative attitudes towards the past. Museums have an enormous 'option demand', as does all heritage, from those who express approval of the idea of preservation but do not currently visit what is preserved. Studies of the value of conserved landscape and townscapes consistently demonstrate that a significant number of people never actually visit but do express great satisfaction that a place is conserved. This option, or opportunity, value is dramatically demonstrated by protest and financial contributions whenever there is a real threat to some heritage site, or artefact, whether locally or even in far distant locations.

### *Exercise Thirty-three*

The three related questions raised by this discussion are, 'who goes to museums and similar collections?' 'why do they go?' 'what do they actually do in museums?' The answers to some of these questions may emerge by just visiting a museum and observing. Do the content and interpretation techniques suggest that either education or entertainment is the main objective of the institution? Which is the main objective of the visitors?

## The use of heritage as a political resource

The deliberate encouragement of support for particular political entities or jurisdictions, and also the strengthening of the identification of individuals with specific political ideologies, would seem to be quite different activities from the assembly and conservation of relict historical artefacts and the products of past cultures, as described above, because they are regarded as having artistic or historical value in themselves. The cultural and political uses would seem to have quite different explicit purposes, motives and historical origins and are frequently being undertaken by different responsible organisations. Many of those involved in the study and care of surviving aspects of the past would go further by denying any political relevance for what they do or political motivation for doing it. The relationship between the conservation of the past and politics is, however, strong, permanent, intimate and quite unavoidable, if less crude and simplistic than is sometimes expressed. Our task here is not to argue for or against the existence of a political role for heritage for it is axiomatic that such a role exists and that all heritage is an actual or potential political instrument whether that was intended or not. The task here is to examine how heritage performs this function and what difficulties and conflicts this creates.

### *National heritage and nationalism*

Nationalism is a political philosophy that identifies the existence of an entity, the nation, to which state structures should necessarily correspond. Central to the whole idea therefore is the discovery and description of this nation and the fostering of an identification of inhabitants with it. Heritage is the most effective instrument for doing this. Heritage has proved to be an integral and necessary adjunct to the idea of the nation-state and developed synchronously with nationalism as a state-building ideology. Although the relationship between nationalism and national heritage is obviously intimate, it is much more difficult to disentangle cause and effect. The nation is an abstraction created by heritage but nation-states need a national heritage in order to survive and thus create it as a matter of policy.

The instruments for the pursuit of such policies may be national museums, art galleries, monument collections or favoured landscapes but all depend upon the prior creation and propagation of a national history. This is the writing, and usually more important, teaching, of an historical narrative that explains the distinctiveness of a nation through time, stressing its longstanding and fundamentally different characteristics from other nations and most usually tracing an unbroken evolution from as far back in the past as possible to the present.

## Exercise Thirty-four

If heritage is used to support currently dominant states and ideas, what happens to the now defunct heritage that no longer supports these? Does it just continue to exist but is ignored? Is it reinterpreted in a way that is appropriate to current ideas? Is it concealed or destroyed? Have you local examples of each of these? The fate of the churches throughout Europe may illustrate the general problem in various ways. Churches are often physically robust, deeply culturally symbolic and thus often preserved buildings. However they may represent an all but vanished religious and political idea, for example Anglican churches in western Ireland or even Methodist chapels in South Wales, or be just irrelevant in a secular society. Are churches in your country or city used for their original pupose, or for some other unrelated purpose, or just left empty?

## Heritage in support of states at other spatial scales

The nation-state has been a demonstrably successful scale for the use of heritage in support of state building where the state has demonstrated its capacity to nationalise heritage. However heritage can be used to support political entities at any other level in the hierarchy of spatial governmental units. Heritage can also be used to demonstrate the unique identities of regions and localities. The national heritage fragments into the heritage of the regions and cities, enhancing the role of heritage interpretation in shaping local identities and even supporting political regionalism and local parochialism. This may or may not contradict the use of heritage at other scales. Regional heritage can be incorporated as a variant upon a national theme or conversely be used in support of regional political separatism, when a new nation is created in opposition to existing national heritage. At the other end of the spectrum of spatial scales, dynasties and multi-national states and empires have also in the past created and promoted a supra-national heritage idea.

Natural and landscape heritage have proved less contentious in this respect, and supra-national cooperation of various sorts is generally easier than with cultural heritage. Concepts such as the Alps, or the North European wetlands, or more generally river basins, obviously require international action for their preservation and there are a number of examples of transnational cooperation in national parks as with the German Bayerischerwald with the Czech Sumava.

## Exercise Thirty-five

It is often much easier to recognise the use of heritage for supporting states and ideologies in countries other than your own. Look back at the history you were taught in school. Did it explicitly or implicitly convey the idea of an almost inevitable progress towards the present? What percentage of the history you were taught concerned countries other than your own? Could it have been differently presented? How do you think history will be taught in the schools in your country in 50 or 100 years time?

## Heritage as an economic resource

The treatment of the past as a quarry of resource possibilities from which heritage products can be created leads logically to the possibility of its commercial exploitation. The commodification of the past can provide tradable products for the economic system. The surprise to many may be that this is only the third of the major types of uses considered here and not the first or even exclusive use discussed; the terms 'heritage' and 'heritage industry' are in practice used by many as synonyms. (Figure 6) The most visible and obvious of such economic uses is in heritage tourism, which will be discussed in detail below as an archetype of direct commodification. However, before considering such direct uses, it is worth noting that heritage has a much broader, if indirect, commercial use in its contribution to place amenity, its exploitation in the projection of place images and thus its influence upon the locational choices of economic actors other than those in tourism.

### *Heritage as a locational variable*

The indirect uses of heritage are most evident in two contexts, within which it makes some contribution to the locational choices being made by enterprises.

**Heritage in place images**

Aspects of heritage can be used within deliberately promoted place images designed to shape the perceptions of a place as a suitable location for investment, enterprise, residence or recreation destination. Factors relating to historical and cultural activities including museum, gallery, concert and exhibition visits, can be related to many other variables so that cities with

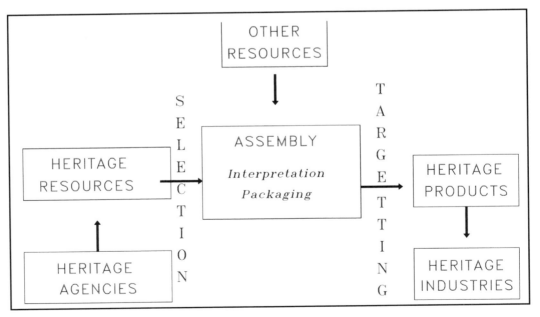

*Figure 6. Commodification of the Past.*

similar synergies of activities can be identified as a cluster competing for similar economic enterprises with a similar mix of attractions. At the local scale, heritage is used in promotional literature specifically designed to attract exogenous commercial investment with no direct link to the heritage industry. History is used to stress continuity and distinctiveness sometimes as a condition deemed in some way relevant to economic production and sometimes as no more than a formal assertion of the unique existence and thus identity of a place.

This use in place images may be an even more important component in the economic value of landscape heritage. Nearness to national parks, heritage coasts, and other designated landscapes is almost everywhere used to attract otherwise footloose industrial investment. One recent attempt to capitalise on the important but vaguely measurable economic value of landscapes is the attempt by the regional government of Tuscany to find ways of charging royalties to advertisers of commercial products who use photographs of Tuscan landscapes in their advertisements. This demonstrates the importance of such images but also raises the difficult question of who owns the copyright to a landscape?

### Exercise Thirty-six

Check some place-promotion advertisements or brochures. A very large number make some, usually implicit, use of the past. Has this any relation to the objective of the campaign, and if so, what exactly?

## Heritage areas and commercial land-users

Heritage expressed through the conserved physical fabric and its interpretation and promotion confer certain attributes upon the specific economic activities that locate in historic buildings or in any premises in historic areas. Such attributes may be advantageous or disadvantageous to any particular activity depending upon its capacity to reap the benefits and its willingness to bear the costs. An atmosphere of historicity confers an aura of continuity and even of artistic patronage upon activities located in it—an inference of reliability, integrity and probity, conferred by association. However, historicity could also suggest 'traditional, old fashioned, and unresponsive to change'. Similarly location in conserved premises or areas imposes costs not only of maintenance of old structures but of vehicle access, structural alteration, and external advertising and display. These uses of the past by commercial enterprises are considered in various urban contexts in Ashworth & Tunbridge (1990). They are reiterated here because it is at this local level that most heritage management occurs and it is undertaken as an integral aspect not of national or regional economic policy but as one element in local land use planning and local economic management. resulting at the urban level in the Tourist Historic City Model (Figure 7).

Heritage conservation in most countries in both Europe and North America is generally executed as a part of an economic strategy in coalition with local commercial interests. Such interests will often discount or be just unaware of the grander cultural or political uses of heritage discussed previously. The fundamental point is that the most important local heritage producers (measured in terms of number of outlets, customers or sales) are not the museums and galleries but the antique, arts and craft shops, and similar

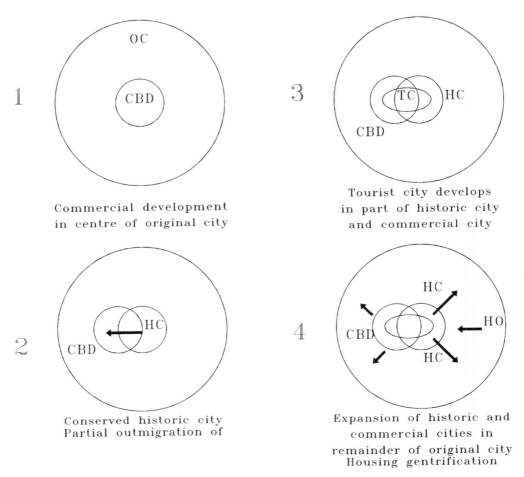

Figure 7. *Tourist, Historic City Model.*

traders of heritage goods and services. Some conflict in messages with the cultural and political users can be expected if only because heritage commerce has a tendency to concentrate upon the rapidly recognisable, and simply reproducible, symbols and associations of the past and can thus be easily accused of bowdlerising aesthetic values and insensitively trivialising political ones. Also the subsequent local management of any such dissonance is most likely to be successful if undertaken with at least the tacit cooperation of this commercial coalition.

The opposite trend to that of mass market bowdlerisation is the deliberate emphasis upon authenticity and rarity and the maintenance of high prices by limited editions and other restrictions on reproduction. Owners of art works and 'collectables' as well as the professions of valuers, authenticators, auctioneers and the like have a vested interest in resisting an expansion in supply.

## Heritage as a tourism resource

The most obviously important use of heritage as an economic resource, at least in its visibility and the support of a vociferous lobby, is as the basis for heritage tourism. This can cover a wide range of activities that use aspects of historicity in various ways. It may include types of 'special interest tourism' where existing interests are continued on holiday; art-culture tourism related to specific performances or collections; more generalised urban historic sightseeing and historic site visiting; and, at its vaguest, just a 'place-specific tourism' where the attraction is the unique identity of the destination to which heritage makes some contribution. Similarly heritage resources may be primary attractions motivating the entire trip or secondary diversions on holidays primarily motivated by quite other attractions. The relationship between heritage tourism and green/eco tourism can be very close, involving the same companies and the same customers. In both instances comparatively small groups of people deliberately profile themselves as individual travellers with strong educational motives rather than mass tourists motivated just by a wish for entertainment. In practice such tourism packages tend not only to be similar but also to include elements drawn from both natural and cultural heritage.

These activities, themselves only one part of a much wider tourism industry, have an enormous quantity of literature as befits their significance in economies at all spatial scales from the local to the international. The questions important to our argument are, 'to what extent is the tourist the same sort of heritage consumer as the other consumers already described?' and secondly, 'does the tourist consume the same heritage product as the other users?'

### The heritage tourist.

The simple question, 'who is the heritage tourist?' and its corollaries, 'what are the distinguishing characteristics, behaviour patterns and attitudes of such a tourist in comparison with either non-tourists or tourists motivated by other types of attraction?', has long received equally simple, not to say simplistic, answers. Consensus suggests that such a tourist is likely to have received a better than average education, to be in the age groups 20 – 30 or 45 – 60, and to be, especially in the older age category, of above average income. The trip to any one set of attractions is likely to be short, a matter of a few days or even hours in any one place, to include a number of different places combined in a single holiday, to be taken as an additional holiday (to be taken throughout the year), or at least to have a less pronounced peak, and stronger shoulder seasons than most other types of holiday. Such a tourist typically travels without young children and with one other companion, is experienced in foreign travel, chooses accommodation which includes catering, and has a relatively high *per diem* expenditure. The holiday is as likely to be independently as collectively organised and has usually been well prepared with a list of pre-holiday expectations and planned visits (Pearce, 1987; Burtenshaw et al. 1991; Dewailly & Flament, 1993; Prentice, 1993).

Such a description of the heritage tourist is a generalisation that emerges from detailed surveys at sites around the world; it is however a poor guide to understanding the relationship of the tourist to heritage and subsequently planning for this encounter. The tourist is more heterogeneous, the trip more varied and the attitudes towards the past more complex than such generalised descriptions suggest. Heritage sites attract a wide variety of different tourist groups, each a minority of visitors but equally collectively too important to be averaged away. Visitors on business or conference trips have a high propensity to include cultural and historic site excursions. Beach holidaymakers frequently include heritage excursions as a diversion from their sea and sand activities, especially in the temporary absence of the sun component. Formal educational trips often contribute a majority of visitors to an historic or archaeological site. Finally 'special interest' holidays attract by their nature small, highly diverse but committed heritage tourists whose aggregate importance is difficult to appreciate because of that very diversity. How can we generalise about the heritage use of those participating in veterans' battlefield tours, seeking Kafka's Prague, Lennon's Liverpool, or Maigret's Paris or following in the footsteps of Saint Paul, Bonnie Prince Charlie or Elvis Presley?

We thus have multi-motivated users of multiused heritage. Visitors to the same museum, historic site or theme park, participating in identical activities, may be tourists, day recreationists, school parties, or local residents and for most practical purposes any distinction will be unimportant. The same heritage facilities can play different roles to different consumers. Secondly individuals may switch roles abruptly, even in the course of a single visit to a locality, being successively or intermittently shoppers, business visitors, beach tourists as well as heritage tourists. Visitors to religious sites may be classified from outside as pilgrims, worshippers or tourists but in practice it may be difficult for individuals to classify themselves into one exclusive category. The heritage consumer is multi-motivated.

### The tourist's heritage

Tourists consume heritage either as an 'escape to fantasy' or an 'escape to reality'. The former (see especially Dann, 1981; Cohen, 1979) argue that the serious realities of everyday life provoke in reaction an attempt to enact various fantasies on a holiday which is basically seen as unreal. The alternative, and contradictory, view sees an increasingly complex and incomprehensible everyday life necessitating a holiday search for a simpler 'more real' world. History as fantasy reaches its apogee in the themed entertainment park, the role play of medieval banquet, 'good old days' sing-along or even participation in battle re-enactments. Heritage tourism as the search for a past that was more real and thus more substantial and satisfying than the present, however, (MacCannell, 1976) is highly sensitive to the perceived authenticity of the object or the place and is repelled by what is experienced as contrived heritage (Cohen, 1979).

From the earlier definition of heritage as customer-defined and the characteristics of heritage tourists described above, it can be expected that their definition of what constitutes tourists' heritage and their uses of that heritage are likely to be significantly different from that of the other groups of users already considered. In part this can be explained by such factors as that the tourist by definition is likely to possess less disposable time, detailed local knowledge and local mobility than the resident. More fundamentally tourist-defined heritage will be selected according to the expectations of the visitor. It can be assumed that these expectations will be substantially different from those of the resident because they will have been shaped by a quite different set of circumstances. The local experience has to be incorporated into the visitor's existing heritage. The unfamiliar is sellable in so far as it can be reached through the familiar; if what is familiar is different then so also is the heritage selected.

The only substantial accumulated body of evidence confirms the general expectation that heritage selected by the tourist is different from that selected by the resident in three ways:

- Quantitatively. All the three major uses described in this chapter are quantitatively selective, in that they make use of only a portion of the possible heritage, but it is demonstrable that tourists use a particularly small portion of the potentially available heritage sites, and resources.
- Qualitatively. Tourism tends to select the large, spectacular or internationally unique over the smaller or more commonplace.
- Spatially. Tourism is particularly spatially selective in that it tends to cluster strongly in relatively compact areas and be located within linked networks of similar attractions at various spatial scales.

All three selectivities are explainable from the characteristics of the tourist sketched earlier. The tourist's behaviour can be seen as a form of collection, which for heritage tourists involves checking off the heritage that has been previously marked by visitor expectations (encouraged by guide books and tourism brochures) as constituting the essential anticipated elements of the holiday experience at that place. Tourists with differing interests, education, experience or even time and mobility will of course have checklists that differ in length and content but the process of collection will be essentially the same.

### *Exercise Thirty-seven*

The study of tourism is made easier by the fact that all of us are sometimes tourists and can therefore observe our own behaviour. When you visit a place for the first time what expectations and preconceptions do you have about it? How were these acquired? Do you have a checklist of 'must do' activities or sites and, if so, who told you? How in particular do you react to the presentation of a heritage that is strange to you? Check some guidebooks or tourism brochures in different languages or intended for different groups of consumers. Are they selling the same past, in the same way for the same reasons?

Of course, for years the media have reported on heritage issues, whether the television coverage of a calamity of international significance such as the Assisi earthquake or a local newspaper reporting on a local monument. However, there is new usage of heritage by the media for it own purposes. So houses, castles and landscapes are used to make films and TV programmes and the visitation that results is as much concerned with the filming and the actors as with the site. Recent films such as *Sense and Sensibility* were an extraordinary collage of heritage sites relating to Jane Austen, the fictive characters, plots and costumes. Places acquire an additional heritage identity by being associated with popular  programmes or famous performers.

## Conflicts between the uses of heritage

The above brief inventory of some of the most important uses of heritage leads to the conclusion, important for the argument of this book, that not only does heritage have many uses but the same resources, facilities, and sites may serve different users at different times or simultaneously. Historic resources were often preserved, and are still managed, by those who value their perceived intrinsic qualities of age or beauty and need no further justification. Public intervention through policies of legal protection and subsidy have depended heavily upon a concept of 'public history' and 'public heritage' that seeks justification in the legitimation of governments, groups and ideologies and in the socialisation of individuals into collective norms. Economic arguments have generally been added to these later and even here the direct commodification of historic resources into heritage products is often less significant than the indirect contribution of the conserved built environment to other urban functions.

The relationship with the natural heritage is very clear. The intrinsic qualities of age or beauty are replaced by the scientific wish to conserve species for their own sake, for the sake of biodiversity or for future human need. Public access is not only unnecessary, it is inimical, but may be one of the prices required by governments to legitimate their democratic credentials. Today there are also enormous economic benefits, to property owners, to biotechnical companies and in the ability of the land to support tourism. Land, however, shares with the outside of buildings a major economic problem, in that it is very difficult to find politically acceptable ways of charging a return for just looking at Mont Blanc, Venice, or Dartmoor.

The uses of heritage may reinforce or contradict each other. Not only is the 'sellable heritage package' for each group of users likely to be different but so also are the motives of the various consumers. The very commodification can divide groups of heritage consumers. Country houses have discovered the need to hold connoisseurs' days, while cathedrals try to separate worshippers from tourists, by no means successfully. People practising their own insider heritage, whether a particular custom or a dance can often clash quite violently with mere spectators. Equally there is rarely a clear-cut distinction between purely economic arguments in favour of conservation for commercial tourism, social arguments justifying conservation for local amenity and political arguments stressing conservation as a vehicle for presenting a political place-identity. Monuments and collections created out of scientific curiosity or love of artistic beauty have become endowed with political significance or found themselves exploited, willingly or not, as resources for important economic activities. The same artefacts, sites and symbolisms are used in differently interpreted products for differently motivated consumers even if the producers are unaware of the ways their products are being used. Multi-use is evident in many guises and at many stages in conservation. All of this is an argument for the necessity for deliberate planning and continuous management. The nature of this management, in various settings, is the subject of the following chapter.

## What you should know

This chapter has dealt with many quite different activities whose only link has frequently been that they are all uses of heritage in some way. This diversity is in itself perhaps the most important point. If heritage has many simultaneous uses, then, in marketing terms it is multi-sold. This is not in itself unusual (nor indeed unethical) but it does imply the need for management to avoid confusion between users with may lead to conflict.

# Further Reading

The various ways that the past has been, and is being, used in creating and sustaining identity with nation-states and other jurisdictional entities is considered from many different viewpoints and with many examples in the chapters in;

B. Graham (ed) (1998) *Modern Europe: Power, Culture, Identity*, London: Mansell.

R. Samuel (1995) *Theatres of Memory*, London: Routledge

S. Pearce (1998) 'The Construction of Heritage: the domestic context and its implications', *International Journal of Heritage Studies*, Vol.4, no.2, pp.86-102.

A more world-wide coverage of the problems of multi-use and its management is found in;

J.E. Tunbridge & G.J.Ashworth (1997) *Dissonant heritage: the management of the past as a resource in conflict*, London: Wiley.

There is an enormous literature on tourism some of which focuses on heritage (or culture) tourism. See for example;

P. Boniface & P.J. Fowler (1993), *Heritage and Tourism in the Global Village*, London: Routledge.

J. van den Borg, P.Costa & G.Gotti (1996) 'Tourism in European heritage cities' *Annals of Tourism Research*, Vol.23. no.2, pp.306-321.

R. Prentice (1993) *Tourism and heritage attractions*, London: Routledge.

The economic impacts of heritage, apart from its use in the tourism industry, has not received much attention from economists. The standard work that attempts to incorporate heritage designations into economic theory remains;

Lichfield (1988) *Economics in Urban Conservation*, Cambridge: Cambridge University Press.

# 6. Heritage Site Management – Comparative Cases

A great deal of this book has been concerned with the ideas and concepts about heritage, which underlie all management and planning. However, the course is intended to help people manage the heritage in particular places throughout Europe. This final chapter, therefore, looks in some more detail at a few of the possible types of heritage sites for which the management strategies and problems may differ. We have chosen eco-museums, 'gem cities', heritage gardens and heritage centres. Of course, the types of site selected owe something to the expertise and interests of the team, and there are many more types. There is little here about natural heritage sites, in nature reserves, national parks or zoos—although nature is significant in garden conservation as well. We deal with heritage gem cities but not with the day-to-day management of built heritage in ordinary cities or in country houses. We deal with heritage centres where interpretation is of major consequence, but much less with theme parks where the accent might be on entertainment. We look at eco-museums but not at the regular civic or national museum or art gallery. There is nothing here about archaeological sites, or industrial archaeology, or maritime sites, all major areas of commitment today.

Nevertheless the sites selected do range across different types of heritage, including artefacts and landscape as well as monuments, and with some attention to heritage centres without original artefacts at all. The examples also consider heritage at national and international and at the local level of the eco-museum, concerned with the conservation of unselfconscious vernacular objects as well as the great architectural work of art. They deal with heritage where the chief aim is visitation, and other examples more concerned with preservation.

Finally there is perhaps a major void, a very considerable gap in our knowledge and understandings. We have referred many times in this book to the wish to conserve activities, and that most people are interested in heritage connected with people. Important as objects and buildings and landscapes are, they frequently are the only things we can save of a disappearing way of life, a way of doing things, a diet, a dance, a sport, a local craft. Heritage experts have become quite adept at conserving the objects; so far they have made very little progress in finding ways to encourage the activity that gave rise to it. Perhaps that is the next great challenge.

## The case of Eco-museums

### *Summary*

This type of heritage site was established as a reaction to rapid change in the European countryside and in rural society. It was an extension and enlargement of the more traditional museum to include a wide definition of cultural and natural heritage. From its inception in the 1970s it has spread to a a number of European countries.

## Change in rural areas

The abandonment of rural areas by millions of country people attracted to the cities by the new job opportunities offered in industrial and tertiary activities, has been a prominent characteristic of the development of industrial societies in Europe. This occurred in different ways and at different times throughout Europe from the end of the 18th century in the UK, after the Second World War in Italy and only at the beginning of the 1970s in Portugal. The face of Europe has been completely transformed by this exodus of millions of families from the rural areas to the great urban-industrial concentrations such as Randstand Holland, the German Rhine-Main-Ruhr or the Milan-Turin-Genoa triangle in Italy. The demographic statistics from the beginning of the century to the 1970s show a large and steady decrease of the population in the rural areas both in absolute and in relative terms. This phenomenon has been particularly apparent in the southern regions of Italy and has concerned the interior and mountain areas of these regions between 1950 and 1970. Millions of people moved to the urban coastal areas (Naples, Bari, Palermo, Catania), or further to the industrialised areas of Northern Italy and the rest of Europe, especially Germany. A similar exodus occurred from other peripheral and comparatively poor parts of Europe, as from Ireland into Britain, from Portugal and from former Yugoslavia into Germany.

Simultaneously as both cause and effect of migration, there has been a profound transformation in traditional agriculture, the main activity and land-use of rural areas. The departure from the countryside has deprived agriculture of its work force, encouraging mechanisation and modernisation, which in turn pushed the surplus labour to the cities. The consequence of these events has been the progressive decline of the European rural world in its economic, social and, even more, cultural aspects. A whole living world has become heritage, i.e. something worthy of conservation as historical evidence of the tools, animals, working spaces and buildings, traditional food, houses and villages, rows and hedges, folksongs and religious traditions. Very often the wildlife, native species of plants, and traditional varieties of fruit and vegetables are also threatened.

The mechanisation of agriculture has led to the disappearance of the traditional tools of peasant work, whether ploughs, sickles, hoes or spades. Similarly with animals as a source of energy or means of transport, tractors have replaced oxen or horses for ploughing and jeeps and pick-ups now threaten the survival of the old, slow donkey, overloaded with baskets and sacks, the former king of Sicilian country roads. Rural handicrafts producing clothes, furniture, carpets, ceramics, jewellery and wood and iron work, have been replaced by homogeneous, industrially produced objects. In much of central and eastern Europe this mechanisation of agriculture and denigration of the rural culture and way of life was the deliberate policy of communist governments. Actual displacement of population only added to the problem, most dramatically in Romania. In many countries there is now a very rapid attempt to reconstruct a local rural identity before it is swept away yet again, and perhaps inevitably, but the new forces of capitalist markets. The Czech village restoration scheme is an excellent example of this (Salasova, 1996).

The rural landscape, the result of the complex interaction between man and environment, has become a matter of the past. In the traditional rural world landscape was, in fact, the main visible product of a local culture, the mirror of the complex interaction between the specific natural conditions and different human activities, especially agriculture, although also other primary activities, fishing, forestry and mining. At the same time the landscape was the result of an equilibrium between natural and man-made components, often in a very dynamic way, but rarely in conflict. Historic landscapes were the product of a material culture that took its sustenance from earth and nature, a culture in which man and nature lived in symbiosis and harmony. The rhythms of life in the fields followed those of nature, especially the succession of the seasons. Many of the human changes and modifications of the natural environment were also highly sensible (for example, terracing in China or Italy) and sensitive to nature; on the contrary they often improved it. The countryman was a landscape builder.

With the passing of the conditions that produced such landscapes, they have become heritage—the main visible and tangible expression of the culture of a place and of its identity which can no longer be produced. Modern and post-modern societies have destroyed local cultures and identities, with their particular values, by creating isotrophic geometric space. The previous culture of co-existence and respect for nature has been replaced with the culture of domination and destruction. Almost everywhere in Europe we have assisted in the destruction of the existing landscape, sacrificed on the altar of modernisation and economic development, and of its natural and man-made elements, such as tree rows, hedges, water channels, water and wind mills, roads and cattle-tracks, stables and cowsheds, farms and small factories. Entire rural settlements have been abandoned, to become 'ghost villages' with the building stock abandoned, decaying, and ultimately ruined. Even where such deliberate or negligent destruction has not been the case, the specific local scene was always a matter of economics, and in particular the economics of transport and of labour. As the cost of transport has plummeted, so it becomes cheaper to move building materials all round a country, rather than use local materials, while town dwellers can also afford to live in a countryside to which they have no particular affiliation. The increase in the costs of labour has forced farmers into capital intensive agriculture, and the growth of the money economy has ensured that rural people need more money, but must travel further to get it.

## Conservation and revitalisation in rural heritage policies

Several new demographic and economic trends are noticeable in rural areas. The previously strong urbanisation process has been halted because of different converging trends, such as industrial decentralisation, the development of information technologies and communications, and mass motorisation that has made it easier to live further away from the city centres. Thus in some ways and in some areas the migration flows have been inverted as every year larger numbers of people and companies decide to move to the countryside, searching for a less congested and polluted environment and a better quality of life. But even in these villages where the population is stable or growing, it is quite a new population.

This 'return to the countryside' brings new problems associated with increasing of development and demand for housing, often beyond institutional control. In Italy and Portugal, for instance, increases in family incomes in the mid-1970s created a capital flow to the building sector, directly managed by the families themselves in an illegal and parallel market. Thousands of old houses, which survived earlier abandonment, succumbed to such family-builders, were demolished and replaced by new modern, international-style houses or, even worse, restored with extensive use of aluminium and high-tech materials. A new very similar landscape often financed from European-community agriculture subsidies, emerged in southern Italy, Portugal and Greece, replacing the previous traditional local landscapes.

The conservation of rural heritage is thus mainly a problem of landscape conservation, as the landscape can be seen to be the principle heritage—the container of other historical and environmental goods, the board on which we can read the tracks and the signs left by human activities. However, landscape conservation is not easy, because landscape is not a painting, and from this may arise many problems and issues. First, if a museum is the place for the conservation of historical objects, it is very difficult to find one large enough to contain landscape; landscape is not a painting if only because it is much larger and just does not fit into a museum. Secondly, landscapes unlike paintings have different owners and users. People normally use landscapes to live, work or recreate and often the goal of conservation may conflict with some of the different uses. That means we need to put constraints upon some uses, which may cause economic losses to the different owners and users. Economic matters play an important role in landscape conservation policies which generally need to be highly financed. A landscape is not the product of a single artist, like a painting, but of a community, of different people that have modelled it over a long period. In this sense landscape belongs to the people that have built it; then we have to decide together what to do with it in order to meet the goals of the people living in it. To conserve landscape, to give back to it a sense of identity, we need the help of the present people to understand the reasons and motivations of the past generations, to recover their collective memory, to rebuild their material culture and identity. However, the local people have often left, and their jobs with them. Sometimes the traditional landscape can be conserved, but only at great cost after the land's economic function has disappeared. The new incoming population may well be prepared to pay this high price to buy themselves an identity and a history, but the new, conserved, landscape is likely to be a sanitised version of the original.

This discussion leads to a focus upon three main issues that need further development:

- the conservation of landscape and associated rural heritage needs an economic base to deal with the multiply generated costs of its conservation;
- the conservation of landscape and rural heritage is tied to the recovery and reconstruction of the material culture that produced it; this means that the goal of its conservation has to do with the rediscovery or reconstruction of local identity and needs the active involvement of local people;
- finally, and consequently, this type of heritage requires a special museological solution.

Contrary to previous policies, in which the role of rural areas has been strongly identified with agriculture, the current policies of the European Union and many national agencies favour recognising the plurality of the possible different economic roles as the basis for a new development of rural areas. The future of millions of people in Europe depends in a large part on the capacity to revitalise rural areas, to stop the decline of their economy and of their local cultures. In 1987 – 1988 the Council of Europe promoted the European Campaign for the Rural World, which aimed at involving European governments in the development of rural regions, in the preservation of their historical continuity and the conservation of the quality of the multiple and different existing resources, from the natural and environmental heritage to historical and cultural values, from architectural and artistic goods to languages, the human dimension, working and living conditions. The Campaign focused on the necessity of a multipurpose policy for rural areas able to reverse their decline. The revitalisation of the rural world was seen as the way to safeguard a unique cultural heritage in which Europe as a whole could trace its roots and identity. In addition the development and survival of the European rural world was seen as the basic condition for a stable and long-term economic development of the whole European Community, to fill the gap between rural and urban regions.

The final meeting of the Campaign, held in Lübeck in 1988, suggested four different and integrated fields of action for promoting the development of rural areas:

- the protection and conservation of natural environments;
- the economic use of local human resources;
- the conservation and reuse of cultural heritage and landscape protection;
- safeguarding local cultural values and developing more active and advanced social relations.

The economic basis for the suggested policy was a combination of traditional activities (such as agriculture or handicrafts) with the development of new tertiary activities, among which tourism would play a primary role because of its positive effects such as:

- stimulating the creation of a market for traditional local products;
- fostering local culture and popular traditions through tourism demands;
- revitalising landscapes, historical centres and architectural heritage, as both a resource and an infrastructure.

In these ways conservation and revitalisation are linked; the conservation of the landscape and its landmarks (hill-towns, farms, rural architecture, etc.) is possible and effective only by means of an overall economic and social revitalisation of the rural world. But at the same time this revitalisation should be based on the conservation of this heritage, which thereby becomes a resource for eco-sustainable development.

There is a problem of levels of identity here. Much rural heritage is perceived as being regional or even more local in character, and Europe-wide solutions may not be seen as immediately relevant. However, it is precisely in areas such as vernacular architecture and rural ways of life that the local can meet the international. Similar environments and economies have called into being similar but not identical responses, perhaps a layout of long-house common across most of the North European Plain and beyond, but with local materials sometimes stone, brick or wood, and with variations in detail. Another similar response is in the mountain regions of the Pyrenees, Alps, Apennines and Carpathians, where similar conditions have produced many styles of dwelling and village, but all obviously with much in common.

Of course, this new rural society is almost certainly self-consciously complicit in the project to save itself. No longer can this be life carrying on in a traditional way, but is life acted out according to traditional rules. The new villager may act out the past, but does so knowingly. This is a re-enactment process as well as a conservational one.

## Exercise Thirty-eight

While we may, nostalgically, regret the passing of an unselfconscious traditional past, is there anything lost from such recreation and re-enactment? Is it valuable to present society to keep the objects and tools of previous economies? Are they only to be kept if they are particularly fine specimens and thus works of art for decorating our houses rather than for use as intended?

## *From the traditional museum to the eco-museum*

A museum is the traditional physical expression of an important function common to all societies, namely the safeguarding and presentation of objects representing their cultural values. In this way museums became tools of discovery and means of saving society's cultural and historical identity. Consequently the museum since its foundation, has been considered not only as a place of exposition but a more complex and multifunctional institution, a place of research, conservation and transmission of national, regional or local cultures and identities. In other words the museum is a teaching institution.

In the last 30 years the concept, role, instruments, use and purpose of the museum has changed drastically and a complete redefinition of its main ideas has been necessary. Indeed the concept of the museum as being a large institutional building itself has been revised. Museums may well be as much outdoors as in, and include many buildings and sites. Until the beginning of the 1960s, museums were visited by a select group of people, but today, with the development of mass tourism, museums have become places visited by thousands and in some cases millions of people every year. This of course has increased their economic role, and today museums represent, because of their capacity to attract tourists and visitors, one of the main resources for sustainable economic development. As part of the development of post-industrial societies, of the conflict between 'space and place' and of economic and cultural globalisation, museums have strengthened their role as teaching institutions, as a way to re-discover, conserve and to spread among the population local culture and traditions. In this sense, local people as well as tourists are the main users of the museums. The third element is represented by the broadening of the heritage concept, as argued in earlier chapters, that today includes not only monuments or fine arts, but almost everything perceived as belonging to a past and contributing to national or local culture, including fauna and flora.

In conclusion, in contemporary societies, museums play different and important roles that include:
* supporting economic development attracting tourism flows;
* rescuing, conserving and rebuilding local culture and identity;
* saving not only objects but also buildings, settlements, landscapes and species.

In the second half of the 1970s Andrea Emiliani and Lucio Gambi, Italian historical geographers, suggested the realisation of a regional territorial system of museums, as a solution for the collection of objects relating to peasant work and early industrialisation. This solution would have increased the role of the museum as a teaching institution, through its territorial spread, assuring, in such a way, better contact with the population of the region, who would have more opportunities to visit museums. At the same time the idea of a new kind of museum was suggested—an 'open air museum', to prevent what Emiliani had called, 'the deportation of the objects of the past'. This avoided their exhibition in a enclosed place divorced from the geographical context in which they had been produced. It was necessary, indeed to give back the lost voice, sense and value to objects and places, through a museological solution able to exhibit and represent the objects in the landscape and in the environmental context in which they had been produced.

The next step in the evolution of the idea was to link the new role of the museum in reconstructing lost culture and identity. To achieve this goal, the proposed solution would have to foster an active participation of the local population. Only through the collective memory and knowledge of people is it possible to pursue the reconstruction process. At the same time, local people become involved and participated in rediscovering their own roots and identity. An eco-museum is thus an open-air museum, built with the participation of the local community, built by the people for the people. Thus an eco-museum involves the conservation and documentation of local material cultures and heritage, mainly based on the relationship with the land and its productive use. It is a museological solution different from the traditional one—an alternative solution able to document clearly the connection between man, land and environment.

The word 'eco-museum' was first used at the beginning of the 1970s by Huges de Varine, General Secretary of ICOM (International Council of Museums). He initiated an awareness of the old concept of the museum as a fortress, a completely closed institution unable to engage in dialogue with the host environmental and social context. 'Eco' comes from Greek *oikos*, house or shelter; the main consideration of an eco-museum is that the history, traditions and culture of a place and of its inhabitants, are for a large part the consequence of their relationship, through the centuries, with the host environment. The whole environment in which a society lives and works is seen as a container of objects (architecture, rural landscape, paths, historical landmarks, etc.) and all the human activities performed in it, are the exhibits in the eco-museum. The eco-museum then shows the whole culture of a people, the material culture of objects and tools, technologies and materials, clothing and buildings, but also religion, folklore and magical beliefs—activities as much as landscape, monuments and artefacts. The eco-museum is thus a museum of time and space; it studies and preserves the material culture of the society, to awaken and rebuild its collective memory. In this aim people are active participants, as the only holders of their own collective and historic memory, the link between past and present.

## Selected examples in Europe
### The French experience:
France is the European country with the most advanced experience of the eco-museum. There are at least 28 associations of museums that include different eco-museums. One of the most important is the *Féderation des écomusees et de musées de société*, including 45 eco-museums in different parts of the country. The *Musée Dauphinoise* is another important association that includes only eco-museums and which has the goal of supporting the information and research functions of the eco-museum. This means that an eco-museum or a 'regional

museum' cannot limit its role to the mere exhibition of objects and tools, but has to involve itself with the collective memory and identity of people living in the area. As a consequence the association promotes the participation of local communities in the setting up, development and management of the eco-museum. Another regional network of eco-museums is the *Réseau régional de la Franche-Comté* whose role is to support the creation of museums of the economy and work in the region, in co-operation with the *Association comtoise des arts et traditions populaires*.

Among the numerous different experiences, the Eco-museum of Ungersheim in Alsace is very significant because it was one of the first developed with the co-operation of the Council of Europe, in an area spreading into three different countries, France, Germany and Switzerland. The creation of the eco-museum was on the initiative of a group of volunteers belonging to the Christian Movement for Peace, who began the rehabilitation of 25 houses in 1971 for families in need, holiday accommodation, community educational facilities, village pubs and the like. A number of houses that could not be rescued *in situ* were dismantled and rebuilt on a site made available by the Ungersheim local authority, where the idea was born to create an eco-museum. Between 1980 and 1984, when the eco-museum was opened, 19 houses were reconstructed. The construction of the Ungersheim eco-museum cost approximately 40 million francs—15 million from voluntary contributions, 13 million from local authorities (Alsace region and Haut Rhin Department), 2 million from Ministry of Culture, 2 million from miscellaneous sources and 8 million in the form of loans. The eco-museum has been one of the most successful in terms of attracting visitors which rose from 140,000 in 1984 to 250,000 in 1990.

**The Italian experience**

*1) Pistoia.*

The mountain area around Pistoia, in Tuscany, though linked in some way to the city, has long been recognised as a place with its own identity and homogeneity, due to the geomorphology, which has profoundly influenced the use of land and the human settlements in the area. The environmental conditions, particularly the high water table and woods, have been a very important resource over the centuries for the development of industrial activities like iron working and ice production. Environmental conditions, settlement characteristics and productive activities, all combined to produce a very particular mixed landscape, worthy of being conserved and visited; the formula of the eco-museum is seen as the best way to do this.

The eco-museum is organised in five sectors, with specific itineraries, that allow an integrated understanding of the different subjects (nature, art, archaeology) and of their interrelations. The five areas are:

- ice production, along the valley of the Reno river, characterised by the ice production factories and a rich network of creeks and ponds;
- the iron production area which is mainly in the municipality of S Marcello and is characterised by the presence of large iron factories mainly built in the 18th and 19th centuries. One of these ironworks has been restored and converted into a museum;
- the green areas, which are a fundamental element in the whole eco-museum and include a Natural Regional Reserve (Campolino) and parts of the original Appennino and Monte Abetone forests;

- the agricultural activities and rural settlements, with all the evidences of the traditional agricultural activities, including stock-raising and wood-related activities like chestnuts and coal production. The Museum of the People of the Pistoiese Appennino has been created in Rivoreta, with a collection of objects and documents of the daily life of the population;
- culture and popular religion, including the sacred art museum in Popiglio. It is possible to visit different churches, in which can be found religious objects and furniture especially of the 16th and 17th centuries.

*2) Po Delta*

The Po, the longest and most important river in Italy, ends in the Adriatic Sea, forming a large delta mostly in the province of Ferrara. The peculiarity of the natural environment consists of mainly brackish areas rich in fish, especially the eels of the Comacchio valley, and varieties of fauna and flora. The area has also been a crossroads of different cultures and civilisations. The whole area has become protected and a large nature park, whose activities include the creation of an eco-museum system, spread over the area. It includes both closed and open exhibitions, and can be visited on foot or using the traditional boats (*barconi*).The system is divided into two different main areas:

- in the northern part, the core of the museum is represented by the Castle of Mesola, the entrance to the park, which accommodates the Centre for Environmental Education, with specific attention to the Great Mesola Forest. Another concentration of the eco-museum is around Pomposa Abbey.
- in the southern part of the system is the Museum of the Valleys of Argenta, which won the museum award of the Council of Europe in 1992. The Museum is concerned with the study of nature.
- the centre of the system is Comacchio and its surrounding hinterland which is presented in different museums; the Museum of Human Cultures, whose purpose is to illustrate the ecological use of the natural resources in the area in all its cultural aspects; the Museum of the Valleys which is located in old fishermen's shelters (*casoni*) and focuses on fishing.

*3) The Gerenzone valley*

Lecco, near Lake Como, is one of the most industrialised areas of Italy, specialised in iron working and silk. There are numerous relics of its long industrial history such as spinning machines and silk-mills, unique in Europe. The eco-museum reflects the long history of this production and the way in which man has used the existing resources. It includes two different itineraries, the Valley of Gerenzone, related to the iron industry, and the silk route.

Water-powered iron forges along the Gerenzone Creek from the Middle Ages to the 19th century have contributed more than 100 industrial archaeology sites now linked in a pedestrian route. The silk route gives the visitor a comprehensive picture of silk production in the area, historically one of the most important concentrations in Europe, and of the associated machinery and buildings. The 33 selected sites include three silk museums, one experimental silk-worm breeding centre, two civic museums (Lecco and Como), the Company town of Valmadrera and 26 silk-mills and dye works, some of which still working.

## The Portuguese experience

The idea of creating an eco-museum in the municipalities of Condeixa, Penela and Arzilla, south of Coimbra, was born in 1979 following research promoted by ICOM and UNESCO and exhibitions and contacts between the local population, elected representatives and leaders of local associations. In addition there have been archaeological excavation, rescue activities for traditional arts and crafts, creation of new crafts, concerts, environmental protection activities, guided tours and in general promotion of rural tourism. All these activities, mostly carried out by professionals joined by elected representatives, leaders of associations and young farmers, led to the improvement of the population's cultural level and encouraged young people to stay in the area, due to the creation of new job opportunities and trades.

Encouraging young people to stay in the area has been the major priority and policies for this have included:

* stimulating tourism-related activities, using the opportunity given by the vicinity of some very important tourist centres like Fatima, Coimbra, and Figueira de Foz;
* improving some of the area's urban and rural landscapes,
* encouraging local historical and archaeological studies;
* stimulating small and medium-size industries;
* developing regional agricultural and forestry potential.

It is hoped that this will result in the reinforcement of local cultural identity. The eco-museum has organised tourist activities, an action programme to improve the existing infrastructure (roads, water supply and sanitation), a social assistance system and created new jobs. All the activities linked to the establishment and the management of the eco-museum have been supported by contributions from the municipalities and from the State Secretariat for Culture.

## The Norwegian experience

*1) The Troms Regional Ecomuseum of the Lapp population.*

This is an important example of an eco-museum created to preserve the culture of a particular ethnic minority, namely the Saami (Lapp) population of Norway. They are today present in six of the nineteen counties of the country, but in the past were more widespread. One of the fundamental characteristics of the Saami's way of life is the ecological use of the earth's resources. The traditional pattern was subsistence farming, supplemented by maritime and forest resources. Potatoes were the main crop, while the outlying fields and the forests were used for grazing, fuel and construction materials, and there were also some cottage industries based on the same resources. The men's main occupation was fishing while women looked after the farm, the animals and craft production and thus created the traditional agricultural landscape of the region. The Saami traditional culture has remained almost unchanged up to the Second World War, when a decline began due to the modernisation of the economy and particularly the destruction of the natural resources, particularly the fisheries, on which Saami based their economy and society.

At the beginning of the 1980s, the local Lapp organisation and the Troms Regional Museums had the idea of building an eco-museum of Saami culture and traditional landscapes, complete with buildings, turf-huts, fishermen's sheds, farmland, pastures and hay-fields. The main goal was to reinforce ethnic and local identity and help cultural traditions and handicrafts to survive. For this purpose the whole area was recorded in the Norwegian national register of heritage and the Holmenes farm was selected as a site for the ecomuseum, whose main goal, apart from exhibiting old buildings, traditions and tools, was to demonstrate the many ways in which populations adapt to natural resources and change the face of the landscape.

The local population has been involved in the process, by gathering information from the elderly about uses, traditions and handicraft skills and also through active participation in the restoration of the buildings. The Troms Regional Eco-museum is engaged in the formidable task of documenting everything that attests to the collective identity of the local Saami community. The involvement of the local population has played a very important role in enabling people to 'communicate with the past, the present and the future' and to increase the economic opportunities, re-establishing traditional processes and using natural resources to develop various forms of tourism and cottage industries.

*2)  The Havratunet – Osteroy – Hordaland eco-museum*
One of the finest surviving examples of rural farming communities in western Norway lies 25km north of Bergen. The clustered settlement consists of eight farmsteads (36 buildings) arranged around the *tungate* (courtyard) set in strip-farming terrain. The strip-farming landscape surrounding the settlement was the outcome of the traditional land management practice, up to the mid-19th century, when large-scale land reallocation schemes caused the old communities to disappear. In Havratunet community the dwelling houses are in the centre and the farm buildings on the outside. The village was first mentioned in documents dated 1303, when the land was undivided and only a farm existed. In 1519 two farms were registered and eight in 1554, a number unchanged to the present. Each farmer owned a small strip of land (*teig*), scattered over the arable area, a system which ensured that each farm had its fair share of good soil. When the land reallocation schemes appeared at the end of the 19th century, Havratunet was not interested in this and remains unaltered to tell the tale of old Norwegian farming, with all its features—the ash trees, the strings used for carrying hay, the stone mounds and the terraces created for growing crops on the step hillsides. It is a landscape that evokes all that 'cultivation' means in terms of horny hands and bent backs. In 1973 a private trust was established to preserve this unique site until it became part of the Osteroy Museum.

**The Spanish experience**
The initiative for creating eco-museums in Spain is about ten years old. In the 1980s the first cultural parks in Spain were due to the activities of people such as Antonio Beltran, an archaeologist well-known for his research into prehistoric art at the University of Zaragoza, who promoted the creation of cultural parks in Aragón. At first, the aim of these was the protection and diffusion of the prehistoric, mainly in the Mediterranean area (Andalucía, Valencia, Catalonia and Aragón). The importance of these artefacts has been recognised by UNESCO declaring them Heritage of Humanity in December 1998.

Legislation about eco-museums has not been extensive developed. The Spanish Heritage Law included prescriptions about sites and archaeological Historical ruins, but nothing creating this new institution. Aragón is the only region that has created a specific law (*Parques Culturales de Aragón*, law 1997, inspired by the experience of Antonio Beltrán of Zaragoza, André Humbert, geographer and director of a cultural park in La Lorena- France, and Adamo, of Novara, and its legislation and experience is now imitated by other communities.

Aragón now has five cultural parks and is expecting a new one, included in the programme *Terra Incognita* of the EU. The objective of all these parks is to protect the rich cultural and natural heritage (including mediaeval villages, landscapes, prehistoric paintings, even dinosaur footprints) and integrate them into the strategies of urban and natural planning and sustained development of these areas. Important heritage has been recovered, protected and interpreted to the population, but more important, these cultural parks have completely changed the life and economy of extensive depressed areas with few inhabitants and a low rents. Visitors to *Río Martín* multiplied ten-fold since the park was created, *Albarracín* is visited by 250,000 tourists per year, and from 200,000 to 400,000 tourists to *Río Vero* and *Maestrazgo* ; this phenomenon provoked the creation of small tourist enterprises (guides, restaurants, hotels, centres of interpretation, etc.) that keep population. For all these villages, heritage is now a real engine powering regional development.

The management of these institutions depends on local authorities, although regional government does support with money and administration. Sometimes other economic resources come from national institutions (Ministry of Industry, for instance) or European programmes.

## Conclusion

There are thus many interpretations of the eco-museum and related ideas for the conservation of rural objects and ways of life. The pioneering role of the collection of typically Scandinavian, mainly Swedish, vernacular architecture at Skansen, near Stockholm as the archetype of a National Museum of Rural Life, is acknowledged. However, regions such as Dalarna (Sweden) or Vestlandet (Norway) have pursued the same policies on a regional scale. Experience in the United Kingdom has taken a slightly different route, and the term 'eco-museum' is not commonly used. There are major collections of vernacular buildings, such as the Weald & Downland Museum at Singleton in Sussex, and also a plethora of Museums of Rural Life, notably that at the University of Reading. The Welsh Folk Museum at St Fagans outside Cardiff is perhaps as close to an eco-museum as is found in Britain, in this case a museum celebrating Welshness by concentrating on Welsh rural life and artefacts. Other cases, such as the Black Country Museum in Birmingham, Ironbridge Gorge Museum and Beamish Open Air Museum, while often having close links with local people, celebrate an industrial proletarian society of about 1900, and the important eco-museum at Le Creusot in France is also partly industrial (Bellaigue, 1999). Mining and industrial remains as well as housing are gathered onto one site, often interpreted by people in costume. The apparent lack of the eco-museum in the UK may be related to the early industrialisation of the country. Consequently a stable rural society is much further beyond human memory than in southern Italy.

# The case of the heritage gem city

## Summary

This type of heritage site management concerns the small or medium-sized town whose heritage endowment is so important, complete and undamaged as to constitute a valued heritage site as a whole. Such towns are produced by a rare accidental set of historic circumstances. They pose particular problems of management. They have few local policy choices and subordinate all other functions to that of heritage, and even the presentation of that heritage involves careful planning for accommodating visitors. Two archetypical cases in western Europe are discussed in detail and two more recent cases in central Europe. A context of cases outside Europe is also discussed.

## What is a heritage gem city?

'Heritage gems' are those, usually small, cities in which the historic resource is both so dramatic, extensive, and complete, and also so valued, as to dominate their urban morphology, their identity and their policy options. They are frequently dominated by structures from a single historical period and contain, at least in their central areas, few architecturally discordant elements. In Europe they are typically medieval or renaissance survivals, whereas in the New World they may appear in various guises associated with pioneer settlement; in the less developed world they are generalisable chiefly in terms of the recency of their discovery as tourism resources. Their endowment has become so appreciated that such towns play important roles regionally, nationally or even internationally as representative archetypes.

Consequently their management is both easier than for multifunctional, multi-period cities and also more difficult. Strategically there are few options or conflicting goals for development—the typical consensus locally, nationally and even in many cases internationally is for preservation at almost any cost. Such a goal will often receive financial support from outside the city, while any development alternative will often be vigorously opposed by individuals and organisations from outside the city. This, of course, raises the question of how many such fossilised gems are actually needed and how many can be afforded? At the tactical level however the very spatial extent and comprehensiveness of the resource, together with the strength of the emotional commitment to its preservation, typically implies that even the smallest deviation from such a policy will be both noticed and provoke opposition. There is thus very little room for the sorts of compromises, allowing the adaptation of old forms to accommodate new functions, that are central to the planning of other cities.

## A model of the creation of gem cities

Gem cities exist as a result of historical accident. This chance survival depended in turn upon a number of historical processes, all of which must occur in sequence and at the correct time to ensure the creation of the gem. The simple fact that of all the cities that have ever existed in the world only a handful have undergone this process, to emerge successfully as today's gem cities, suggests that the process of their creation depends upon a rare, even bizarre, set of circumstances. Figure 8 suggests that these circumstances can be summarised in a simple four-phase model. Most cities, it can be assumed, develop through time, building and adapting their urban forms in response to changing demands. Growth, of course, can vary through many short-term vicissitudes, and the overall tempo of growth will vary greatly in different historic time-periods. However the whole urban system can be generalised to a regularly rising line; the important point is that gem cities deviate sharply from this norm and it is this

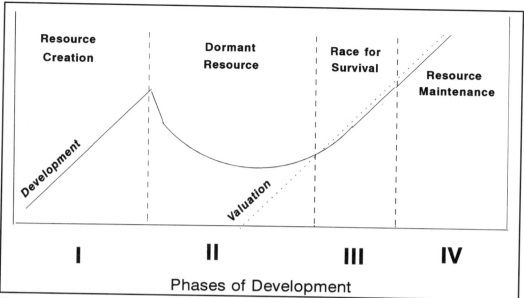

*Figure 8. 'Gem City' Model.*

deviation that creates the gem, in four successive phases. In the real world, of course, some gems are purer than others, and elements of variation from the model may occur.

**The resource creation phase**

The potential gem city commonly experiences a period of exceptionally rapid growth compared with other cities. This may well be a result of the exploitation of a sudden economic windfall such as a discovered advantage of fortuitous location, or equally the chance endowment of a specific strategic military or political importance. Such growth is generally not only intense but of short duration, often also associated with powerful or creative individuals and bounded therefore by their life-times. This growth is reflected in a burst of creativity, leading to the creation of architectural and other morphological expressions and even historical events and personalities associated with this short 'golden age'. This period stops, often as suddenly as it began, with the evaporation of the initiating economic, political or strategic advantage and the absence of a substitute. Not infrequently the powerful individual who created the town falls from grace and power. Such evaporation may arise through human or natural environmental agency.

**The resource survival phase**

There now follows a long period of stagnation or even population decline which may extend over many centuries. The structures created earlier may well be neglected, reused or just ignored but critically they will not be subjected to demolition and replacement because there are few pressures for development, as the city as a whole is just by-passed by new economies and transport or even in exceptional cases abandoned.

**The resource appreciation phase and the race for survival**

At some moment, and for any of the various reasons discussed earlier, the surviving relics may begin to be valued as a socio-economic resource (a metamorphosis typically diffusing outward from European origins). Now begins what can be seen as a race for survival. On the one side the growing valuation of the historic structures and associations leads eventually to pressures for preservation through protective legislation. All this takes time to be effective. In the European case, as argued in Chapter Three, it took as much as a century for the campaigns of an eccentric minority to be expressed in legislation and planning practice. During this period the pressures for development can be assumed to be growing, not least because the conservation movement itself can be seen as a product of growth and in part a reaction to aspects of it. If the protective measures are in place before substantial growth occurs in the town, and again this is often the result of the initiative of specific individuals, then a gem city will have been created. If not, then important parts of the endowment will have been demolished or damaged and the comprehensive integrity, the hallmark of such cities, will have ceased to exist before it could be saved. The race will have been lost, as has been most often the case.

**The resource maintenance phase**
Having been created, the gem city must now be maintained; and the very fact that it is now valued in this unique way itself creates many pressures for change. The resource endowment becomes an exploitable tourism resource and the highly appreciated urban environment becomes a desirable location for many commercial and residential functions. This is a universal condition, as discussed earlier, but the specific problem of gem cities is that their value lies in the completeness of the ensemble. They therefore face the twin threats of creeping demolition or visual intrusions on their peripheries to accommodate growing new functions, thereby removing the 'settings' and isolating the jewels, and also insensitive 'heritagisation' of their centres as a result of the very growth of the appreciation of them.

Each gem city is unique, not only in the same general way as are all cities but specifically because gem status is only conferred on the exceptional. However we will now examine some cases in more detail which we regard as representative, not in terms of their creative endowments which remain individual works of art, but in terms of their history of development and most important their management problems and solutions.

## Cases in Western Europe
### Ribe (Denmark)
Ribe is a small compact town of only some 8,000 inhabitants surrounded by open meadows. It lays claim, however, to being Denmark's oldest city (incorporated around AD 700) and having the largest concentration of nationally listed historical buildings (103) outside Copenhagen. It is thus quite clearly recognised, both nationally and in terms of local identity and function, as an historic gem city by our definition. The chronology of its creation accords well with our model. Steady if unspectacular development as a regional market town accelerated in the 16th century, when it became a major entrepot centre linking the Baltic and North Sea trade routes across the base of the Jutland peninsula. Little more than a century's economic prosperity resulted in almost all of the currently conserved buildings. A combination of local, national and even intercontinental factors removed the basis of prosperity by the 17th century. Local navigation difficulties, the shifting of the trade route northwards, the declining significance of the Baltic trade, all contributed to the economic

collapse. The loss of Schleswig/Slesvig in 1864 which placed Ribe on the new international frontier, further restricting its local hinterland, merely confirmed and continued an existing long period of stagnation.

Although some notable buildings were demolished in the course of the 19th century, a local antiquarian society was formed in 1855 and a local tourism association as early as 1899. These pressed for the recognition of the need for systematic conservation and the development of a town plan to manage it. The national Protection of Historic Buildings Act was passed in 1918, a significant date, symbolically in the 'nick of time', as North Schleswig was returned to Danish sovereignty in 1919 and Ribe resumed a regional service function. More realistically however there were few pressures for serious morphological change until the 1960s; and an awareness of the value of architectural preservation and subsequent implementation through appropriate protective measures just predated the encounter with such pressures. A local plan of 1963 imposed general controls on change in almost the entire area of the old town, including no fewer than 550 buildings. This was followed in 1969 by a comprehensive building-by-building survey and the adoption of a conservation plan (Bevaringsplan Ribe), which significantly predates the national enabling legislation of the 1977 Municipal Planning Act for the designation of conservation areas.

The small compact extent of the town, together with the completeness of its architectural ensemble and its visibility as a result of its setting in open country, raised a number of special problems and justified quite rigorous detailed measures. For example, not only are roof lines carefully controlled but so also are the types and colours of tiling used on them. Again the small size of the town has made it relatively easy to consign non-conforming uses, such as large scale modern retailing and car parking, especially for the million-plus annual visitors, to the periphery. Perhaps the lesson of Ribe is that even in a country with a relatively long tradition of regulatory land-use and acceptance of planning constraints, the survival of the historic gem city owes much both to chance and to local initiatives and is by no means inevitable.

### Rothenburg (Bavaria)

Rothenburg ob der Tauber repeats the critical elements of gem resource creation and survival, with variations. Founded as a castle town in the early Middle Ages, in common with many other German towns, it achieved the status of a Free City of the Holy Roman Empire in the 13th century, when its economic and political importance were sufficient for the Imperial Diet to be convened here in 1377. It remained significant through the Thirty Years War (1618 – 1648) but its free status was lost with 19th-century incorporation into Bavaria, whereafter it was functionally marginalised relative to the major cities in the strategic Rhine and Main corridors. Rothenburg's site and morphology provide a further constraint upon its contemporary functional possibilities but also a highly distinctive scenic and historic tourist resource; it shares with Ribe (and most European gems) a high visibility but in a quite different physical context. It is a completely walled town on an escarpment overlooking the Tauber valley, the contours of which are precisely reflected in the alignment of the walls. Modern functions serving some 12,000 inhabitants are necessarily concentrated in the limited suburban development beyond the walls; the historic town is highly constricted in its ability to handle vehicles, or activities other than some of those geared to serving the tourist trade. This has been generated by its fame as an exceptionally complete medieval/renaissance gem, both in its internal streetscapes and in its aggregate townscape as seen from its fortifications and from across the Tauber valley.

The survival of Rothenburg's historic resource was dependent upon its economic and political eclipse before the industrial period. Its discovery by 19th-century Romantics as a symbol of a vanishing Germany, led to early heritage awareness, the founding of the Verein Alt Rothenburg (a conservation society) in the 1890s and the enactment of civic controls in 1900 which, as in Ribe, largely forestalled insensitive redevelopment. Rothenburg's eclipse is particularly critical in the context of recent German history. It was, none the less, substantially damaged in 1945 and its emergence from this national trauma is credited to the forbearance of an American general who halted his attack when he saw the town's quality, and who is duly remembered as a vital figure in the town's history. This survival through a single military decision to respect historicity is not unique, other famous examples being Savannah and Heidelberg. There is a likely factor in the tourist-historic survival of Rothenburg that could be labelled the *Student Prince* phenomenon, although it is Heidelberg that can actually claim Romberg's operetta. The relevant point in these two German cases is that artistic fiction shapes expectations which a city may fortuitously fulfil, or a role model for the city to emulate. Cause and effect, reality and myth are impossible, and for our purposes unnecessary, to disentangle. What is important is the popularity of the H.C. Andersen images in Ribe or the Brothers Grimm in Rothenburg, however subconsciously, among potential users of the historic resource.

Maintaining, enhancing and capitalising upon the historic resource has been the principal preoccupation of Rothenburg's recent planning and management. The municipal controls ensured that post-1945 reconstruction adhered to the historical character. As in Ribe they predated higher authority but were reinforced at the Land level by the Bavarian Denkmalschutzgesetz in 1973 and by tri-level cost-sharing provisions, including the federal government, for related urban management. The entrenched preservation of historic Rothenburg has provided a fertile centre-piece for abundant tourism services and sophisticated marketing. Tourism success has a predictable price, however; there is a concern to balance tourism with suburban industrial development without visual intrusion, and to spread tourists more evenly through the historic city. As in Ribe, major parking facilities are provided in relatively unobtrusive locations outside the walls and moat, where tourist information is available. In this way tour buses, which cause particular environmental stress, are deflected from the narrow gates and streets. Note that Rothenburg is marketed in a wider regional framework, which as we discuss below is common elsewhere; here there is a particularly linear dimension since it is a prime attraction on the Bavarian Romantische Strasse.

## Cases in Central and Eastern Europe

The implications of the dramatic political changes in Europe since 1990 have had major consequences for heritage and for tourism. A decade ago the cities of central and eastern Europe were more or less severely constricted in terms both of tourist access and amenities, and of funds, enterprise and incentive to sustain and develop their often pristine, if neglected, historic resources. The transformation since has been radical. The 'golden horde' of western tourists, ever eager to extend the repertoire of tourist-historic experiences beyond the familiar western cases, arrived first in Prague, Budapest and Krakow and then dispersed to the smaller gems such as Cesky Krumlov, Levoca or Sentendre. This is proving to be a mixed blessing for conserved cities. On the one hand the value of the historic gems is being more widely discovered and appreciated and opportunities for western investment in their enhancement and development are being exploited. On the other hand tourism requires modern facilities for accommodation, transport and entertainment which increase pressures for development, at precisely the moment when many public planning controls are being relaxed and public management agencies being dismantled.

Case studies at different scales have appeared in various contexts akin to the present focus, such as the Czech cities in Hammersley & Westlake (1994) and Gdansk, Kraków, Budapest and even the remnants of Königsberg (Kaliningrad) in Tunbridge & Ashworth (1996). These are not repeated here; rather the two cases of Eger and Weimar have been selected.

### Eger (Hungary)

This small town has not only a remarkable ensemble of Baroque buildings of international importance but also a unique symbolic significance to the identity of the Hungarian nation. It is thus an archetypical historic gem city for which the questions when and how was it created can be answered quite precisely. It developed as a small unremarkable medieval market town between the mountains (Matras / Bükk) and the great plains (Puzta). However its strategic position contributed a major castle whose defence in 1552 provided both a potential epic tale of desperate Christian resistance to the Asiatic hordes and also a hero in commandant Istvan Dobó. However it subsequently fell to the Turks, the villains of the tale, and was occupied for more than a century. The liberation from Turkish rule in 1687 began a renaissance in which the conquering Hapsburg state and the post-Tridentine counter-reformation Catholic church played the initiating roles. The population rose from 1,200 to 15,000 in little over a century. In particular Eszterházy (Bishop from 1762 to 1799) created what amounted to a new Baroque city around the small medieval core with episcopal palace, lyceum as proto-university, library and numerous ecclesiastical administrative buildings. Also notable was the preservation and even reconstruction of some relics of the Turkish period, no doubt as a reminder of conquest and reconquest. These include the most northerly minaret in Europe, now crowned symbolically with a cross.

The end of the 18th century marked a quite abrupt end to these developments and the pretensions of the town. No longer on the frontier of a resurgent Christendom, it was by-passed by the major east-west road and later railway links. Its only major economic activity, the wine trade, became concentrated in a valley outside the town (Szépasszonyvölgy).

The valuation of the resource can be dated to the last decades of the 19th century, corresponding to the burst of self-conscious Hungarian nation-building that was released by the Imperial 'compromise' of 1867 and which culminated in the celebration of the millennium of the Magyar state in 1896. The critical role for Eger was played by the novelist Geza Gárdonyi whose account of the heroic siege in the book *Stars of Eger* became the best-known children's story in Hungary. The mythologising of the 16th-century siege became linked to the 18th-century architecture in a powerful synergy to which was also added the local wine (Egri Bikavér), skillfully marketed under the *Bull's Blood* label that links it with acts of heroism. The already existing spa tourism was thus extended to pilgrimage tourism, to the reconstructed castle and millennium statues of the now legendary national heroes, with the addition also of gastronomy.

The post-Second World War period witnessed the implementation of systematic preservational measures, but also some major threats to the resource. On the one hand the new communist government had a programme of planned industrialisation and extensive social housing provision for a rapidly growing population, which rose from 38,000 in 1960 to 60,000 in 1980; both led to unsightly high-rise intrusions in both the Medieval and Baroque towns. On the other hand, while having little official interest in monuments to either bourgeois nationalism or baroque Catholicism, both local and national governments had a considerable interest in legitimating their rule and associating themselves with Hungarian self-identity as purveyed through the state-building mythologies. Significantly, they also had the authority to introduce protective measures, including quite detailed regulations about material use and colour schemes in the main Baroque thoroughfares (Széchényi and Kossuth Avenues).

The post-1990 period opened up such towns throughout central Europe to western tourists eager for new horizons. This has led to an increased local appreciation of the economic value of the historic resource, but also to its commercialisation. The potential tragedy illustrated by Eger is that this has occurred at precisely the moment when local planning has been largely dismantled, property privatised and most of the detailed management controls either relaxed or just no longer enforced. The gem created by historic accident, the fortuitous existence of individuals and the popularity of a novelist is in very real danger of destruction by an equally chance combination of circumstances.

**Weimar (Thuringia, Germany, former DDR)**

As a former Residenz city, Weimar (population c.60,000) more closely resembles western German counterparts such as Coburg (Bavaria) than the smaller Rothenburg. However, within the former DDR it is the most comparable claimant of 'gem' status and its consideration with the latter is instructive. In 1990 the contrast was glaring, reflecting the ubiquitous identity of the DDR; buildings were typically blackened to several metres from the ground by two-stroke engine emissions and domestic use of lignite; the town centre was decayed and the market-square buildings still incompletely reconstructed after 1945 bomb damage; traffic and parking management were conspicuously absent; hotels and restaurants were a fraction of Rothenburg's and the standard of food facilities often inadequate. The city's cultural significance was, however, not merely appreciated but promoted as the real German heritage, as opposed to that of West Germany. Yet neither public resources nor tourism revenues were adequate to sustain it and the DDR in its last days was obliged to appeal to UNESCO for help to this end.

Weimar is a monument to German culture of the Renaissance period, during which the local nobility were outstanding patrons of the arts. Later Goethe, Schiller, Herder and Liszt are among the outstanding cultural figures supporting Weimar's claim to be the intellectual focus of Germany. The city's association with the founding of German democracy in 1919 both reflected and augmented its stature as a centre of enlightenment. Conversely, however, the aggrandisement of German culture under the Third Reich created a Nazi veneration of the city, with devastating consequences for its subsequent associations. The DDR government in turn co-opted Weimar's heritage, creating a national research centre of classical German literature in Weimar Castle.

The Nazi lionisation of Weimar led directly to the creation of a traumatic paradox in its identity which was persuasively marketed by the DDR as expressing the essential contradiction of German heritage. On the Ettersberg, overlooking Weimar to the north, was built one of the first concentration camps of the Third Reich—Buchenwald. It was out of sight but close enough to bring in prisoners to maintain the city, and has thereby indelibly stained it. The heritage of atrocity which Buchenwald represents has been extensively discussed elsewhere (Tunbridge & Ashworth, 1996) and it is unnecessary to reiterate it here. The following points are germane to the present purpose, however. First, the DDR identified itself with the humanist resistance at Buchenwald and projected this as the legitimate heir of the Weimar enlightenment, a heritage interpretation subsequently in flux. Secondly, the future status of Weimar as a tourist-historic gem is inseparable from the Buchenwald paradox because of both the political imperative to remember and the economic incentive to capitalise on the magnetism of atrocity heritage. Thirdly, the global (especially pan-European) significance of Weimar as a tourist-historic city is enhanced by the international victimisation which is memorialised by Buchenwald.

In the 1990s Weimar's historic resource has been significantly reshaped in both structure and symbolism. This has involved both the rehabilitation of decayed elements and some reinterpretation such as street renaming. In particular there has been a difficult reconceptualisation of Buchenwald, the joint marketing of which with Weimar continues however to project the German paradox. There has been a rapid upgrading of transport and tourism facilities. Planning control has devolved to Thuringia, the new *Land*, but with the assistance of Western counterparts and federal resources this has not involved the capitulation to development pressure encountered elsewhere in former Eastern Europe, although resolving who owns privatised property is also a vexatious issue here. Marketing is no longer politically or financially constrained, and is able to exploit the regional reunification with Hesse as the old German heartland. Standards of tourist-historic provision and control (such as of parking) are converging with those of Rothenburg. As a net result of its resurgence, Weimar was designated European Capital of Culture in 1999.

## An overview

The fullest gem expressions in the cases reviewed above are typical of many such historic gems that were created and have survived largely by chance occurrences, are maintained by detailed regulatory planning, and now enjoy wide public esteem for their undisputed historical value. What is also clear, however, is that such cities are comparatively rare, and that this very rarity confers a substantial consensus about the objectives of their planning. Equally, though, the range of development options open is severely limited and such cities can be regarded as being locked into the valuation of their past. The planning problems tend to be technical and architectural rather than political or economic. Functions other than those directly related to the historic city, even those concerned with tourism, will only be tolerated so long as they conform with, and offer no threat to, the preserved historic fabric. The town's economic viability, retailing structure and the social and demographic balance of its residential population have all in effect been sacrificed to the single goal of preservation. Most countries consider themselves fortunate in possessing a few such gems, but would not be prepared to pay the price, in terms of urban fossilisation, of too many.

Although there are many categories of such cities, two are especially prevalent. Fortress towns are often built in one historical period to meet a particular military threat; reassessment of defence needs and abandonment of the military function, and failure to find an alternative, may then result in stagnation and ultimately valuation and preservation. Many of the most renowned gems fall into this category, including Willemstad and Bourtange (Netherlands), Palma Nova and Citadella (Italy), Neuf-Brisach and the Bastide towns of France, Terezin in Bohemia, and even the New World contains a few, such as reconstructed Louisbourg (Canada).

Secondly, a recurrent geographical environment in which historic gems tend to be found is the obsolete port location, if only because ports are particularly vulnerable to technical innovations or natural processes that can abruptly terminate periods of prosperity. Sluis in Belgium, Rye in Sussex, England, Aigues Mortes in the south of France and Dubrovnik in Dalmatia illustrate this type. This classic gem location again occurs also in the New World (Portobello, Panama; Nantucket, Massachusetts) and to varying extents in colonial gateways elsewhere, as in Asia (Goa, India; Malacca, Malaysia; Macau, China).

---

### Exercise Thirty-nine

How many historic gem cities can any country afford to have? To what extent do such towns sacrifice important characteristics of towns through their focus upon the heritage values of their built environments? To what extent are they still towns? In particular, gem cities are likely to be dramatic illustrations of the process of gentrification. Property prices are likely to rise and property be transferred progressively into the hands of those who can afford the costs of conservation and value the benefits. If the purpose of the eco-museum discussed earlier was to benefit the local people, who benefits from the creation of gem cities, and their exploitation, largely for tourism?

---

## The Case of Heritage Gardens

### Summary
The conservation and management of gardens require significantly different skills from those needed for the built heritage, a result both of the living nature of plants and from the variety of heritage functions gardens are required to provide, from seed bank to aesthetic historical exemplar. Restoration is often made difficult by the extinction of species and the lack of documentary evidence.

### Garden Heritage
Gardens are different from buildings. These differences lead to one of the most fascinating problems of conservation and management in the whole field of heritage—and one of the most holistic. Gardens cross at least three of the fields of heritage which were discussed at the beginning of this book. In Europe at least, gardens nearly always include plants (and animals

too) so that nature is an important element; second, they are designed landscapes so all the problems of landscape aesthetics are involved; and third, they almost always include significant built elements. In addition, gardening is, for many, a most important activity, a traditional hobby often passed down through the generations, so that there is an important behaviour involved also. Some gardens are conserved because of their associational importance with famous people—the prime example perhaps being the garden of Monet at Giverny, on the Seine below Paris. So the heritage of people is also deeply involved.

Perhaps the fundamental difference between the management of gardens and the management of buildings is that plants grow, and stone does not. In many cases even the original designer never saw the garden which he planned through to the stage he imagined in his head. He planted saplings; a century later we see a forest. Much building conservation is predicated on the presumption that we know what the architect intended, and that that vision is the appropriate condition to which the building ought to be kept. In the case of a garden we only rarely know what the original designer intended. Sometimes we do, for example, Humphrey Repton left detailed pictures of what he wanted in his Red Books. But many gardens never had a named designer—the garden was laid out by the owner and his workmen, not on the drawing board, but actually out on site. Even where there was a named designer, research into garden history is in its infancy, and we probably know very little about the designer or the plan. In any case good designers would automatically assume that gardens will change over time, and will allow for the fancies of future generations. One of the most famous gardens in England is at least three gardens in one. At Stourhead there is the original 18th-century landscape garden with a lake and a lawn backed by beech trees, and decorated with buildings and statuary. To this has been added a rhododendron garden in the 19th century and a major arboretum in the 20th. None of these is 'wrong'. Some visitors come to see one, and some another. Like most gardens, it evolved.

The designer has been assumed to be male, but one of the unusual features of garden design is that, at least in the last century, women have been as important as men as gardeners and landscape architects. It may be also that there are significant differences between gardens made by men and by women. The former often tend to openness, with vistas and panoramas stressing land ownership. This may be more obvious in the French style formal garden than the English style landscape, but actually the latter stresses land ownership just as firmly, if rather more subtly, with concealed bounds and open views. Women's gardens often tend to be a series of outdoor rooms, a compartmentalised view of the world, intimate and smaller in scale.

Private owners of gardens (and many public owners too) do not expect to maintain it as inherited. The plants intended to be in the garden grow, and die. Other plants, not intended, weeds, grow and smother the whole area. So gardening is a constant process of pruning woody plants, mowing, weeding, slashing and strimming, lopping and chopping and, just occasionally, planting. The cost of making a garden is usually less than a building, but the cost of maintenance is always high. Stop the maintenance for a year, and the garden will transform itself from cultural to natural heritage. Two identical plants may be set to form a pair or a group forming an avenue. Fifty years later one has died and the other is a rampant tree, twice the size intended. Similarly, plants will not grow anywhere, so that to replace a few dead trees in an avenue or clump is often a major problem. Ideas basic  to building conservation, such as 'conserve as found' 'repair but do not restore' rapidly cease to have any meaning, when applied to the living garden.

The occasion when we can return the garden to what was intended, how it 'ought' to be, the 'proper' appearance, is a very rare situation. With some of the great formal gardens, including lots of architectural features, and lots of carefully trimmed plants used as architecture, it may be possible; though even there, replacing plants with identical varieties may prove very difficult indeed. While most species of garden plant remain available, the particular varieties are often a matter of fashion and old ones are frequently unobtainable.

## Garden Legislation

Management systems designed for buildings cannot be extended to gardens and made to fit. However, there are many examples where legislation designed for buildings has been extended with little change to include gardens and parks. The result can be that only certain kinds of garden, especially those with an architectural and formal style get conserved. Informal plant collections get overlooked. In France, perhaps the main support system for gardens is the regulation insisting that 'nothing can be altered without permission within a perimeter of 500 metres from any monument that is *classé* or *inscrit*.' (Pitté p.10). This means that gardens are often regarded as merely the setting for, and subordinate to, the built monument. With the desperate attempt to find more parking space, the protection is somewhat less than absolute. There are now in France an increasing number of gardens classified in the historic monuments register in their own right, but the distribution of these owes as much to historical accident as to a careful survey of quality. In Britain the system of Listed Buildings is replaced by Registered Gardens, and such registers were drawn up during the 1980s, by English Heritage and with the support of local County Gardens Trusts. Although some of the built elements in the garden may also be listed buildings, making alterations in the registered garden does not usually require consent from the authority. All requests for new development have to 'take into account' the existence of a registered garden, but there is little to stop owners from developing the garden in any way they like, provided it remains a garden. Most countries have recognised the different nature of gardens in their preservation legislation, accepting that questions of authenticity and conservation are much more difficult to resolve. So far this has meant that the legislation is much weaker than for building.

Gardens and parks had some protection in Italy as long ago as 1912, though this mainly applied to the environs of villas. Since 1939, however, green spaces could be protected in their own right. Italy took a lead in the production of The Florence Charter, the International Charter for the Restoration of Historic Gardens which dates from 1981, although that document again faces the problem of 'the original state' of a garden. The German protection for gardens again shadowed monument legislation, being the responsibility of the *länder*, with Baden Würtemberg being the first to include gardens in 1971. Hungary reached a similar position in 1976 listing 140 parks and gardens as national monuments.

## Garden Functions

Gardens may be defined as designed space. Landscape architects look at space in a different way to architects, often as a simple reversal of vision, they see places 'inside out'. The architect designs a 'light well', a negative space intended to illuminate the building; the landscape architect sees a 'courtyard', a positive space to be used. Indeed it is that concept of use which is fundamental to the garden. Many gardens, especially public squares, parks, sports fields, and leisure gardens have very clear functions—although nearly always more than one, and sometimes purely scientific functions—such as the physick gardens, the earliest of which was at Padua. The great city open parks, such as Hyde Park in London, are often called 'lungs'. This of course is meant metaphorically, places for people to relax, to breathe good air, and to rejuvenate their lives. It is also true literally. The trees and plants take out carbon dioxide and convert it to oxygen—a vital fact always to be considered even when putting the most elegant building or sculpture on previously green sites. Japanese gardens, sometimes built with no plants at all, merely an arrangement of raked gravel, sand, water and rocks, may be some of the most advanced aesthetic constructions made by people—but they do not produce much oxygen!

The concept of function is most useful also for the private garden. The Japanese garden is designed for contemplation, not for children to play! The great French gardens of Le Notre, as at Chantilly, Vaux le Vicomte and Versaille, were places in which to be seen, not quite complete without a large crowd of gentry, music and perhaps fireworks. By contrast the classic English landscape garden is more designed for physical activity, for playing games, including hunting. Many modern gardens are designed as hobbies, to provide a place for the activity of gardening to take place in. Others, including the traditional cottage garden, were intended to grow food, originally as necessity and perhaps later as a pleasurable activity.

Heritage gardens may come in many kinds with many functions. Only through the 1980s did inventory and designation begin to give way to conservation in any organised way, and the history of the movement has largely defined the kind of garden protected. These are overwhelmingly the ornamental parks surrounding major aristocratic buildings—royal palaces, castles, country seats, city parks which had originated as private grounds, and just a few public parks. The gardens of the Alhambra and Generalife at Granada, the Villa d'Este at Tivoli, Versaille, Schönbrünn, and the landscape gardens of Blenheim or Stourhead are all such aesthetic high points. These are those which dominate the world heritage lists, and very often the palace attached to the garden is also of great significance. These are the gardens which figure in histories of art, and which indicate so clearly the attitude of human beings, or at least the aristocracy, to nature and to the land.

The great aesthetic gardens present almost a full cycle. As human beings struggled to assert their power over nature the small, formal, symmetrical garden, enclosed behind walls and with the few plants clipped and trimmed in line with human attitudes to geometry slowly developed into the greater gardens designed with 'wildernesses' of carefully planted trees and few fences. As the agricultural revolution, first in England, gave landowners more or less complete mastery over nature, so the formality could be discarded, and nature be allowed to appear itself—though within strict control. In recent years the circle has been completed. With natural and even semi-natural land reduced to a tiny remnant over most of Europe, so we are encouraged to introduce wild nature into our gardens. From a small outdoor rectangle demonstrating human control in a vast ocean of nature, so we now have a small rectangle of nature in a vast ocean of human control.

The conservation of plant collections, vernacular gardens, the gardens of the poor or even of the suburbs has scarcely begun, and there are just a few attempts to conserve kitchen gardens and other kinds of open space. But these other types of heritage gardens apart from the aristocratic are at least beginning to be recognised and inventories made. Some are heritage gardens because of their plants.

Killerton House in Devon is indeed a country gentleman's residence, with a large landscape garden, though it is not known who designed it. However, for a period in the early 19th century the head gardener was the Scotsman James Veitch, who sent out explorers over many parts of the globe to return with new shrubs and trees, many of which were planted at Killerton for the first time in Europe. Some originals even survive, and the greatest care is taken to continue the cultivation of the many species with the Latin name *Veitchii*. The conservation of plants can itself be a major national effort.

The voluntary sector can be of considerable benefit, and the National Council for the Conservation of Plants and Gardens is a British group of enthusiasts who are concerned less with garden design and aesthetic history than with trying to preserve species and varieties of garden plant. This organisation nominates many National Collections for each genus of plants. Even the local university has a National Collection—of azara, and many of these collections are in the small gardens and greenhouses of enthusiasts, sometimes obsessives, all over Britain. Such groups also host shows of alpine plants, of roses and of many other plants. This is an aspect of heritage conservation so often overlooked by those concerned with an aesthetic history—but without it the varieties needed in the great gardens would soon disappear.

The great English gardener Gertrude Jekyll developed the gardens of Hestercombe House near Taunton in Somerset in the early years of the 20th century. When the house was abandoned they became overgrown, and were later purchased by Somerset County Council as the headquarters for the Fire Brigade. By an extraordinary coincidence the Chief Fire Officer was not only a keen amateur garden historian, but actually found all Jekyll's letters and plans relating to the garden. The garden was then meticulously restored to her designs - so far as possible. In the restoration of Hestercombe the landscape architects had detailed written evidence of the many varieties of lily, a favourite plant of Gertrude Jekyll, and where in the garden they should be planted. Unfortunately more than half the varieties were no longer in cultivation, and often there was no evidence what they looked like. There were other trees and shrubs which were not part of her design but far too attractive to be destroyed.

Most European gardens of the 18th century were far from colourful, and a determined attempt to remove the flowering trees, shrubs and flower beds which have been planted since would result in much criticism from visitors. A particular case is that of the 16th-century knot garden which originally only had coloured gravels and sands between the little hedges of box (*Buxus sempervirens*) which constituted the lines. Today they are usually a riot of coloured bedding plants.

To many people gardening is a pleasurable activity. Almost by definition gardening will flourish when there is wealth, leisure and peace, and since 1945 there have been all three in much of Europe, so all over the continent people are busy digging, planting, harvesting, pruning. In England this is probably in their back-gardens of their suburban houses, or sometimes on the plots of ground called allotments largely for the growth of vegetables. The Dutch front garden is equally notable, while Italians may be busy with their patios and their vines, Danes and Czechs with their leisure gardens and garden colonies, groups of gardens with some accommodation and used especially at weekends. Indeed gardening is such a universal activity in Europe that one is tempted to view it as a distinctively European feature. Such people are much more concerned with the conservation of a traditional activity than they are with the restoration of the gardens of the wealthy. Very often they are more concerned with plants than with design. Are these heritage gardens? Certainly there are demonstrations and strong objections when such gardens are threatened, and they are places where not only plants are conserved and bred, but which now act as important havens for wildlife, especially birds, and also where many types of fruit and vegetable, which have features which do not appeal to the professional grower, are maintained and propagated. Just as there is a heritage of rare breeds of pig, so there are rare varieties of apple. There are even traditional methods of pruning to be conserved and the Ecole Nationale de Paysage at Versaille maintains an extraordinary collection of different ways of pruning fruit trees. In the main, however, we have not yet developed successful legislation for guaranteeing that the heritage of gardening techniques, the activity itself, will survive, though eco-museums make a determined effort to do so.

## Garden Visitors

This raises another very significant difference between architecture and gardens. Only a small percentage of visitors to a palace are architects or builders, but gardeners form an important element in the garden-visiting public. Most of the great gardens open to the public have realised that garden visitors want to see the back of the garden. They like seeing the greenhouses where the plants are propagated as much as seeing the garden itself. They take great interest in all the plant names, which need to be discreetly displayed, and the most respectable-seeming visitors often come armed with a knife. Removing a cutting seems so much less reprehensible than scratching one's name into the stonework. Much more than with buildings there is interest in the 'back-stage'—and the sale of plants is an important source of income.

Visitors also create major problems of wear and tear. Grassy walks intended for twenty people per week cannot take 200 people per day. Japanese gardens in particular have had to cope with huge numbers visiting parks which are now public, but even more robust European gardens have had to be re-designed. What was intended to be a narrow winding grassy walk, for a romantic evening stroll, has to be converted into a paved or gravelled straight strip, two metres wide, intended for a thousand people per day. Something gets lost in the conversion! If hand rails have had to be added there is an added loss of authenticity. The problem of providing effective facilities for disabled visitors is a problem outside as well as in, although there are determined attempts to provide special odoriferous gardens for the blind.

Because plants grow, the maintenance of the garden is expensive and unremitting. Garden labour is skilled though comparatively cheap (and many of the old skills are in danger of disappearing), but is still much more expensive than when these gardens were made. The invention of machinery has not entirely made up for this enormous difference though it is certainly vital in another problem of garden restoration, erosion and deposition. All too often terraces have collapsed and lakes have been silted up—as at the restoration at Seregélyes in Hungary. Hence keeping gardens open to the public is an expensive business, and the more formal and stylised the garden, the more expensive it is. Glasshouses are perhaps the biggest problem, adding to the heavy capital costs of restoring a huge glasshouse such as that at Lednice in the Czech Republic, are the maintenance costs of looking after a building which is overgrown with plants and soaked in condensation. The English-style landscape garden is less heavy on labour than the French or German baroque garden.

The most expensive of all is a traditional vegetable or kitchen garden. Despite this, there have been a few highly successful reconstructions of the kitchen gardens of big houses, which have proved immensely popular with visitors, who can learn techniques of gardening often applicable at home. Perhaps the most famous is that at Villandry near Tours, which was built in 1906 'inspired by the designs of de Cerceau'. The lost gardens of Heligan in Cornwall represent one British example, where bus loads of amateur gardeners arrive to learn about techniques of Victorian fruit and vegetable rearing. Mostly the great walled kitchen gardens still lie unused, covered in weeds, or in concrete and used as a car park. Even in Scotland, where the walled garden is something of a symbol of national identity, many lie unused because of the cost of labour.

Then there are the public parks and open spaces. With the growth of tourism these often become foci of attraction. In Brussels the Parc Royal, Ludwig-Kirchplatz in Berlin, the Royal Parks of London, in Paris the Bois de Boulogne and the new gardens of Les Halles. Some are significant for historical reasons also—in Birkenhead the Victorian park is by Loudon and is the direct forerunner of Central Park New York and all the other works of Frederick Law Olmsted, the town planner and leader of the City Beautiful Movement. Almost all urban open spaces are under threat, from motor vehicles, and very few have really effective legislation to protect them.

Cemeteries are a case on their own. Paris has to maintain Père Lachaise, now a major tourist attraction, as is Highgate cemetery in London. But interest in many other nineteenth-century cemeteries has been growing recently, as for example with the Friends of Nunhead Cemetery in London, and from many directions. Local people use them as walks and lungs, children as places to play. The interest in genealogy means a steady stream of visitors looking for the graves of ancestors. Naturalists, seeing the cemetery as a refuge for birds and mammals, fight against the conservator's wish to tidy it all up. Teachers even teach geology there. As the people buried there pass into history, many see the great municipal cemetery as a major heritage concern. In Hannover the graves of the Jewish cemetery, An Der Strangriede are being meticulously restored by students of restoration at Hildesheim.

Gardens which are freely open to the public, whether the grounds of great houses, public parks or cemeteries are quite different from those which the visitor pays to see. In the latter case it is a reasonable assumption that the visitor's aspirations are focused on the garden itself. There will be plenty of variety in detail, just as there is for visitors to the building, perhaps on the same ticket. But visitors to free parks go there for every possible purpose and for none. A period of careful people-watching and asking lots of questions, not just on a sunny summer afternoon, but right through the day, week and year, will soon yield an astonishing number of responses. This is where small group research can be best used. For every one interested in the history of the design there are ten interested only in the plants, twenty there for a picnic, others cutting through on their walk to work, walking the dog, or looking for somewhere suitable for a romantic assignation. We have only mentioned the legal users. People-watching can be dangerous, but is a remarkably useful counterpoise to the academic conservator determined to produce an authentic restoration! The demands are endless—although in Central Park New York they have not completely yielded to loud demands to fell every tree and shrub so as not to provide hiding places for muggers.

At least there is now rapidly developing interest in the subject at academic level, with journals such as the *Journal of Garden History* and the Institut für Geschichte der Gartenkunst at Hannover. These complement the rise in significance of landscape architecture and the new professional garden designers. It may well be that future garden historians will be describing and tracing the enormous rise of the garden in the late twentieth century, a boom of interest and activity which simultaneously guarantees that the garden heritage of Europe will be taken seriously, but also that significant parts of the vernacular garden heritage will be lost in the wish to make new gardens. The British suburban garden of the 1930s is at last meriting some academic attention. Very few are left in anything approaching an original condition. The growth of plants, the ever-changing nature of the garden, means that it is perhaps the most transient and vulnerable as well as the most sensitive indicator of social attitudes and habits. Here more than anywhere, there is the danger that heritage conservation can be a deadening activity, desperately attempting to preserve the unpreservable, while the more popular heritage —the heritage of the traditional activity of gardening—is stifled. The difference between heritage as a static spectacle and as an active pastime is made quite overt in the garden. Our management techniques work quite well for the spectacle, and hardly at all for the pastime—although Heligan garden in Cornwall now charges people to visit and work in the garden. You may purchase a holiday course, working hard and learning from professionals. In doing so the garden is, inevitably, altered.

### *Exercise Forty*

Visit an historic garden or park. What are its functions? Have they changed and what do people do there nowadays? How similar is the garden to the original conception of the designer? What conservation legislation is in force for it? How many gardeners are employed? Is there a distinctive annual change?

# The case of theme parks & heritage centres

## *Definitions*

In several places, particularly in the discussion concerning eco-museums, the point has been made that the definition of a 'museum' has undergone very considerable change in the last few decades. Today's museums may well be out-of-doors though usually only in part, and they not only welcome, but actively encourage visitors. They probably have considerable educational programmes and operate in quite a commercial way, with shops and restaurants and some knowledge of the profitability of their exhibitions. Clearly, however, the term 'museum' has not expanded its meaning to include Euro Disney outside Paris, the Canterbury Tales visitor centre at Canterbury or even Jorvik at York. There are now many places which call themselves Heritage Centres and others Theme Parks, so that some debate about terminology is useful.

People in the tourist industry avoid this debate about terminology by referring to Visitor Attractions, including within that term any identifiable place, of an institutional nature, where visitors are welcome. Cathedrals count, even though they may not charge. Beaches do not count as they are not, usually, institutional organisations. The trouble with 'Visitor Attraction', however, is that the word assumes that attracting visitors, especially tourists, is the sole *raison d'etre* of these institutions; while this may be true of Disney World, it is not true of the Prado, for example. Visitor Attraction management does remind heritage specialists that for many people, if not most, the conservation of objects is of much less importance than access. Also most visitors to most heritage sites, heritage centres, theme parks, are not specialists. Only occasionally do people travel hundreds of kilometres specifically to view a particular painting, or exhibition, a particular animal, a particular building. Most people going through the turnstiles at any of these Visitor Attractions, visit many sites in a particular area. Today they are going to the cathedral, tomorrow to the zoo, and the day after to a theme park. So that all these three types of places are in competition with each other. A custodian of a wonderful art gallery, or of a palace, if he is concerned with visitor numbers at all, needs to be very aware of the local 'Family Fun Day Out' or 'Animal Sanctuary', of how much they charge, when they are open, what kind of marketing they are involved with. The Duke of Bedford, who opened his home at Woburn Abbey long before such places were common, reminds other owners that visitors 'do not come to see the Rembrandts ... they come because they have a motor car.'

So there are no simple distinctions between museums, heritage centres, theme parks. There is a continuum, with at one end the museum which makes no attempt to attract visitors, and perhaps Disney World at the other. Nevertheless some important points can be made. One thing that changes along the line is funding. At the museum end funding is usually at least partly from public, governmental sources, or occasionally from private benefactions, with comparatively minor direct contribution from visitors. At the theme park, decisions on everything, on exhibitions, on car parking, on opening hours, will be dictated largely by profit, and that will often be closely connected with sheer numbers of visitors. A further consequence is that the museum will expect to serve many more constituencies than the tourist. It will expect to have a significant local relevance, with many local people returning many times, and usually a major educational provision. Most heritage centres too will have a significant educational provision. Theme parks are likely to put much less emphasis on such visitors, and are likely to charge for educational services.

Such an emphasis on visitor numbers will usually lead to a visitor profile which is much less educated, less wealthy. Heritage tourists tend to come from the upper social groups, theme park visitors do not. The only significant exception to this class differential is the zoo, which has a visitor profile much more akin to a theme park than a museum.

The most obvious academic distinction is that of perceived authenticity. The extreme case at the museum end of the spectrum is the collection of selected and ordered artefacts authenticated by scholars, carefully conserved, and possessing very little interpretation beyond documentation. At the other extreme there are may be no artefacts at all. There may be lots of interpretive material, lots of things to do and little evidence of academic involvement. Even this is assuming that there is still a significant connection with heritage, with something to be conserved. There are, of course, some theme parks which have no heritage connection whatsoever, or at least only of the most tenuous kind. This book is not really involved with the management of such institutions as the Parc Asterix in France, or Alton Towers in England, which may be Visitor Attractions but make no pretence to be either curatorial or educational. They cannot reasonably be regarded as part of the heritage business.

Perhaps this release from educational or curatorial roles, is what distinguishes a theme park from a heritage centre. In the heritage centre there is a determined desire to teach, that the visitor goes away having absorbed some knowledge, discovered a skill, enhanced some understanding. Someone, perhaps a city council or a heritage organisation, is determined to impart knowledge and understanding. A theme park, however, is customer-driven; entertainment takes precedence over education, and here the customer, the visitor, is king.

To reduce this to its most simple position, the museum is driven by an academic and curatorial motive, the heritage centre by an educational one and the theme park by an entertainment motive. But these categories are not watertight. Flambards, in Cornwall, has water slides and roller-coasters, but also conducts a significant educational programme and the owner is a keen collector of artefacts from the Second World War. Equally there are places calling themselves museums, and galleries within existing museums, where there are few artefacts and a heavy emphasis on amusement. Some of the new breed of science 'exploratoria' are full of interesting activities which may have an educational intent, but this is far from overt.

## The academic debate

While it may be useful to make distinctions between the three types of institution, it must be stressed that these are different in kind and not in quality, still less in moral superiority. There is a great deal of academic snobbery, which presumes, for example, that 'heritage tourists' are the opposite of 'beach tourists', presuming that beaches are not heritage, simply because they are popular. Heritage is a consumer product with many purchasers, some of whom want to 'buy' academically authenticated artefacts, and they go to museums. Some want to buy education and they visit heritage centres; some want to be entertained, and they go to theme parks. Those who visit theme parks are much less likely to cause wear and tear on monuments or the countryside, and put much more money into the economy than those visiting archaeological sites. Heritage tourists damage much more heritage than others!

Scholars of the academic disciplines which are concerned with heritage artefacts, for example historians, art and architecture historians, ecologists, are used to controlling knowledge in their fields. They have done so ever since the invention of printing. Now they see non-specialists taking knowledge into their own hands and disseminating knowledge through heritage centres, theme parks and the internet in ways which academics find it very difficult to control. So academics do not like theme parks.

Just as with museums, heritage centres and theme parks will have policies dictated by the organising institution. This may well be a city council or a regional or national government. Sometimes it is a heritage organisation, whose main job is conservation, and the heritage centre is the public face. This is especially true in rural heritage, where most national and regional parks and major nature reserves have Information Centres, which combine interpretation with information, advice and warnings, and usually a shop. Even in those heritage centres and theme parks where profit is a major motive, there will be a policy relating to the aims and objectives of the original funding body.

Civic heritage centres tell a limited version of history, which is inevitably local and partial. Just as National Museums tell a national story, so Plymouth Dome heritage centre tells a story of Plymouth which concentrates on those times in Plymouth's history when it has played a major national role. There are displays about Sir Francis Drake and Elizabethan England, and on the destruction of Plymouth in the Second World War. Not surprisingly Drake is portrayed as maritime hero and explorer rather than a pirate. National Park information centres give lots of information about the landscape and nature of the national park, and a lot more information about the National Park Authority, and what it does—so that interpretation and education imperceptibly become public relations. There are frequent silences. Cities prefer not to tell the whole story about incidents in history of which the city is not proud. It would be difficult to find much reference to slavery in the cities of Bristol or St Nazaire, although several of Bristol's important monuments honour benefactors of the city who acquired their wealth in the slave trade. Civic history is often one of continual progress. There are many silences for other reasons too, some of them entirely honourable. The national park centre prefers not to divulge too much information about where the eagles nest, in order to protect them. The location of many important works of art in private houses is obviously information best not disclosed, and with underwater archaeology this becomes a very major issue. However worthy the motive, such interpretations are always partial and a vital part of management.

## Exercise Forty-one

Visit a Heritage Centre in your area and examine its purposes. Who funded it? Who is being addressed? Which discipline provided the educational information? Could it have been another discipline? What is not said? Is there a collection of artefacts? How much is given over to entertainment, without any educational intent (playparks etc)?

## Interpretation

Our ideas about interpretation, about the ways and means of presenting heritage to people stem largely from those of Freeman Tilden, writing in 1967. While his principles are still often quoted, it is important to remember that such principles were written thirty years ago and concerned American environmental education in their national parks. Tilden assumed that to a very considerable extent there was one story to tell, stemming from an accepted 'expert' in an appropriate discipline. In interpreting the Grand Canyon he assumed that a geologist might write a script about how the Canyon came to be like that, perhaps supported by an historian to describe how it was 'discovered' and used. Before the post-modern revolution in thinking, he did not really consider disputes between geologists, nor that a different ethnic group, such as Native Americans, might have a different history to write, nor that visitors might be more interested in last week's murder than the geology. In writing about American national parks he was also involved in a uniformed organisation, which had strong links with the military, in a country which at the time had a powerful determination to weld many different peoples into one nation. Not only have times changed, and everyone today accepts that there are many versions of the truth, but the European tradition has much more difficulty with 'simply telling history as it was'. In any group of tourists there are likely to be French, Germans, British let alone Japanese and Arabs, all with different versions of history, so such simplicity is rarely acceptable.

Interpretation is not always required, nor is it always desirable. Much heritage management, especially the conservation of the built heritage, makes little use of interpretation. The buildings are conserved for their own intrinsic value, they are not open to the public, and those who wish to look at the outsides can do so largely without mediation. The heritage centre lies at the other extreme where the whole centre is based on interpretation, and management is largely concerned with choosing what to say, to whom to say it, how to say it, where and when.

In the early days of many museums, interpretation of even the simplest kind, such as labelling exhibits, was frequently regarded as an unnecessary distraction. If visitors had not the knowledge to know what they were observing then they had little justification for visiting. However, more recently interpretation has been elevated to one of the most central tasks of museum staffs and has even become something of a profession in itself. Interpretation may range from simple labels to complex multi-media presentations requiring great technical expertise, demanding from the visitor every response from passive reception of information through to active participation.

**What to say?**

Any interpretation has to select some themes. This is much more problematic than it sounds, because selecting any one theme automatically ignores several other possible ones. For any piece of heritage, especially any building, there are many 'stories' that could be told, just as there are many different groups of visitors. There may be different histories. At Bayeux the story of the Bayeux tapestry is explained twice. One gives the Norman view of the story, and one the Saxon view. One stresses William's just claim to the throne of England, the other denies it. Both stories are given in both French and English. This is clearly good practice, enabling both French and English visitors to consider another perspective on their national histories, but there is little there about the cloth itself and the stitch work and the nature of textile art in the eleventh century. Telling one story prevents new interpretations coming forward, deters new investigation. The visitor to the portrait gallery may be an art historian interested in the painters, or an historian interested in those depicted, or someone investigating historical costume, or a chemist interested in paint, or a carpenter interested in picture frames.

The ideal, which is almost certainly unobtainable, is that all visitors can find the information they wish to find, at the academic level they want, without being obliged to find any information at all. If someone wants to visit the church simply to get out of the rain, or visits a garden just to have a picnic, there is no reason why they should be forced to learn. Compulsory education is neither popular nor very effective.

**How to say it? Interpretation techniques**

There are many ways of getting information to people. Apart from books, the two principle categories are live interpretation and interpretation by design, the latter including computers, maps, leaflets, signage and displays. Live interpretation can vary from using a guide to fully costumed reenactment. In general, people clearly learn much more from good live interpretation than from the most outstanding displays. Guides can vary their approach for different groups, they can respond to the moment, and they can foster enthusiasm like no sign board. A good guide even knows when to keep quiet! Children especially remember for life having a snake on their shoulder or operating a sheerlegs to move a piece of cathedral stone. But guides are expensive, unless volunteers are available, and volunteers, however enthusiastic, bring with them significant management problems.

The guide may don a costume of a period appropriate to the place, and then may act either as a third-person interpreter, wearing costume but still speaking as a modern person, or as a first-person interpreter, speaking in the voice and style of the appropriate period. These are difficult decisions. To what extent should this be like a theatre where people suspend their disbelief? At one abbey people are shown round by a resident monk, at another by a young actor dressed as a monk. Does it matter? Some people love being asked to act a part, others are utterly embarrassed and will take care never to return. At the extreme end of live interpretation lies reenactment, often of battles, but also of 'life in Tudor times' as at Kentwell Hall in Suffolk. Many people get great enjoyment from such enterprises, and there seems little doubt that many young people develop a fascination for the past from such events. The great advantage of live interpretation is that the interpreter does not have to tell one story, but can answer all the questions, whereas design inevitably tells people what is the 'correct' way to think about this object.

But the ethics involved are, of course, modern. This wonderful old building has to meet fire safety regulations. Usually women in these '16th-century' armies fight alongside men. No-one gets killed. Actual human excrement is not poured on your head. Children experiencing the 19th-century school-room, are not whipped and thrashed with canes. There is a problem with empathy. It is not possible to step into the past. This was most neatly put by a professor of music, talking of the fashion for playing baroque music on 'authentic' instruments and in a style of the period, he said 'But you are listening with twentieth-century ears'.

The citadel in Halifax, Nova Scotia, has developed a renowned 'animation' event involving the Scottish highland regiments that formed its nineteenth-century garrison. A meticulously detailed reconstruction of dress, arms and drill is now somewhat compromised by the inclusion of not only black, but female, 'highlanders' that current non-discriminating employment legislation cannot exclude from the ranks. One regular participant in 17th-century re-nactments proudly boasted that in his 'regiment' promotion to officer rank was strictly on merit—which would certainly have been unusual in 17th-century England.

Designed interpretation is usually cheaper, and the ability to brief a designer is a critical skill for a heritage manager in this field. Sometimes the brief is so detailed that no room is left for a good designer's creativity. There is little point in hiring a great architect if you have already designed the building! Some other managers write briefs that are so vague that the designer has no idea what is intended, for what kind of audience at what cost.

## Exercise Forty-two

Some understanding of the problems of interpretation technique is essential. There are many pitfalls, and a few visits to heritage centres will demonstrate them very clearly:-

Find examples of the following or similar problems on visits to heritage centres.

a) When you  arrive at the heritage centre you are given a leaflet which tells you how you should have got there!

b) At the start of the trail there is a huge map to tell you where to go. You remember some of this for about 100 metres; thereafter you are lost.

c) There are excellent instructions explaining how to use the computer programme for a virtual display. Unfortunately there is nothing to tell you how to switch it on.

d) You decide to use a slide show rather than a video, but either you cannot see the slides because it is too light, or people keep falling over because it is too dark.

e) The exhibition board cost a great deal of money and time. No-one even stops to look at it because just ahead there is a live animal or something much more interesting.

f) The displays look wonderful. Unfortunately they are not written in any language which you can understand.

Such mistakes are very common, but there are many much better examples. Find a really good interpretation and explain why it works.

---

The critical issue is constant evaluation, always watching people react, asking questions, getting people new to the place to visit and report. Context is of great importance. Many people might wonder why anyone today would use a slide show when video is so cheap. The answer is context.  The production quality of a video must reach the standards of a major national television station, or it will just look second-rate. A slide show only has to be better than the geography teacher back at school, and it will look wonderful—and a lot cheaper. The same is very true with pictures, especially photographs. If pictures are carefully framed, and hung individually on a white wall, with very little text, then people will read them, and judge them, as works of art, with the content of very secondary importance. That may be exactly what is required, in a gallery for instance, but for teaching purposes, whether about the history of a building, or about fauna and flora, the pictures must be presented differently.

**To whom?**

The stories to be told inevitably depend on the audiences. This opens the entire field of communication theory, and two paragraphs here stand as an introduction to a complete subject. Already the question of nationality and language has arisen. There are also questions about people with disabilities—not only about access, and the use of braille for the blind or sign language for the deaf, but perhaps special gardens for the blind. There are major issues about gender stereotyping also. Many science and technology museums have been accused of presenting 'toys for the boys', and certainly the typical aircraft display concentrates more on engines and on navigation than on cabin service—though that in itself could be another form of gender stereotyping. Big country houses have only just begun to tell the story of the servants who worked below stairs, and people's interest is obvious. Such issues are the practical problems which arise from the theoretical debates about political messages intrinsic to heritage which were discussed in Chapter Five.

   In a museum or large building various aspects can be presented to various different groups. In a heritage centre the interpretation generally has to cover all visitors—the general public, as well as specialists, and educational parties of all ages. Educational interpretation is particularly difficult. Where there is a National Curriculum, as in the UK or France, special interpretive packs can be provided for different subjects at the appropriate ages. Children age rapidly, and all too often there is just one set of educational material, aimed at average eight-year-olds. A party of undergraduates can present a real problem! As for the general public, whenever they are investigated they become less and less general.

**Where and when to say it?**

Having decided what to say, to whom and how, there are still important questions left. The location of the heritage centre is critical and can be the most important management tool, especially at sensitive sites. Many archaeological sites now put the information centre beside the car park, and quite a long walk from the actual heritage material. A surprising number of people will not make the extra effort and this saves considerable wear and tear. At Lidice, near Prague, the site of the erasure of a village by the Nazis, the museum display and visitor centre is right beside the car park and entered by almost all visitors. To get to the remains of the village itself, with the memorial garden, is perhaps 200m walk, and many visitors do not bother. The graves of the victims are at least another 500m, and they seem to be visited by few other than relatives, left largely in peace.

This question of location raises the important issue of the role of interpretation centres in managing visitor behaviour. Vulnerable structures or areas can be protected by deflecting visitors to high-capacity centres whose interpretations become an acceptable, and even in terms of the visitors' experience, more authentic, alternative for the site being protected. Careful planning of location and management of visitor routeing can be observed, for example at the Vindolanda Centre on Hadrian's Wall in northern England.

Timing is also important, especially in the case of live interpretation. Time can be used to differentiate between different types of visitor. The summer exhibition may be largely aimed at tourists and quite different from winter for locals. Tours for specialists and connoisseurs may be in weekday evenings while the weekend caters for families. A common technique is to have good general design interpretation backed up by specialist staff for specific audiences.

---

## Exercise Forty-three

Report on a site where the location of parking and interpretation facilities has been carefully managed. For what purpose? Report on an interpretation strategy which separates visitors by time, providing different facilities for different groups at different times.

---

## A Code of Interpretation

Any form of interpretation brings problems in its train, not least it inevitably acts as a form of advertising, and the option of silence, of saying nothing, should always be considered. Where a site is quite sensitive, easily worn away or liable to damage, the best interpretational policy is possibly none at all, provided the site is not in full view. There are many other cases where any interpretation is likely to cause offence to some, so that silence may well be the best policy. But such policies only work where the heritage product itself can tell its own tale. Fine for a cathedral, or a battlefield cemetery or town centre, but not a policy suitable for an information centre in a national park, or town's heritage centre.

There has been a great deal of debate at many conferences (Uzzell, 1989) about a professional code for interpretation. Museums in particular are immensely authoritative, and heritage centres not much less so. Modern design and communication systems are very powerful so it is only too easy for visitors to go away fully convinced of the truth of what they have learnt. It may be only one version of the truth; it may be heavily biased; it may be from only one point of view; it may even be lies. But the weight of authority and the quality of the communication techniques will mean that what is learnt will be difficult to erase.

In the post-modern world we are well aware that there are many different truths. Every struggle had two sides, at least. The difficulties of interpreting the Bayeux tapestry are just normal, and to a considerable extent the natural heritage is no less contentious. Good interpretation should read 'This is the latest theory....' or 'These are two separate species (we think)'. Nevertheless the fact that there are many versions of truth does not mean that anything is true. There are still untruths. So how many versions of the truth can an interpreter provide? Unlike books, there are no footnotes in displays so that the audience can check the information. Unlike the lecture, there is no chance for questions or contrary views. This places on the interpreter a heavy responsibility for honesty of purpose. A determined attempt to allow visitors to access any information they want, or none at all, together with an honest assessment of the intellectual position of the interpreter are the only defences there are against indoctrination.

Many scholars are so concerned about the dangers of interpretation that they criticise all heritage centres and all interpretive efforts. But such a policy of silence draws upon it the charge of elitism. Heritage would be kept for those already in the know, for experts only. These days support from taxpayers' money implies access to the heritage by those who are paying for it, who also expect some explanation of the importance of this heritage. Heritage centres often perform this role with considerable success while simultaneously protecting the heritage itself.

All of this assumes that a complete revelation of all the possible truths about the past is an ideal to which the interpreter should aim. However, sophisticated interpretation needs to consider that the message received by the audience may not necessarily be that intended by the sender. Audiences bring to the site their own mental constructs which filter the messages and may blank them out. At sensitive sites, such as battlefields or sites of atrocities this may be a matter of great significance. The interpretation may deliberately and carefully promote multi-racial tolerance, reconciliation, and peace, with messages intended to stress the inhumanity of all humanity, but some visitors may well experience a thrill from the reported violence, and go away with their existing prejudices, whether anti-semitic, anti-German, anti-Islamic, or even sado-masochistic, not only intact but exaggerated. The option of making no interpretation, of silence, may exacerbate such tendencies.

## Exercise Forty-four

Do you think there are some historic events which should be forgotten? Are there some sites which should just be ignored because the consequences are too awful?

## *A few Heritage Centres:-*

In Dorchester, England, a few yards away from the county museum there is a Dinosaur Museum, in a county famous for its Jurassic geology and the discovery of many fossil dinosaurs. This institution has no authentic objects of its own, except for a few fossil dinosaur footprints on loan from the county museum. There are many well-designed panels of information, and lots of large plastic models, as well as interactive exhibits and a well-stocked shop. Such an institution comes within this book's definition of a Heritage Centre rather than a museum. In fact, the educational motive seems subordinate to profitability, which would suggest that it is really a small Theme Park

Dawlish Warren is a sandspit across the mouth of the river Exe. It has a large golf-course, and is a very popular beach with large caravan sites, and is home to many rare birds, especially avocets and Brent geese. The heritage centre is run by volunteers from Devon Wildlife Trust. It contains identification of all the special plants and the wildlife, games for children, books and maps for adults. It runs bird-watching trips. Its success not only in enthusing adults and children but also in helping to manage and protect a delicate ecosystem is immense. Since its opening the dunes have been recolonised by marram grass without disturbance, and the whole area is largely now self policed.

Disney's 'Mainstreet USA' was created at just that moment in development when the main street in US towns was losing its economic and social functions. However, visitor nostalgia for a vanishing past fostered by Disney, led to the Main Street conservation programmes in North America which to an extent recreated in real towns that which was exhibited in the theme park.

The cases of Eurodisney, Disney World and Disneyland also raise questions of the relation of reality and pastiche. Of course, Disneyland is an authentic theme park, which has something of importance to say about the late twentieth century. It resembles a stage set. But many heritage gem cities are also stage sets, built by wealthy burghers to impress their neighbours with facades which had no economic function, and nowadays are restored (often using completely new materials) for the benefit of visiting tourists who pose for photographs against the backdrop of the buildings. Perhaps the differences are not so absolute.

# What you should know

There is a distinction between museums, which have significant collections of artefacts, heritage centres with fewer real artefacts, but driven by a need to educate and heritage theme parks, where entertainment is the primary purpose. There may be an academic case in favour of the former and opposed to the latter, but that is because museums are academically driven, heritage centres education driven. There is a real danger of assuming that using the heritage for education is morally superior to using it for entertainment.

There is a powerful academic case urging caution about interpretation, which tends to provide only one storyline, and to have a hidden agenda, often national or representing the owner. Interpretation is the main management policy in heritage centres, and there is a major distinction between techniques of live interpretation which are more effective and flexible but very expensive, and design which is cheaper but inflexible. The evidence of the educational effectiveness of interpretation is weak and most cases for its use are based on socialisation, and entertainment value.

# Further Reading

G.J. Ashworth  & J.E.Tunbridge (1990) *The tourist-historic city*, London: Belhaven.

S. M. Goulty (1993)*Heritage Gardens: care, conservation, management*, London: Routledge.

ICOFOM Study Series 10, (1986) 'Museology and Identity', Buenos Aires: ICOFOM.

R.J.P. Kain (ed) (1987)  'Conservation of historic gardens and parks on the continent of Europe', *Landscape Research*, Vol.12, no.2, Summer, special issue including articles by Margherite Azzi Visentini & Lionella Scazzosi on Italy, Jean-Robert Pitté on France, Piet Lombaerde on Belgium, Klaus von Krosigk on Germany and József Sisa & Károly Örsi on Hungary.

J. Roberts,(1996) 'The Gardens of Dunroamin: history and cultural values with specific reference to the gardens of the inter-war semi', *International Journal of Heritage Studies*, Vol. no.4, pp.229-237.

F. Tilden (1967)*Interpreting our Heritage*, Univ. of N. Carolina Press.

J.E. Tunbridge & G.J. Ashworth (1996) *Dissonant heritage; the managenent of the past as a resource in conflict*, Chichester: Wiley.

D. L.Uzzell (ed) (1989) *Heritage Interpretation*, 2 volumes, London: Belhaven.

# 7. Reflections

The material in this text is not, of course, the last word in understanding the nature and meaning of heritage and even less the end of a process of heritage education and training. It is, however, an important stage *en route*. There are many specialist areas of training which may follow, some in both town and country planning, some in museums, some in the tourism industry, some in national parks and in theme parks, dealing with buildings, gardens or objects, either in conservation or in interpretation. All of these areas will require further training, and all provide enough material for life-long learning. However, the stage has been set. Some principles have been elucidated which will provide the basis for future development of ideas and further training in any part of Europe and beyond. It is so easy, when deeply involved in the detail of a particular restoration project, to forget to ask 'Who is it for?'

Heritage, we have discovered, is a process. It is a process which happens to some things, and can happen to almost anything. While it is interesting to list all the kinds of things which can be heritage, from whales to palaces, from beer to a painting, the list is never complete. Anything can become heritage, can acquire a particular set of meanings which give it heritage value. It follows that heritage is not a very rare commodity, although individual items may acquire enormous value through their scarcity or uniqueness. Throughout history people have found different things to regard as heritage, whenever they need them, so things which are within the heritage process are saleable commodities, and if more are needed, more can be found or created.

They are sold to many different people and organisations for many different reasons. Most pieces of heritage can be multi-sold, and the heritage manager's job is to ensure that all possible legitimate demands on the product are met optimising the total use value without detracting from the long-term vitality of the resource. This is no easy task, with simple guidelines, as different user groups need to be satisfied with compromises and balances. There are also, of course, illegitimate demands on the product to be resisted; security against thieves, vandals and other misuses is often important. Knowing who wants the product, and what they want from it, and attempting to satisfy their needs is critical. Most in the museum business would now assume that every visitor has a right to find out about every object in words they can understand, and from the perspective they choose. Many would also accept that visitors also have the right, not only to be told everything, but also to be told nothing. Some people just enjoy the ambience, and that is also legitimate.

Among the major groups who should be considered are: governments, at various levels, seeking identity and prestige; visitors seeking education and entertainment; potential purchasers seeking a variety of advantages some of them financial; academics seeking to preserve the materials on which their discipline is founded; and local insiders with a host of memories and meanings invested in the site. A text such as this has been involved, inevitably, with the public purposes of heritage, with society's needs and demands, whether that society is represented by a government office, an academic department or a bus load of tourists. But

134

we must never lose sight of the reality that all sites and most objects carry quite different, and much stronger, private meanings to somebody. This photo-album heritage, a list of places, buildings and artefacts with deep meaning for oneself or members of one's family can be compiled by us all. For most people such meanings and such things are much more important than things of public importance. When the house is burning down, many people will rescue the photo album rather than the valuable object. As managers,we may not be able to cater, on every occasion, for such special meanings, which are so diverse, but we must always be aware of them. Tread softly for you tread on someone's memories and dreams.

There are others who purchase heritage. Just as famous paintings fall into the hands of the rich, by an inevitable market process, so restored buildings will fall into the hands of those who can afford them. Rich individuals and museums in rich countries will acquire a disproportionate share of the world's heritage treasure. This may or may not matter as accessibility is more important than ownership. But if, as frequently happens, heritage objects are collected as a financial investment rather than for their symbolic values, security considerations may prevail over public access and heritage locked in a vault is, in terms of its potential users, hardly heritage at all. Setting about the refurbishment of run-down old housing, converting the old warehouses along the dockside into housing, will change the social mix there with equal inevitability. This gentrification is a process which has to be accepted from the start. There have been many attempts to counter it, but few successful in the long term, as the price mechanism will take over and someone always has to pay for restoration and maintenance so the investment of individuals for their own profit and enjoyment is generally essential. Good planning requires that such consequences have been considered and accepted in advance, and that those displaced have also figured in the calculations. Heritage has social implications and as with any commodity, amenity or enjoyment those with greater economic or political power will acquire or gain access to more of it.

Heritage is conserved for reasons which include the social, the cultural and the economic. It is a major constituent of identity, and that comes at many levels. Family identity is vital to many, but largely beyond the scope of this book— indeed largely beyond being managed. But there are sub-national levels for the parish or the neighbourhood, the town, district or region. The creation and maintenance of national identity may have been responsible for the preservation of a huge percentage of official heritage, but this has always been challenged by those lower levels of identity. These are now joined by pan-European identity, sought by many, and by the notion of a world heritage. In addition to such identities which have geographical components, there are others which have few spatial elements, various groups within society, but scattered throughout it. Such scattered groups are particularly easy to overlook. Consequently heritage is always dissonant in ways that may be serious or trivial, affecting few or many. Someone always feels threatened, someone excluded, degraded or just ignored. Battles had losers as well as winners. Every building conservation had objectors and every interpretation is to a degree tendentious and partial.

Societies throughout Europe are coming to terms with being multi-cultural or inter-cultural. Either societies accept that they are kaleidoscopes of various groups each entitled to their own, possibly separate, development, or that the kaleidoscope of groups needs to converge into one society, or at least to develop some common links. Heritage is obviously deeply implicated in these debates and struggles. Every time a museum opens its doors or a building is conserved there is a political implication. Managers need to be aware of such implications and to have considered them carefully. There are many who have seemed totally surprised when an entirely predictable political argument developed around the latest exhibition. Such pluralist views are part of the post-modern world. Luckily many heritage buildings and sites are themselves multi-faceted and can be used for many purposes. The church can be used for a debate about architecture or history, or even geology, as well as one about religion. The battle-field can be interpreted from many points of view.

Yet there lies the opportunity. When both sides can see the battle from both points of view (and there may be many more than two sides), some common understanding may emerge. If we now understand that to all things there are many different truths, we also know that lies still exist. Truth is as difficult a concept in interpretation as is authenticity in conservation. To both there is no absolute answer, but a determination never to deceive is sound policy. Heritage planners and managers can rarely change the world in any substantial way; they can, however, understand what is happening and the implications of what they do. It may not be possible to do it perfectly; we can at least do it better.

# Appendix 1
# National Policies towards Heritage

## Summary

This appendix describes briefly how various selected countries became officially concerned with the recognition, designation and protection of the built environment deemed worthy of conservation. Each description is written by an observer from the country concerned and therefore reflects not only the detail of the particular national histories but also the definitions, assumptions and approaches that characterise each country.

## Spain
by Ascension Hernandez

The history of Spanish conservation of heritage is little different to that of the rest of Europe, although it does present certain peculiarities which are a result of the country's specific history over the last two centuries.

### A few important events

The need arose to conserve cultural heritage in Spain, as in the rest of Europe, during the Enlightenment and with the appearance of historical consciousness with respect to the past, reflected in the creation of the Royal Academies of History (1738) and Fine Arts (1752), the first institutions charged with guardianship of a national heritage, especially in reaction to such problems as pillage. To prevent looting, an order of 1779 (repeated in 1801, 1827, 1836 and 1837) prohibited the illegal export of works of art, clearly demonstrating that this was one of the negative problems for Spanish heritage.

At the beginning of the 19th century the Guerra de la Independencia (1808-1814), provoked by the Napoleonic invasion, had terrible consequences for Spain's heritage through destruction and looting. Some cities, such as Zaragoza and Gerona, besieged by Napoleonic troops on several occasions, lost a large part of their architecture (up to 70 per cent in Zaragoza) and took more than thirty years to rebuild their urban structure. A second important event was the effect of the Leyes Desamortizadores (Disposession Laws) introduced by successive governments between 1820 and 1837 which confiscated a large number of inactive agricultural and urban properties, mainly from the Church. The laws were prompted by the need for building land in the cities which were growing due to the nascent industrial revolution which was to make itself felt towards the end of the century. As a result of these laws of dispossession, many religious communities were closed, many of them fortunately located in the old parts of Spanish cities and making this event supremely important for the nation's heritage. The collections (paintings, sculptures and other objects) from these religious orders formed the starting-point for the provincial museums of fine art. In addition, the demolition of many of these monastic complexes, some in a state of disrepair after the Guerra de la Independencia, facilitated the process of urban reform, making possible the opening up of spacious streets, squares and boulevards in accord with the 19th century, bourgeois vision of town planning.

Although these urban reforms meant improved hygiene and sanitary conditions in Spanish cities and their modernisation in general, they also had serious consequences for the conservation of heritage. Important parts of the historical layout of cities, dating back to the Roman Empire, disappeared. Likewise, in common with the rest of Europe, the city walls were demolished, reflecting a modern spirit which considered it necessary to remove the old limits constricting the traditional city, although it really implied the elimination of important material tokens from the past. In the 20th century, the Civil War (1936 – 1939) had effects that were felt practically up until the restoration of democracy upon the death of General Franco in 1975. Apart from the human loss, a report from the Dirección General de Regiones Devastadas, an institution created at the end of the war to rebuild and repopulate areas damaged during the war, listed 150 churches which had disappeared, 4580 damaged, and of these, 1,850 were irredeemable. These figures not only implied the disappearance of buildings but also the objects they housed, which were stolen, illegally sold or destroyed as a symbol of one of the warring parties during the conflict (similarly, there were numerous cases of the burning of convents and churches).

Another historical phenomenon during the period 1939 – 1975 (the Franco dictatorship) which should be taken into consideration is the rapid industrial development in Spain in the 1960s and 1970s coinciding with a world-wide economic boom, the results of which were, in some respects, negative for heritage. With the improvement in the Spanish economy, there was a demographic explosion which caused many villages to be abandoned, and uncontrolled growth in the cities. This in turn fueled the disappearance of important historic buildings and the modification of traditional urban spaces in many Spanish cities.

The arrival of constitutional democracy (1978), established a new order and the division of the state into self-governing Comunidades Autónomas which normally took responsibility for heritage. Moreover, the new local administration's need for symbolic government buildings has led to the restoration of numerous buildings and historic complexes which were either abandoned or in disuse, marking a notable acceleration in the process of conservation of Spanish cultural heritage. At the same time, institutes and local centres for restoration such as the Instituto Andaluz de Patrimonio Histórico play a vital role in the management of heritage, both in aspects strictly related to conservation and restoration and in research and the spread of new values.

## Legislation
### Background
There is a long tradition in Spain of laws for the guardianship of heritage which goes back to the Middle Ages (see table 1) and begins in the Modern Era with Carlos IV's Novìsima Recopilación (1803) in which instructions are given on how to conserve ancient monuments, but the problem which has dominated these two centuries of regulation has been that the laws, in general, have not been accompanied by the administrative support and funding

which would guarantee their implementation, and not only has the protection of heritage by the citizens not been encouraged, excessive financial costs and limitations in the use of these objects have been imposed. Also, with few exceptions, the laws have commonly lagged behind reality (See Table 1).

Although space forbids a study of all the legislation up until the Ley de Patrimonio Histórico Español (PHE) of 1985, special note should be made of some pioneering regulations such as the 1915 Ley de Conservación de Monumentos Histórico-Artistico in which limitations of epoch or style in relation to heritage were eliminated. The 1926 Law dealing with the Artistic Treasure of the Nation, included the very modern concept of heritage understood as the sum of objects deserving of being preserved for reasons of art or culture, giving the idea that heritage was exclusively made up of objects of historical and artistic value; this idea was not widely adopted elsewhere in Europe until the 1931 Athens Charter.

Spain did not remain at the margin of debates in Europe on the criteria to be used in the restoration of works of art, and Spanish legislation reflected this. When the continent was dominated by Viollet-le-Duc's school of thought, a regulation was introduced in 1850 by which buildings should by restored 'respecting the original idea' and that the old and modern parts should resemble each other and appear to be of the same epoch, thereby seeking that unity of style which Viollet-le Duc sought. The international meeting in Athens in 1931 also had repercussions in Spain, all the more so because of the attendance of important Spanish architects such as Leopoldo Torres Balbás. The 1933 Ley de Patrimonio Artístico Nacional, drawn up during the Second Republic, included prohibiting the rebuilding of monuments, limiting interventions to consolidating and preserving.

Cultural heritage is subject to different regulations (Table 2), although the two basic regulations which affect a great part of the country are the 1978 Constitution and the 1985 PHE law.

The Spanish Constitution of 1978 established a new political regime, democracy, and a constitutional monarch. It refers to heritage in articles 46, 148 and 149, although indirect allusions are made when public access to culture is mentioned in articles 9, 44, 48 and 50. Important questions which appear in these articles are:

- the State must guarantee conservation and promote the enrichment of the nation's heritage.
- the Constitution recognises access for all as a right, to further the harmonious development of the Spanish people.
- the distinction between collective enjoyment and private ownership of heritage is included. This disassociation of the public interest from property (public or private) guarantees free access for all Spaniards to heritage, or in other words, public interest prevails over the ownership of heritage.

A fundamental landmark in Spanish legislation was that the power to protect heritage, which since the 18th century was reserved to the State, passed to the Autonomous Communities. The administration of heritage was decentralised.

Responding to the growing importance given to heritage as an element helping to integrate the Spanish people, in June 1985 the Patrimonio Histórico, Artístico e Cultural (PHE) was introduced. A new Royal Decree of 1987 established the regulation of state

## 18th century
1738  creation of the Royal Academy of History
1773  creation of the Royal Academy of Fine Arts of San Fernando
1779  Royal Decree against the export of works of art

## 19th century
1803  Carlos IV's Novìsima Recopilación, with instructions for the preservation of ancient monuments.
1814  Inauguration of the Museo del Prado
1836/7 Dispossession Laws.
1844  Creation of the Provincial Monuments Commissions
1850  Royal Decree dictating the rules to follow in restorations inspired by the theories of Viollet-le-Duc
1857  Ley Moyano de Instrucción Pública. This law gave the Royal Academy of San Fernando responsibility for the protection of Spain's artistic heritage.
1866  Royal Decree concerning the care of public buildings as the responsibility of the local authorities

## 20th century
1900  Creation of the Ministry of Public Education: produces a Royal Decree ordering the undertaking of the Spanish Catalogue of Monuments.
1911  Royal Tourism Commission and the Archaeological Excavations Law is drawn up.
1915  Conservation of Historical and Artistic Monuments Law
1926  Artistic Treasure of the Nation Law
1931  Spanish Constitution (2nd Republic)
1933  National Artistic Heritage Law
1939  Devastated Regions Office created.
1944, 1963, 1973    regulations concerning the protection of castles, emblems and coats of arms and the traditional buildings known as *horreos* and *pazos*.
1977  Ministerio de Cultura created (the State Fine Arts Office takes over responsibility for Spain's cultural heritage)
1978  Spanish Constitution (Democracy)
1985  Spanish historical heritage law, the Ley de Patrimonio Histórico Español or PHE.

*Table 1. The evolution of Spanish heritage legislation*

museums and Spanish museums system of which the Instituto de Conservación y Restauración de Bienes Culturales now called the Instituto Español de Patrimonio Histórico forms a part. This centre is responsible for drawing up plans for the conservation and restoration of Spanish heritage, research and studies in criteria, methods and adequate techniques for conservation and restoration, as well as training technicians and specialists.

A Royal Decree of 1994, modified the PHE, in line with the 1991 Supreme Court

Judgement which recognised the right of Autonomous Communities to designate objects of Cultural Interest. Likewise, from 1990 onwards, Autonomous Communities have powers to pass their own heritage laws (table 2).

**The Law of 1985**

This law is the culmination of an historical process which goes back to 1779 and has as its aims, the unification of legislation (repealing all previous laws and decrees) and the adaptation of Spanish regulations to the new situation of Spanish heritage in the contemporary world, and in the new decentralised political situation.

The aims of the law were to consolidate existing varied regulations, to include Spanish law in international directives and to respond to problems caused by the new distribution of powers. The participation of city and town councils in the defence of heritage is encouraged through the drawing up of General Plans and subsidy regulations, and the need to communicate with the central and autonomous administrations when they identify some object in danger.

The law has 79 articles which deal with the following points:
* the definition of objects of cultural interest including both immovable (land, buildings, monuments etc) and movable objects (furniture, paintings, machines, books etc.)
* the protection of movable and immovable objects.
* Archaeological Heritage
* Ethnological heritage
* Documentary and bibliographical heritage of archives, libraries and museums.
* Means of promoting heritage.
* Administrative offences and their sanctions.

The conservation, growth and transmission of heritage is viewed as 'the principal witness to the historical contribution of the Spanish people to World civilisation and also to its contemporary creative capacity. The Spanish Historical Heritage is a collective wealth which contains the most worthy expressions of the Spanish people's historical contribution to World culture. Its value is derived from the esteem which, as an element of cultural identity, the people's sensibility merits.'

The law defines heritage as 'immovable and movable objects of artistic, historical, paleontological, archaeological, ethnological, scientific or technological interest. Documentary and bibliographical heritage, archaeological sites and areas, are also to be included in the above, as well as natural spaces, gardens and parks, which have artistic, historical or anthropological value.'

Once the limits of the material reality known as heritage were defined, it was necessary to set up a legal framework to control its management. This is an important concept to keep in mind because the law states: the relevance of the object is a value, which is determined by someone.

The law establishes two legal categories, *bienes inventariados* (listed objects—a category which only applies to movable objects), and *bienes de interés cultural* (objects of cultural interest—a category which applies to immovable objects and the movable objects they contain). The duties and obligations are basically as follows:
* If listed objects (*bienes inventariados*) are private property, the owner can ask for them to be

---

## 1. Directives of an international nature (EU, UNESCO etc.)

## 2. State regulations.The 1978 Constitution

**Direct:**
> 1985 Ley de Patrimonio Histórico Español
> Ley de Patrimonio Nacional

**Indirect:**
> Regulations covering the environmental impact of public works.
> Coasts Law
> Land Law
> Protected Natural Sites Law

## 3. Other laws: museums and national archives etc

## 4. Legislative output from the Autonomous Communities
> 1990 Castilla La Mancha and Basque Country
> 1991 Andalucia
> 1993 Catalunya
> 1995 Galicia

---

*Table 2. Regulations concerning Spanish Cultural Heritage*

included on the inventory but must allow their study by researchers and lend them to approved bodies for the purpose of their exhibition and should also report their transference to third parties by inheritance or sale. Movable objects belonging to the church, whether listed or not, cannot be sold to private citizens or commercial institutions, only to the State or to other ecclesiastical institutions. Neither can the listed objects belonging to the State pass into private ownership.

- Objects of cultural interest (*bienes de interés cultural*) are designated by the Autonomous Communities and are incorporated into a General Register. The owners of BICs are obliged to facilitate their inspection by approved bodies, their study by researchers and public entry at least four days a month and for movable objects, put them in a suitable place for viewing for a period of at least five months every two years.

Immovable objects declared BIC are classified into monuments, gardens, historical complexes and sites, and archaeological areas. These objects may not be moved, renovated nor may their immediate surroundings be altered. The council for the area in which the BIC is located must draw up a Special Protection Plan for Historical Complexes, Historical Sites and Archaeological Areas. The BICs can never be demolished, except with the authorisation of the relevant administration.

The law clearly states that the objects making up the Historical Heritage of Spain must be preserved, maintained and cared for by their owners although situations are included in which the State can maintain heritage if the owner has not done so. The legislation also defines the duties of the State Office of Administration with respect to heritage—guarantee its conservation, promote its improvement, encourage and care for public access, protect it from export and illicit removal, facilitate collaboration with the other public bodies, recover illegally exported objects and exchange cultural information on these objects with other States. The law does not restrict itself to establishing this legal framework, it also includes financial and tax measures to stimulate the conservation and growth of the PHE (one of the most notable being the obligation to commit one per cent of the budget for each public works project, to the work of conservation and restoration of heritage) and with administrative offences which follow up and punish the destruction of PHE.

**The law's criteria for restoration.**

Article 39.1 states that 'public authorities will try, by all possible technical means, to preserve, consolidate and improve the objects declared to be of cultural interest, as well as the movable objects included in the General Inventory'. In the second part of the same article, for immovable objects, the rebuilding of historic buildings is prohibited 'except when original parts of the same are used and their authenticity can by demonstrated' and the additions only permitted if they are indispensable for the building's stability, must be recognisably modern, thereby avoiding mimicking the originals. Another point is respect for all parts of the building, even though they might be from different periods, only removing those pieces which obviously degrade the building or impede its correct interpretation.

All these considerations allow the law to be seen as a regulation reflecting internationally accepted criteria for restoration which have two basic points. They give priority to conservation over restoration, categorically eliminating restoration and they mark the materials and shapes of necessary new additions and respect all periods in the building or object. These are the criteria established by the international charters, later included in Spanish legislation and help us to understand and evaluate contemporary restoration.

## A summary of the history of monument restoration in Spain

An overview of the conservation of Spanish cultural heritage should include some reference to the history of restoration which runs in parallel with events in the rest of Europe. In Spain, as elsewhere, buildings and artistic objects have been modified since antiquity for very different reasons but restoration as understood today did not begin until the middle of the 19th century, slightly later than other European countries but due only to the coincidence of certain events. Amongst these were the need to restore important monuments, given the pitiful state of many Spanish buildings and sites, damaged during the War of Independence, to which were added those expropriated from the Church due to the Dispossession laws, passing into the hands of the State; the re-evaluation of a large part of Spain's medieval heritage as a result of romanticism, historicism and neo-medievalism; the influence of the views of Viollet-le-Duc and his followers; and lastly, the better understanding of Spain's artistic heritage being acquired through the work of the Provincial Monuments Commissions and the cataloguing and study of the country's works of art.

All these elements favour the appearance of a restoration mentality and tendency, aiming to complete the building, just as Viollet had described, and receiving the sanction of the Spanish administration with the introduction in 1850 of a Royal Decree which laid down guidelines for restoration, thus paying homage to Viollet-le-Duc. The Royal Decree specifically prohibited variations in style and aimed to prevent differences between the old and modern parts, thereby consolidating the view that style was the necessary tool for restoration. The law was no more than an expression of the ideas of the times which were put into practice in the restoration of important medieval monuments in the second half of the last century, given that, in the first half, when intervention was necessary in a building, it was completed with contemporary neo-classical architecture. As a result, important Spanish Romanesque and Gothic buildings, often unfinished, were completed by long restoration campaigns. Such is the case, for example, of León Cathedral (the first National Monument in 1844) where the west and south façades were rebuilt (Architects: Juan de Madrazo, Demetrio de los Ríos and Juan Bautista Lázaro), Seville Cathedral, the transept of which had collapsed in 1888 and which was completed, Barcelona Cathedral, which was presented with a new façade towards the end of the last century (work of the architects Oriol Mestre and Font i Carreras) and many other cases which profoundly affected important historic buildings. Consequently Spanish medieval architecture cannot be understood without the restorations undertaken in the last century.

Critical voices were raised at the time, denouncing the excesses committed, but the 19th century was dominated by the followers of Viollet and not until the 20th century did a new opposition appear, the Conservatives. During the first 30 years of the 20th century, a confrontation developed between two contemporary and radically opposed movements, corresponding to the struggle taking place, some years before all over Europe. The restoration school, whose leading figure was the architect Vicente Lamperez Romea, the 'Spanish Viollet'. Restoration, for Lamperez, aimed at finishing unfinished buildings or correcting altered buildings, as at Burgos and Cuenca Cathedrals. The Conservative school echoed the views of John Ruskin and the international Athens Charter (1931). Its most important figure was the architect Leopoldo Torres Balbás, responsible for the Alhambra complex between 1923 and 1936. Torres Balbás is not unique as there was contemporary criticism of 'a la mode' restoration in the previous century. Notable here was the well connected and well travelled Marquis of Vega Inclán, a disciple of Ruskin, and the historian Manuel Gomez Moreno who, in 1900, was made responsible for drawing up the Historical and Artistic Catalogue of Spanish Monuments.

The triumph of the 'scientific' criteria represented by the conservative school occurred after 1931, with the proclamation of the 2nd Republic and, specifically, in the 1933 Ley de Patrimonio Artístico Nacional which accepted the principles of the 1931 Athens Charter. However, the Civil War (1936 – 1939) cut short the country's modernisation in the field of restoration as the scientific criteria, politically associated with the defeated Republican regime, were abandoned, producing a notable step backwards in the ideology of intervention, with a return to much more traditionalist postures, reconstructing many buildings for ideological reasons (associated with Catholicism of the Middle Ages and the starting point of the Spanish State) or political reasons (the Alcázar de Toledo, which had been under siege from Republican troops, for example). Also between 1939 and 1975 buildings were frequently altered on historicist criteria (the restorations of Luis Menéndez Pidal at the Guadelupe Monastery or of Rafael Manzano in the Alcázares) added to a lack of organisation and clear criteria. Nonetheless, there did exist architects who acted with greater respect and historical rigour with respect to monuments (amongst them Manuel Lorente Junquera, who worked on Huesca and Barbastro cathedrals) but they were not dominant. A notable example of this treatment of historic buildings was the 'Paradores' policy of the Ministry of Information and Tourism, which created luxury hotels in monumental buildings. The result, in the main, was to create Olde Worlde pastiches designed to attract a specific sector of the tourist market at a time when recognition was dawning that this was one of the country's main economic assets.

With the arrival of democracy upon the death of Franco (1975) and the new Spanish Constitution in 1978, a substantial change was brought about in restoration practice. Spain rapidly tried to bring itself up to date, both in theory and in practice. This translated into an increase in activity, amongst other reasons due to greater awareness of heritage and to the need for public buildings such as legislative buildings, libraries, museums, and universities. The 1985 law repealed the previous regulations and from 1990 onwards, new laws have appeared from the Autonomous Communities. In theory, there has been a broad acceptance of the ideas expressed in the international charters and a Spanish contribution is being made through such Spanish theorists as Ignase Solá Morales, Antonio González, Dionisio Hernández Gil etc. With respect to practical efforts there is no single attitude and there are basically three postures. Two of them continue the 19th century confrontation between the schools of conservation and restoration, although their boundaries are not as clear as in the previous century. The argument centres around the limits to the project and the design of new elements with respect to the original.

Historicist approaches continue the restoration school of thought in examples such as the work of the architect Fernando Cueca Goitia in the San Fernando Royal Academy of Fine Arts building in Madrid or that of Rafael Manzano Martos in the Alcázares Reales in Seville.

Conservationist approaches include a variety of attitudes, ranging from the supporters of consolidation and minimal intervention (Ruskinian architects such as Susana Mora and Salvador Perez Arroyo) to those who introduce contemporary design into historic architecture. This is not just a question of taste; it is about functional needs if one wishes to give the building a new use, which is one way of guaranteeing its existence. This attitude can be summed up by a respect for historic architecture plus an interest in new design as demonstrated by the examples of Dionisio Hernández Gil in the Templo de Diana in Mérida, Juan Navarro Baldweg in the Molinos del Río in Murcia and Antonio Fernández Alba in the Madrid General Hospital, now the National Museum Centro de Arte Reina Sofía.

Modernist approaches support the insertion of contemporary architecture in historic buildings. There are some architects working along these lines, such as the much-criticised work of Manuel Portacoeli and Giorgio Grassi in the Roman Theatre in Sagunto (Valencia) or Alejandro de la Sota's project for the Bishop's Palace in León. A generalised model of conservation in Spanish cities is given in Figure 9.

# France
by Christian Prioul

France was one of the foremost countries in Europe to recognise, list and legislate to protect the heritage of both the built and natural environments. The focus has been upon the national importance of heritage, aided perhaps by the centralised character of the French state.

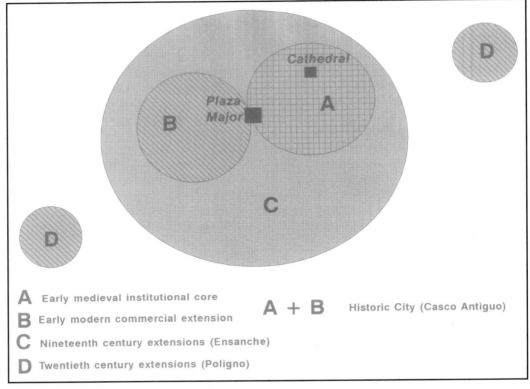

*Figure 9. A model of conservation in Spanish Cities.*

## Inventorisation

The French revolution produced a concern for the national heritage reflected in the Commission des Monuments (1790) and the establishment of the major museums and *conservatoires nationaux* in 1794. An Inspection Générale des Monuments Historiques was established in 1830 (under the leadership of L.Vetet and P. Merimée) and in 1836, a Commission des Monuments Historiques. The law of 1913 added the notion of *classement* (i.e. registration) and funding was provided by the 1914, Caisse Nationale des Monuments Historiques. This system of inventorisation has continued largely unchanged with the addition of an Inventaire Général des Monuments et Richesses Artistique de la France in 1964 which collects basic information available to all interested parties in heritage management. In 1974 the national system was supplemented by an Inventaires Régionaux du Patrimoine.

## Legislative protection

The 1790 – 1815 revolutionary / Napoleonic periods nationalised heritage lands, buildings and artefacts and the Law of 1830 instituted a classification procedure for *monuments historiques*. The Law of 1906 (Protection des sites et des monuments naturels) provided legal protection, extended to a protection zone around monuments in 1913. In 1927 an additional inventory for each *departement* was required, the general protection was extended to *monuments naturels* in 1930, to the protection of archaeological sites in 1941, and the prohibition of advertising near classified sites and monuments in 1943.

The establishment of the *parcs naturels nationaux* in 1960 and the Loi Malraux of 1962 developed the idea of ensembles and area conservation and management (*les secteur sauvegardés*). These ideas were extended to coastlines in 'Loi du conservatoire du littoral', 1975, and the 'Réserves naturelles' of 1976.

### Consolidation and development

Protection was extended to regional parks (Parcs naturels régionaux, 1969), coastlines (Conservatoire du littoral et des rivages lacustres, 1975), and mountains (1985) which included the possibility of land purchase. Area conservation was reviewed in 1983 (Zones de protection du patrimoine architectural et urbaine), 1986 (Law for the planning, protection and development of shorelines), 1989 (Grands sites nationaux), 1993 (Law for the protection and development of landscapes) and 1996, (Creation of *fondation du patrimoine*).

# The Netherlands
by Gregory Ashworth

The Netherlands is a small, compact, governmentally and socially centralised, densely peopled country, sandwiched between the major European cultures of Germany, France and Britain. It has enjoyed relative prosperity, at least in the past 50 years, and a much longer tradition and public acceptance of planning intervention. Although there is only a population of about 15 million, the country has occupied a central position in European history since the 16th century, has been open to the wider European trends, movements and fashions but nevertheless has a distinctive national cultural and political identity. All of this would seem to favour the creation of an effective, nationally sponsored system for the conservation of the built environment but equally suggests the existence of some paradoxes or at least balances that would need to be reflected in policy.

### History of concern

Despite the long acceptance of the necessity for collective action in the public interest in many spheres, the dominance of the Liberal state and its concern for the inviolability of private property delayed effective action here as in other European countries. Enthusiastic, influential individuals similar to, and usually in contact with, the prophets of preservation discussed in the text, also promoted a concern for a rapidly disappearing past in the Netherlands in the second half of the 19th century. The two most notable names were Victor de Steurs who wrote an influential polemic in 1875 condemning the small-minded attitude of the government, and Cuypers who became the Viollet or Gilbert Scott of the Netherlands with his enormous influence on medieval church restoration. As in the rest of Europe the most important organisations were Royal Academies, especially Koninklijk Instituut voor Wetenschappen, Letteren en Schone Kunsten, 1808, (Royal Dutch Institute for Science, Letters and Fine Arts), private organisations, such as the Koninklijke Nederlandse Oudheidkundige Bond (Royal Dutch Antiquities Society), 1899 and 'Heemschut' (Society for

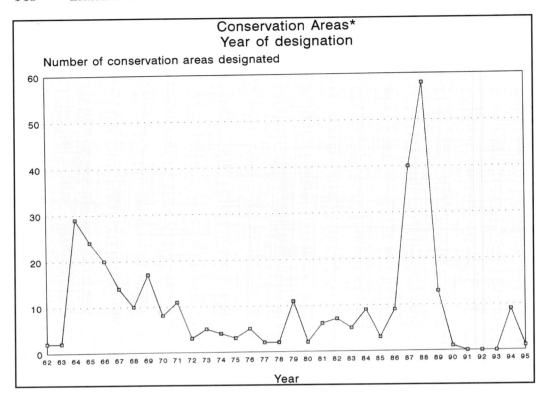

*Figure 10. Designation of conservation areas in the Netherlands.*

the protection of cultural monuments in the Netherlands), an organisation in some ways similar to the British National Trust, founded in 1911.

Governments were slow to react to such pressures, but in 1875 a Rijksdienst voor Monumentenzorg (National service for the care of monuments) was established to inventorise the most important national architectural monuments. There was, however, little effective preservational legislation, the 1814 Act of the Napoleonic kingdom was never enforced and a number of Acts in the first 50 years of the 20th century extended only a partial protective cover and minimal public economic support to monuments, although the category of 'state monument' (Rijksmonument) was established and pressures from both the Rijksdienst and private pressure groups, some for bell towers (1919), windmills (1923), military architecture (1932) and castles (1945), grew.

As in most of the rest of western Europe, it became apparent in the 1960s that a new and broader approach was needed. This resulted in the Monumentenwet (Monument Act) 1961. This Act consolidated previous legislation about individual monuments, increased the possibilities of governmental subsidy for restoration but also recognised the importance of ensembles by creating the 'beschermde stads(dorps) gezicht' (Protected urban (village) scene).

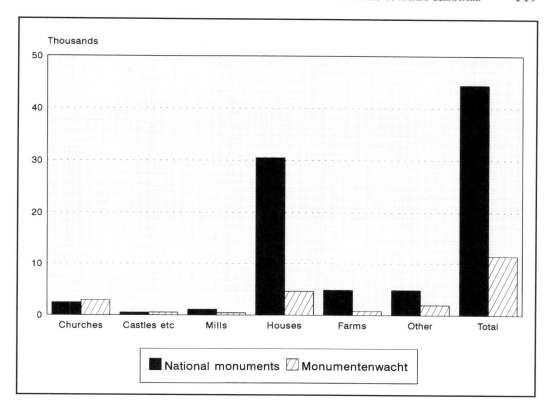

*Figure 11. Care of National Monuments in the Netherlands.*

It also initiated the tripartite division of functions between national, provincial and district authorities.

Over the next 25 years the consequences of the Act were evident in a steady increase in the number of National Monuments designated, in the number of local authorities instituting their own monument protection policies and designating a separate category of local monuments, and in the number of towns and villages creating conservation areas (see Figure 10). In addition a national service monitoring and reporting upon the physical condition of monuments (Monumentenwacht) was established available to both public and private owners of state monuments (Figure 11). A number of local authorities funded a revolving fund for the purchase, renovation and resale of historic property (*stadsherstel*).

A revised Monument Act in 1988 made few fundamental changes to this pattern with the exception of decentralising much of the national responsibility to the Provinces and local authorities. Furthermore lists were considerably lengthened by a national inventory of more recent monuments (Monument Inventorisation Project) and the inclusion of an additional category of Young Monuments, that is those less than 100 years old which included many *arts nouveau* (Jugendstijl) and interwar (Amsterdam and Delft School) buildings.

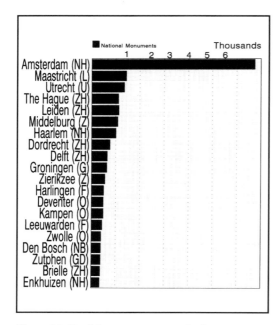

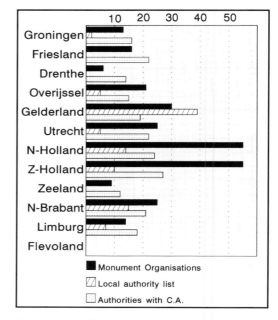

*Figure 12. Top 20 monument towns in the Netherlands.*

*Figure 13. Local monument protection in the Netherlands by province.*

## The problems of success

Almost 40 years of government-financed and -encouraged conservation of the built environment and a growing public consciousness of its importance has led to a proliferation of monument designation, of various categories and the extension of conservation areas to cover the central areas of most Dutch towns. That is not to argue, however, that in a densely populated country with enormous pressures upon land for residential, industrial, commercial and transport uses, actual or potential monuments are not still threatened or even demolished. There is also a considerable variation in the spatial impact of the conservation effort. Some towns, provinces and regions are still much more conservation-conscious than others (see figures 12 and 13). Even more evident are the many problems that success itself has created.

Amongst the most important of these is to find economically viable uses for preserved premises. The expanding lists of monuments, and the designation of extensive conservation areas has included a higher percentage of small residential properties while the group in the population prepared to live in, and finance, historic houses has not expanded proportionately. Similarly the commercial and governmental functions favouring location in historic premises or areas is much smaller than the increasing supply of such locations.

The expanding number of preserved buildings and areas and the increasing role of conservation within local planning has shifted the focus from architectural preservation to the place of fostered historicity within much wider issues. In the Netherlands these have included sharp debates upon the social consequences of area designation and the role of built-environment conservation within the functioning of inner cities in particular. In terms of political legitimation, the origins of the Dutch preservation movement, as in most western European countries, lay in the discovery and propagation of a dominant national ideology to encourage the identification of citizens with the prevailing ethos of the state. A liberal, mercantile, protestant, bourgeois, orangist ascendancy is evident in the stress upon the 17th century (the concept of 'the golden century') and upon the warehouses, modest residences and trading cities of this period. The difficulty with this 'Vermeer image' of the Holland of a particular period is, as with all heritage, its selectivity. There are now calls for a wider variety of heritages, including the 15th-century heritage of the Catholic Burgundian southern provinces, and Hansa-oriented Northern and Eastern provinces, as well as industrial and working class heritages, and ultimately also the contributions of more recent immigrant groups, to be included.

# United Kingdom
by Peter Howard

In the United Kingdom official heritage is generally protected at the level of the constituent countries, England, Scotland, Wales, and the province of Northern Ireland, although the legislation itself is largely centralised in Westminster. National policies are locally administered. Real policy-making powers of the county authorities are very limited. There are many clashes of identity within and between these countries:

- the Isle of Man and the Channel Islands are outside the UK in heritage terms, and organise their own affairs.
- the Scots and Welsh regard themselves as nations, not merely regions, and Scottish and Welsh heritage agencies tend to gloss over significant different identities within their countries, while emphasising the differences with England. For example, some Welsh nationalists regard World Heritage Sites such as Caernarvon Castle not as Welsh heritage, but as symbols of English oppression.
- within these countries there are some regions or counties which consider themselves significantly different from the rest, Shetland from Scotland, Pembrokeshire from Wales, Cornwall from England. In all three countries, England, Wales and Scotland, there are very important differences between north and south.
- there are also many important minority groups, some of them immigrants from former British colonies. These include large communities from southern Asia (India, Pakistan, Sri Lanka, Bangla Desh), and also from the West Indies. In some cities such groups are sufficiently numerous to be jealous of their identity and heritage.
- the situation in Northern Ireland is even more problematic, with a Roman Catholic group stressing a heritage similar to that claimed by the Republic of Ireland, while the Calvinist Protestant group has a significantly different heritage, though still not an English one.

## *Nature*
Conservation of the natural heritage (fauna, flora, geology) is looked after at country level by English Nature, Scottish Natural Heritage and the Countryside Council for Wales. They have

no responsibility for the conservation of nature in zoos, which operate independently, nor for museums. The Department of Environment has overall responsibility.

The major designations are:

- Sites of Special Scientific Interest (4729 covering 1,517,536 hectares). Protected geological, fauna and flora sites.
- National Nature Reserves (224 number covering 160,044 hectares).

There are also European designations – e.g. Special Protection Area, – and world designations – e.g. Ramsar site.

Environmentally Sensitive Areas are administered by the Ministry of Agriculture where farmers can receive cash payments for farming using methods approved as being capable both of preserving nature, and of conserving landscape.

Within the UK the Nature sector has always prided itself on operating from a scientific basis. This was most marked in the Nature Conservancy Council, the UK-wide predecessor to the country organisations. There has been a degree of tension between this scientific view and the wish to conserve landscapes for aesthetic reasons, especially in England. Hence it makes much sense to divide Nature from Landscape, which in some other countries would seem an absurd division.

## Landscape

In England the conservation of landscape for aesthetic reasons is separated from the conservation of nature for scientific reasons, and the government advisory body is the Countryside Commission, based at Cheltenham. In Scotland and Wales the same bodies are responsible for both sectors. The major Act of Parliament for landscape conservation was the 1949 National Parks and Access to the Countryside Act. The 1981 Wildlife & Countryside Act and the 1990 Environmental Protection Act were also significant.

The ten National Parks, plus the Broads Authority, are administered by committees with members from the county councils in whose territory they are, plus other members. Each National Park operates as a planning authority, and has considerable authority to control new developments. The Parks are charged both to conserve natural beauty and to encourage public access. National Parks are inhabited, farmed and forested for economic gain, and are largely in private ownership. Most of them are upland areas. There are no National Parks in Scotland, though there are designated Scenic Areas.

Areas of Outstanding Natural Beauty number more than 35 covering 11.3 per cent of Britain. They have been selected for landscape beauty at national level, and are administered by the local county council, who remain the planning authority. Heritage Coasts (43 sections) have been designated since 1966 and are managed in a way similar to Areas of Outstanding Natural Beauty

The Countryside Commission are currently exploring methods of securing the future of non-designated areas by investigating the landscape character of the whole of Britain. This is an attempt to safeguard the landscape of areas outside the official designations. Most county councils have also designated Areas of Great Landscape Value (or others with a similar title) which are areas where development is limited.

## Built Monuments

Buildings and monuments are looked after by English Heritage, responsible to the Department of Culture, Media and Sport in England, by Historic Scotland, responsible to the Scottish Office, in Scotland and by CADW, responsible to the Welsh Office, in Wales. Some major monuments and buildings are owned, or managed, by these organisations and are open to the public. They also offer advice to owners of other historic buildings.

In the UK, heritage conservation is closely tied to Town & Country Planning. All significant new development requires planning permission from the District or City Council. This dates largely from the Town & Country Planning Act of 1947. These councils keep the Lists of Historic Buildings, and also often employ a Conservation Officer. Historic Buildings are Listed as being of architectural or historical importance. There are three lists, and all alterations to buildings on the lists must have Listed Building Consent from the county council:-

List 1     5000 buildings
List 2*   50,000 buildings
List 2    450,000 buildings of lesser significance.


Listing means that all significant changes to the property, whether inside or outside, within the curtilage of the property (so including all fences and outbuildings) require Listed Building Consent. In buildings Listed Grade 1 such permission would be a rare event, but Listed Grade 2 buildings have the same basic rules, but a lesser level of enforcement. Where a Listed building requires repair, this can be ordered by the Council, and it is possible for the Council to do the work, and then charge the owner.

Many centres of old towns and villages are designated as Conservation Areas, first permitted under the Town & Country Planning Act 1971 section 277. Although not all of the buildings within them will be Listed, special consent is required for all alterations to the outside of all properties and streets within them.

Ancient monuments (which are usually unroofed) are Scheduled, and a Scheduled Ancient Monument is equivalent to a list 1 building. Ancient Monuments have been scheduled since 1882 and are usually archaeological in character rather than architectural, though some structures are both. There are 14,000 Scheduled Ancient Monuments. The Royal Commission on Ancient Monuments maintains details and started listing buildings as early as 1908.

Historic Gardens can be Registered. All development proposals which affect a registered historic garden must take account of their impact.

Note:- apart from very many voluntary organisations, some of considerable size, e.g. Landmark Trust, National Trust, there are several amenity societies, such as the Victorian Society, the Georgian Group, Ancient Monuments Society, Society for the Protection of Ancient Buildings, Twentieth Century Society which have the statutory right to be consulted about applications which affect buildings in which they are interested.

The National Trust is a very well-known organisation, which is now over 100 years old with nearly two million members. It was set up to acquire beautiful landscape and places at risk, and from 1945 – 1970 acquired a large number of country houses with their collections, their estates and their villages. More recently they have expanded their holdings to include, for example, the municipal house where Paul Macartney grew up in Liverpool. This is a very powerful organisation, the third largest landowner in Britain, and founded in 1885. The aristocratic country house is perhaps the archetype of heritage in England, where land-ownership remains socially very important, with many mansions being owned by the National Trust. Such properties often contain very significant collections of artefacts, as well as the building and the extensive gardens and landscape parks. This may have encouraged an holistic sense to the study of heritage in England.

A second British characteristic is the enormous role played by voluntary societies, some of them so large and powerful, that their votes are assiduously courted by politicians. This applies not only to the built heritage but also in the field of Nature, some organisations such as the Royal Society for the Protection of Birds having their own bird reserves.

# Italy
by Giuseppe Fera and Marina Arena

### The pre-unification states.
Some legislative measures for the protection of cultural heritage, already existed in the first half of the 19th century in the different States into which pre-unification Italy was divided. These measures were often concerned with the export and trade in antiquities as for example from 1745 in the Austrian State of Lombardo-Veneto. Similar measures had been adopted in the Dukedom of Parma (1760) and Modena (1857). In Tuscany, an act of 1854 prevented the moving or destruction of all works of art. But the most important and relevant measures in this field were those of the Papal States from the end of 18th century. In particular the Act of 1820 for the safeguarding and conservation of the great masterpieces of art and classical monuments in Rome, arguably the richest concentration of artistic and historical heritage in the world, represents the most complete and advanced legislative measure in this field at that time. This Act, in addition to regulating archaeological excavations and the export of arts and antiquities, included an inventory of objects of heritage in the possession of the church.

### From the Kingdom of Italy to Fascism
After unification there was little progress in this field. The reason for this lack of interest and legislation is explained by the prevailing liberal ideology which considered heritage protection to be undue state interference with private ownership. An Act of 1865 allowed expropriation in cases of dangerous neglect but the incorporation of Rome in 1870 led to a weakening of the restrictions on export.

The first attempt at new national legislation started in 1872 but the new act was not approved until 1902. It was, however, substantially strengthened by a more comprehensive Act in 1909, which controlled export, forbade the alienation of public heritage property and controlled archaeological research. This Act was expanded in 1913, 1917, 1923, 1927 and 1937.

In 1939 the Minister of Education introduced the so-called 'Bottai reforms', influenced by the aesthetic philosophy of Benedetto Croce. These reforms, which are the basis of present legislation, resulted in two Acts, one for natural and the other for artistic heritage. They include measures for:

- broad definition of natural, historical and artistic heritage;
- inventorisation;
- the compulsory notification of demolition, alteration, restoration or incompatible use;
- state action including compulsory purchase in the event of deterioration or destruction;
- the prohibition of export;
- rights of public access;
- state ownership of archaeological finds;
- the preparation of a landscape conservation plan for protected landscapes.

## After the Second World War

The 1948 constitution recognised that, 'the Republic promotes the development of culture, scientific research and the conservation of the landscape and of the historical and artistic heritage of the Nation.' This statement makes heritage conservation a constitutional duty of the State, with the goal of promoting the cultural development of Italian people through the conservation of heritage. However this responsibility was not always implemented in the period of post-war reconstruction and industrial transition.

The implementation of the 1939 Acts were often in conflict with the emerging free-market economy and urban development. Only during the 1960s did national public opinion became concerned and international concern was focused by the disastrous floods of 1966 in Florence and Venice. In 1964 a national parliamentary committee enquired into the condition of national heritage and suggested ways, 'to save cultural heritage in Italy' in the face of the ineffectiveness of public policies.

In 1973 some special Acts for the protection of Venice were approved but only after 1975 were relevant measures adopted by the Ministry of Environment and Cultural Property. The introduction of regional government in 1977 transferred some powers to the regions and especially to the autonomous regions, such as Sicily and Sardinia. The 1978 Conservation of Heritage Act introduced urban conservation plans in historical centres encouraged by the example of Bologna. This represented an important evolution of the idea of conservation from the single historical monument to the whole urban centre, as had occurred in most of Western Europe a decade earlier.

The 1985 Galasso Act represented an important development of the 1939 Act for landscape conservation now defined as more than natural beauty, as an 'environmental good', or 'resource', not only to be conserved but also, if necessary, developed. From this different notion of landscape came an extension to wide areas of national territory, for example large parts of the Alps, the Apennines, all volcanoes, the wet-lands, the banks, major rivers and lakes. This wide concept of landscape requires efficient planning, going beyond mere protection, especially by the regional governments. Therefore the Galasso Act required the regions to prepare large scale landscape and environmental plans.

## Some final considerations

Finally there are remaining issues. These include the shift from an aesthetic view of heritage (the 1939 Acts), mainly inspired by Croce's philosophy, to a more recent idea of heritage as 'every material evidence having cultural and historical values' (as in the Franceschini report) which has increased the amount of heritage thought worthy of conservation. The shift in responsibility to the regions has not been matched by adequate regional legislation. The transition from policies of constraint to a more flexible and active planning approach to conservation has been only partly successful in combining preservation with the management of heritage as a development resource.

### Main Legislative Acts

1913  Implementation of the 1909 and 1912 Acts concerning antiquities and fine arts.
1918  Foundation of the National Institute of Archaeology and History of art.
1923  Regulations for the inventorisation of monuments and works of historical, archaeological and artistic interest.
1939  Protection of historical, artistic and natural heritage.
1958  Approval of The Hague International Convention for the Protection of Cultural Heritage in case of war
1964  National committee of enquiry into the conservation of historical, archaeological, artistic and landscape heritage.
1972  Regulation of the export of historical and artistic artefacts.
1974  Founding of the Ministry of Environment and Cultural Property.
1975  Emergency protective measures.
1977  Transfer of some powers to the Regional Governments.
1978  Urban conservation and restoration plans for historic centres.
1982  New tax regime for heritage property.
1985  Environmental and Landscape conservation

## What you should know

Each of these very different national studies has been a selection and summary by a 'local' expert which therefore represents in itself a national, as well as a personal, vision. Two sorts of comparison are possible. First, a consideration of the common features and links between the national summaries. This raises the question of what features and timings, and what problems and solutions, can be regarded as European. Secondly, and conversely, to what extent do quite different and specifically national policies emerge?

## Further Reading

G.J. Ashworth (1984) The management of change: conservation policy in Groningen, *Cities*, pp.605-616.

G.J. Ashworth (1991) *Heritage planning; conservation as the management of change*, Groningen, Geopers.

L.R. Ford, (1985) 'Urban morphology and preservation in Spain', *Geographical Review*, Vol.68, no.3, pp253-273

R. Kain (1975) 'Urban conservation in France' *Town and Country Planning*, Vol. 43, pp.428-433.

R. Kain (1981) *Planning for conservation: an international perspective*, London: Mansell.

P.J. Larkham & A.N.Jones (1993) 'The character of conservation areas in Great Britain' *Town Planning Review* Vol.64, no.4, pp.395-413.

Nationale Contactcommissee Monumentenbescherming (annual) *NCM monumentenjaarboek* Amsterdam.

G. Pearce, L.Hems, & B.Hennessy (1990) *Conservation Areas of England*, London: English Heritage.

V. de Steurs (1875) 'Holland op zijn smalst' *De Gids*, Vol.37, no.3, pp.320-403.

J.E. Tunbridge (1981) 'Conservation trusts as geographic agents: their impact upon landscape, townscape and land use' *Transaction, Institute of British Geographers, N.S.* Vol.6, pp.103-25.

E.E.Viollet-le-duc (1875) *Histoire de l'habitation humaine, depuis de temps historiques jusque · nos jours*, Paris.

## Some useful web-sites include:

| | |
|---|---|
| Countryside Commission | <http://www.countryside.gov.uk> |
| Countryside Council for Wales | <http://www.ccw.gov.uk>. |
| English Heritage | <http://www.english-heritage.org.uk> |
| English Nature | <http://www.english-nature.org.uk> |
| Historic Scotland | <http://www.historic-scotland.gov.uk> |
| National Trust | <http://www.nationaltrust.org.uk> |
| Scottish Natural Heritage | <http://www.snh.org.uk> |

# References

G.J. Ashworth & P.J. Larkham (eds) (1994) *Building a New Heritage: tourism, culture and identity in the New Europe*, London: Routledge.

G.J. Ashworth & J.E.Tunbridge (1990) *The Tourist-historic City*, London: Belhaven.

Bedford, Duke of (1971) *How to Run a Stately Home*, London: Deutsch.

M. Bellaigue (1999) 'Globalisation and Memory', *International Journal of Heritage Studies*, Vol.5, No.1.

P. Boniface & P.J. Fowler (1993), *Heritage and Tourism in the Global Village*, London: Routledge.

D. Burtenshaw, M.Bateman & G.J.Ashworth (1991) *The European city: a western perspective*, London: Fulton

E. Cohen (1979) 'A phenomenology of tourist experiences' *Sociology*, Vol.13, pp.179-201.

G. Dann (1981) 'Tourism motivation: an appraisal' *Annals of tourism research*, Vol.8, pp.187-219.

N. Davies (1996) *Europe, a History*, Oxford: Oxford University Press.

J.M. Dewailly & E. Flament (1993) *Geographie du tourisme et loisirs*, Paris: SEDES.

L.R. Ford (1978) 'Continuity and change in historic cities' *Geographical Review, Vol.68, no.3*, pp.253-73.

N. Graburn (1977) 'The visitor and the museum experience', in L. Draper (ed) *The visitor and the museum*, Berkley: American Association of Museums, pp.5-26.

J. Greenfield (1996) *The Return of Cultural Property*, Cambridge: CUP.

T. Griffiths (1987)*Beechworth: an Australian country town and its past*, Melbourne: Greenhouse.

R. Hammersley & T.Westlake (1994) 'Urban heritage in the Czech republic' in G.J. Ashworth & P.Larkham (eds) *Building a new heritage: tourism, culture and identity in the new Europe*, London: Routledge, pp.178-200

R. Hewison (1987) *The Heritage Industry: Britain in a climate of decline*, London: Methuen.

E. Hooper-Greenhill (1992) *Museums and the Shaping of Knowledge*, London: Routledge.

D. Horne (1984) *The Great Museum: the Re-presentation of History*, London: Pluto.

P. Howard (1991) *Landscapes; the artists' vision*, London: Routledge.

K. Hudson (1987) *Museums of Influence*, Cambridge: Cambridge University Press.

D. Lowenthal (1985) *The Past is a Foreign Country*, Cambridge University Press.

K. Lynch (1960) *Image of the city*, Cambridge MA: MIT Press.

D. MacCannell (1976) *The Tourist: a new theory of the leisure class*, New York: Schoken.

D. Pearce (1987) *Tourism Today: a geographical analysis*, London: Longman.

S. Pearce (1998) 'The Construction of Heritage: the domestic context and its implications', *International Journal of Heritage Studies*, Vol.4 , no.2, pp.86-102.

J-F. Pitté (1987) in R.J.P. Kain (ed) (1987) 'Conservation of historic gardens and parks on the continent of Europe', *Landscape Research*, Vol.12, no.2.

R. Prentice (1993) *Tourism and heritage attractions*, London: Routledge.

J. Roberts (1996) 'The Gardens of Dunroamin: history and cultural values with specific reference to the gardens of the inter-war semi', *International Journal of Heritage Studies*, Vol. 1, no.4, pp.229-237.

A. Salasova, (1997) 'Village Restoration in the Czech Republic',*International Journal of Heritage Studies*, Vol.2, no.3, pp.160-171.

R. Samuel (1995) *Theatres of Memory*, London: Routledge

N. Smart (1997) 'The Maginot Line: an indestructible inheritance', *International Journal of Heritage Studies*, Vol.2, no.4, pp.222-233.

F. Tilden (1967)*Interpreting our Heritage*, Univ. of N. Carolina Press.

J.E. Tunbridge (1981) 'Conservation trusts as geographic agents: their impact upon landscape, townscape and land use' *Transaction, Institute of British Geographers*, N.S. Vol.6, pp.103-25.

J.E. Tunbridge & G.J.Ashworth (1997) *Dissonant Heritage: the management of the past as a resource in conflict*, London: Wiley.

L.J. Turner & J. Ash (1976) *The golden horde: international tourism and the pleasure periphery* London: Constable.

D.L. Uzzell (ed) (1989) *Heritage Interpretation, 2 volumes*, London: Belhaven.

D.L. Uzzell (1996) 'Creating Place Identity through Heritage Interpretation', *International Journal of Heritage Studies*, Vol. 1, no.4, pp.219-228.

P. Vergo (1989) *The new museology*, London: Reaktion Books.

J.A. Wright (1985) *On living in an old country: the national past in contemporary Britain* London:Verso.

L. Young (1998) 'Museums, Heritage and the things that fall in-between' *International Journal of Heritage Studies*, Vol.3, no.1, pp.7-16.